What's in a Name?

*The origins, meanings and significance
of Steam Locomotive Names in the
British Railways Era*

Part 1 – LNER

David H. Baldwin

 www.trafford.com

North America & international
toll-free: 1 888 232 4444 (USA & Canada)
phone: 250 383 6864 ✦ fax: 250 383 6804 ✦ email: info@trafford.com

The United Kingdom & Europe
phone: +44 (0)1865 722 113 ✦ local rate: 0845 230 9601
facsimile: +44 (0)1865 722 868 ✦ email: info.uk@trafford.com

10 9 8 7 6 5 4 3 2

ACKNOWLEDGEMENTS

I am grateful to my friends and former work colleagues Sue Coulson, Janet Gregory and Mark Harrington for their invaluable assistance in the compilation of this book.

I am also indebted to the Director and staff of the National Railway Museum, Leeman Road, York, particularly John Clarke, Assistant Curator, and Sarah Hammond, Library Assistant, for their kind co-operation in facilitating access to the nameplates held at York as part of the National Collection and for their consent to the use of photographic images of those plates in the preparation of the bookcover.

FOREWORD

The social, political, military and cultural history of the nineteenth and early twentieth centuries is broadly encapsulated in the names given to British steam locomotives. To understand the origins, significance and meanings of those names is to understand much about the fabric and development of life in Britain during that period: the names fit together like some huge, interlocking jigsaw puzzle and, in one way or another, make reference to virtually everything that was important and of significance to those generations for whom steam traction was a commonly accepted part of life and living.

As a boy, in the fifties, I spent countless hours – as did so many others of my generation – "copping" named locomotives, particularly on the ECML, without ever really knowing, or even wondering, why the likes of **Persimmon** or **Meg Merrilies** or **Sir Ronald Matthews** were so named.

A named locomotive was not merely one of several with shared characteristics but, through its name, acquired a unique identity outwith the class to which it belonged; some even acquired "celebrity" status.

So, for the tens of thousands of schoolboys in the fifties and beyond whose passion was train spotting, "namers" were everything and the subject of much excited and animated conversation following a visit to a faraway railway

'Mecca' such as Doncaster or Tamworth. Yet, whereas virtually all schoolboys would have known where to see **Sir Herbert Walker**, **Sir Keith Park** or **Sir Daniel Gooch** and the classes of locomotive to which they belonged, few would have known much, if anything, about the history, origins or achievements of the name behind the treasured 'cop' carefully underlined in their compendium of British Locomotives.

It may be difficult for subsequent generations to understand the obsessional nature of the train spotting hobby and its continuing fascination for a substantial and significant number of the boys who were "hooked" on it. Perhaps not surprisingly, with the passing of the steam era interest in the nature of this obsession has increased rather than diminished, with a seemingly insatiable demand for photographic essays and other books on the subject. I hope that those who continue to be ensnared by the hobby will, through this book, share my fascination in discovering and exploring the origins and meanings of some of the names which were the focus of their youthful attention and "gave life" and added interest to the pursuit of collecting engine numbers.

David H. Baldwin
Sheffield
March, 2008

CONTENTS

CLASS A4

INTRODUCTION AND GENERAL CHARACTERISTICS

But for the early exploits and achievements of the Gresley A3 Pacifics, the A4's might never have been built.

Impressed by the performance of the streamlined "Flying Hamburger" diesel-powered train in Germany during the early 1930's, Nigel Gresley and the LNER Board briefly contemplated the purchase of similar units for an accelerated London – Newcastle express service.

In the event, high speed running by the A3's persuaded the Board that the four-hour target was achievable with steam traction. Most notably, on 5th March, 1934, No.2750 *Papyrus* clipped several minutes from the scheduled times (with a top speed of 108 mph). The LNER subsequently proceeded with the construction of streamlined train sets and the locomotives to haul them. In September, 1935, the first streamlined locomotive, **Silver Link**, achieved a new British speed record of 122.5 mph on a demonstration run to publicise the new "Silver Jubilee" Service.

The rest is, as they say, history.

The success of the A4 was due not only to its streamlined casing, adopted as a means of reducing air resistance, but also to internal design features, from regulator valve to blastpipe, intended to allow steam to flow freely. In March, 1938, **Mallard** became the first A4 to be equipped with the Kylchap blastpipe and double chimney. Only four of the Class were similarly equipped when first built but the eventual adoption and fitting of this device to all A4's between May, 1957, and November, 1958, gave them an extended lease of life and greatly improved their performance on the East Coast Main Line.

DAVID H. BALDWIN

Withdrawal commenced in December, 1962, and was completed in December 1966. No fewer than six of the original 35 locomotives have been preserved.

THE NAMES

The first four locomotives of the Class were built to haul the streamlined "Silver Jubilee" train and were named appropriately. It was the intention to name all the remainder after British birds that were noted for being "swift or strong of flight". In the final analysis, however, only 23 of the class carried bird names and just 14 were to retain them to the end.

THE CLASS

A total of 34 locomotives (originally 35) numbered 60001 to 60034

60001	Sir Ronald Matthews	60018	Sparrow Hawk
60002	Sir Murrough Wilson	60019	Bittern
60003	Andrew K. McCosh	60020	Guillemot
60004	William Whitelaw	60021	Wild Swan
60005	Sir Charles Newton	60022	Mallard
60006	Sir Ralph Wedgwood	60023	Golden Eagle
60007	Sir Nigel Gresley	60024	Kingfisher
60008	Dwight D. Eisenhower	60025	Falcon
60009	Union of South Africa	60026	Miles Beevor
60010	Dominion of Canada	60027	Merlin
60011	Empire of India	60028	Walter K. Whigham
60012	Commonwealth of Australia	60029	Woodcock
60013	Dominion of New Zealand	60030	Golden Fleece
60014	Silver Link	60031	Golden Plover
60015	Quicksilver	60032	Gannet
60016	Silver King	60033	Seagull
60017	Silver Fox	60034	Lord Faringdon

"STREAKS AHEAD"

60001 SIR RONALD MATTHEWS

Originally named Garganey, this locomotive was re-named in March, 1939, after the then Chairman of the LNER.

Sir Ronald Matthews (1885 – 1959) was educated at Eton and saw service in the Great War as a Captain in the *King's Own Yorkshire Light Infantry*. Closely associated with the City of Sheffield, he held the Office of Master Cutler in 1922/23 and was President of the Sheffield Chamber of Commerce from 1929 to 1931.

Sir Ronald succeeded **William Whitelaw** as Chairman of the LNER in 1938, having joined the Board in 1929, and remained in that office until nationalisation of the railways in 1948. He successfully maintained a sense of direction and cohesion despite the fact that most of his stewardship was in wartime and the immediate postwar prelude to nationalisation. A more extrovert personality than Whitelaw, he is remembered for the interest he took in those around him and, by some, for the poker schools which frequently took place at the conclusion of Directors' meetings.

The locomotive which bore his name had the distinction of being the only one of its class to be allocated (as 4500 Garganey) to just one shed (Gateshead) for the whole of its working life (1938 to 1964).

60002 SIR MURROUGH WILSON

Originally named Pochard, a diving duck, in April 1939 this locomotive instead acquired the name of the Deputy Chairman of the LNER.

Lt. Col Sir Murrough John Wilson (1875 – 1946) was educated at Marlborough College and was in the service of the North Eastern Railway Company from 1893 to 1902. He became a Director of the Company in 1912 and ultimately, following Grouping, Deputy Chairman of the LNER in 1934 in succession to **Lord Faringdon**.

Sir Murrough served with the Yorkshire Regiment during the Great War and was Member of Parliament for Richmond (Yorks) from 1918 to 1929.

60003 ANDREW K. McCOSH

This locomotive was originally numbered and named 4494 *Osprey* until July, 1942, when it was re-named after the Chairman of the LNER Committee responsible for locomotive building and repair and one of only five Directors who served on the Board of the Company for the full 25 years of its existence.

Andrew Kirkwood McCosh JP, DL, (1880 – 1967) was educated at Fettes School and Trinity College, Cambridge (BA Mechanical Science Tripos 1902). A mining engineer by profession, and a former Director of the **North British** Railway, he was President of the British Iron and Steel Federation 1936; Deputy Controller of Iron and Steel, Ministry of Supply 1939 –42; President of the Mining Association of Great Britain 1944; and President of the British Employers Confederation 1945-46.

The displaced name *Osprey* was subsequently carried by Class A1 Pacific 60131.

60004 WILLIAM WHITELAW

Grandfather of the Conservative politician of the same name, William Whitelaw (1868-1946) was educated at *Harrow* and at Trinity College, Cambridge. He was MP for Perth City 1892-95 and a Director of the Bank of Scotland. He became a Director of the Highland Railway soon after his 30th birthday and, later, its Chairman. In 1912, he was appointed Chairman of the **North British** Railway. He was the first Chairman of the newly-formed LNER and remained in that Office until 30th September, 1938, when he was succeeded by **Sir Ronald Matthews**. His name had originally been carried by A3 Pacific No. 2563 (subsequently re-named *Tagalie)* before being transferred in July, 1941, to A4 Pacific

No. 4462 (originally 'Great Snipe').

Although possibly somewhat paternalistic, Whitelaw was highly regarded for his unfailing courtesy, his wisdom in dealing with difficult problems and his insistence on strict financial management and accountability.

Under his capable leadership, and with the enthusiastic support and encouragement of **Sir Ralph Wedgwood** as Chief General Manager and H.N. (later, Sir Nigel) Gresley as Chief Mechanical Engineer, the LNER became the undoubted leader in setting new standards of speed and comfort for railway travel. Imaginative and far-reaching developments included the introduction of the non-stop "Flying Scotsman" Service between London and Edinburgh, streamlined train sets and all-Pullman Services such as the "Queen of Scots".

60005 SIR CHARLES NEWTON

Originally 4901 Capercaillie, this locomotive was re-named Charles H. Newton in August, 1942, in recognition of the Chief General Manager of the LNER (who had succeeded **Sir Ralph Wedgwood** in 1939). Ten months later, the engine was again re-named, becoming Sir Charles Newton to reflect the Knighthood bestowed upon its namesake.

Charles Henry Newton (1882-1973) entered the service of the Great Western Railway in 1897 at the age of 15 and retired fifty years later as Chief General Manager of the LNER. During his long and distinguished career, Sir Charles held the posts of Assistant to the Comptroller of the Great Eastern Railway 1916; Chief Accountant, Great Eastern Railway 1922; Chief Accountant, LNER 1928; and, for the three years prior to his appointment as Chief General Manager in 1939, Divisional General Manager (Southern Area).

Following his retirement in 1947, he became a Director of the LNER during the final year of its existence.

60006 Sir Ralph Wedgwood

Sir Ralph Lewis Wedgwood (1874-1956) was a great-great-grandson of Josiah Wedgwood, founder of the celebrated pottery firm, and was related by marriage to Charles Darwin.

A man of formidable intellect, Sir Ralph was educated at Clifton College and at Trinity College, Cambridge, following which he joined the staff of the *North Eastern* Railway, becoming District Superintendent at Middlesbrough in 1902. In 1905, having briefly held the post of Secretary to the NER, he returned at his own request to the Traffic Department as Divisional Goods Manager at Newcastle. In 1911, he became Assistant Goods Manager, and then Goods Manager, at York. His responsibilities were subsequently extended to include Passenger Management.

Following war service as Director of Docks, GHQ, France, 1916-19 (during which period he held the rank of Hon. Brigadier-General), Sir Ralph became Deputy General Manager of the North Eastern Railway during the period 1919-21, and was appointed General Manager in 1922. Following Grouping, he held the post of Chief General Manager of the LNER from 1923 to 1939, and was knighted in 1924. When the railways were brought under Government control during World War II, Wedgwood became Chairman of the Railway Executive Committee, effectively in control of all the railways in Britain. He was succeeded in 1942 by Charles H Newton and was created a baronet.

The adoption by the LNER Board of a decentralised system of management based on Area headquarters located in London, York and Edinburgh left the Chief General Manager free to concentrate upon board matters and major policy issues, although it is known that Wedgwood favoured a centralised system – at least initially – along NER lines. He was firmly opposed by those Directors, including **William Whitelaw** and **Lord Faringdon**, who believed that over-centralisation at the outset would be counter-productive and adversely affect attempts to promote closer integration and cohesion among the constituent bodies of the LNER.

By common consent, Wedgwood was masterly in handling external relations and was widely respected, although he was to some a remote and awe-inspiring figure. His diplomatic and negotiating skills were particularly evident in his representation of the collective interests of all railway companies before parliamentary and other committees.

Sir Ralph was personally responsible for the policy of introducing Britain's first high-speed streamline train, the "Silver Jubilee". His collaboration with his close friend and colleague **Sir Nigel Gresley**, Chief Mechanical Engineer of the LNER, was crucial in making this and other express services such as the "Coronation" and "West Riding Limited" the outstanding successes which they undoubtedly were.

Originally 4469 Gadwall, this locomotive was re-named Sir Ralph Wedgwood in March 1939. On 29th April, 1942, the engine was damaged beyond repair in a German air raid on York. The tender only was salvaged and eventually fitted to Thompson Class A2/1 Pacific *Highland Chieftain*. The name Sir Ralph Wedgwood was transferred to 4466 Herring Gull in January, 1944.

60007 SIR NIGEL GRESLEY

Appropriately, the one hundredth Gresley "Pacific" to be built was named after its designer, arguably Britain's most celebrated and accomplished locomotive engineer, at a ceremony on 26th November, 1937.

Born in 1876, Nigel Gresley grew up in Netherseal, Derbyshire, where his father was the rector. Educated at Marlborough College, he was apprenticed to the LNWR at Crewe, later holding a series of posts on the Lancashire and Yorkshire Railway. In 1905, he moved to Doncaster as Carriage and Wagon Superintendent of the GNR, succeeding *H.A. Ivatt* as Locomotive Superintendent in 1911. Appointed Chief Mechanical Engineer of the LNER shortly after Grouping at the age of 46, he continued in that post until his death in 1941, a few weeks before his 65th birthday.

The single type of locomotive most associated with Gresley's name is, of course, the 4-6-2 "Pacific". The first appeared in 1922 as Class A1 No. 1470 and appropriately named *Great Northern* followed shortly afterwards by what may arguably be the world's most famous steam locomotive, *Flying Scotsman*, which has been in virtually continuous service from early 1923 to the present day. A total of 113 Gresley Pacifics were built.

Other forward-thinking products of the Gresley era included the celebrated fleet of V2 mixed-traffic 2-6-2's and the big rotary poppet-valved Class P2 *Cock o' the North*.

60008 DWIGHT D. EISENHOWER

Formerly 4496 Golden Shuttle, this locomotive was re-named in September 1945.

Dwight David Eisenhower (1890 – 1969) American general and 34th president of the United States, commanded Operation 'Overlord', the successful Allied invasion of Europe during World War II which led to the subsequent defeat of Nazi Germany.

Eisenhower spent his first 50 years in almost total obscurity. A professional soldier, he was not even particularly well known within the U.S. Army. His rise to fame during World War II was meteoric; a lieutenant colonel in 1941, he was a five-star general in 1945. As supreme commander of the Allied Expeditionary Force, he commanded the most powerful force ever assembled under one man. He is one of the few generals ever to command major naval forces; he directed the world's greatest air force; he is the only man ever to command successfully an integrated multinational alliance of ground, sea, and air forces. He led the assault on the French coast at Normandy, on 6th June, 1944, and held together the Allied units through the European campaign that followed, concentrating everyone's attention on a single objective: the defeat of Nazi Germany, completed on 8th May, 1945.

Eisenhower's position has been compared in some respects to that of a constitutional monarch: the power vested in him being less important than the fact that his possession of it denied it to others.

His success as Supreme Commander lay in the way in which he dealt with tensions in the Anglo-American relationships and his generosity of spirit towards difficult subordinates.Whatever criticisms may have been made of his qualities as a military commander, he showed great personal courage, judgement and decisiveness in taking the decision to launch the D-Day invasion on 6th June, in the face of hesitant or contradictory advice from subordinate commanders.

The locomotive was withdrawn from service in July, 1963, and is now preserved in the National Railway Museum of America, Wisconsin.

THE "CORONATION" EXPRESS

In 1937, following the success of its "Silver Jubilee" express, the LNER decided to add to its prestigious streamlined trains and, in June of that year, introduced the "Coronation" (journey time London – Edinburgh 6 hours) to commemorate the Coronation of King George VI and Queen Elizabeth (later to become Queen Mother).

The bird names originally intended for A4's 4488 to 4492 were changed to represent the Dominions and other major parts of Empire.

No. 4489, originally named Buzzard but (thankfully!) changed before service to **Woodcock**, was altered again and emerged from Doncaster Plant in June, 1937, in Garter Blue livery with red wheels as **Dominion of Canada**. The front of the locomotive carried a bell presented by the Canadian Pacific Railway Company. This locomotive (subsequently 60010) is now preserved at the Canadian Railroad Historical Museum.

In addition to their nameplates, each of the locomotives in the "Empire" group carried coats of arms on the cabsides.

9

60009 Union of South Africa

The Colony of the Cape of Good Hope was founded by the Dutch at Cape Town in 1652 and remained a Dutch Colony until Britain took possession of it in 1795. Restored briefly to Dutch rule in 1803, it was again taken by Britain in 1806.

A rejection of British liberalism and the desire to keep slaves led to the movement of large numbers of Boers, (the descendants of the Dutch settlers) north-eastwards in the years after 1834. This "Great Trek" led to the foundation of the Orange Free State and Transvaal republic by the Boers, which were recognised by Britain in 1853-4. Natal was annexed to Cape Colony by the British in 1844 and then formed as a separate colony in 1856, to which Zululand was added in 1897 after the British victory in the Zulu Wars. Transvaal and the Orange Free State (renamed the Orange River Colony) became British Colonies after the Boer defeat in the Second Boer War 1899-1902. The self-governing colonies of the Cape of Good Hope, Natal, the Transvaal and the Orange River Colony became united in 1910 under the name of the **Union of South Africa.** Independence within the Commonwealth was gained in 1931.

60010 Dominion of Canada

Canada was originally discovered by Cabot in 1497 but its history dates from 1534, when the French took possession of the Country. The first permanent settlement at Port Royal (now Annapolis), *Nova Scotia*, was founded in 1605, and *Quebec* was founded in 1608.

In 1759, Quebec was captured by British forces under General Wolfe and in 1763 the whole territory of Canada became a British possession. Nova Scotia was ceded in 1713 by the Treaty of Utrecht, the provinces of *New Brunswick* and *Prince Edward Island* being subsequently formed out of it. *British Columbia* was formed into a Crown Colony in 1858, having previously been a part of the Hudson Bay Territory, and was united to Vancouver Island in 1866.

The constitution of Canada has its origins in the British North America Act of 1867, which formed the **Dominion of Canada** from the four provinces of *Ontario*, Quebec, New Brunswick and Nova Scotia. The other provinces and territories were subsequently admitted to this federation; *Manitoba* and North West Territories (1870), British Columbia (1871), Prince Edward Island (1873), Yukon (1898), *Alberta* and *Saskatchewan* (1905) [and *Newfoundland* (1949).]

60011 EMPIRE OF INDIA

Muslim, Hindu and Buddhist states developed from the Seventh Century onwards until the establishment of the Mughal dynasty in 1526. The British East India Company established settlements throughout the 17th Century; clashes with the French and with native princes led to the British government taking control of the company in 1784 and gradually extending sovereignty over the whole sub-continent. Queen Victoria was declared Empress of India in 1877.

The separate Dominions of India and Pakistan became independent within the Commonwealth in 1947 under the Indian Independence Act. In 1948, 60011 apparently carried the name 'DOMINION' **of India** for little more than a week while in the Paint Shops, but returned to traffic with its original name. The re-naming of 60020 **Guillemot** as 'Dominion of Pakistan', although apparently planned, never took place.

60012 COMMONWEALTH OF AUSTRALIA

Australia was discovered by European explorers in the 17th Century. Its eastern seaboard was claimed for Britain by Captain James Cook in 1770 and became a penal colony ("Botany Bay"). *Tasmania, Western Australia, South Australia, Victoria* and *Queensland* were established as colonies between 1825 and 1859. The colonies were federated as the **Commonwealth of Australia** on 1st January, 1901, at which time Australia gained dominion status within the British Empire. Australia became independent within the British Commonwealth by the 1931 Statute of Westminster.

60013 DOMINION OF NEW ZEALAND

The discoverers and first colonists of *New Zealand* were Polynesian people, ancestors of the modern-day Maori. The 9th Century is generally considered to be the date of the first settlement; by the 13th Century or 14th Century settlements were well established.

The first European to discover New Zealand was a Dutch navigator, Abel Tasman, who sighted the coast in 1642 but did not land. It was the British explorer James Cook who circumnavigated New Zealand and landed in 1769. Largely as a result of extensive emigration, the country was annexed to Britain in 1840. The British Lieutenant Governor, William Hobson, proclaimed sovereignty over the North Island by virtue of the Treaty of Waitangi, signed by him and many Maori Chiefs, and over the South Island and Stewart Island by right of discovery. In 1841 New Zealand was created a separate colony distinct from *New South Wales* (a state of South East Australia which originally contained over half the continent but between 1825 and 1911 was reduced by the formation of other states); in 1907 the designation was changed to the **"Dominion of New Zealand"**.

A King's Cross engine for most of its life, No. 60013 was frequently rostered to ECML expresses, its most notable exploit being in the Summer of 1937 when it worked the non-stop "Flying Scotsman" for 44 consecutive days.

THE "SILVER JUBILEE" EXPRESS

60014 SILVER LINK

Within three weeks of emerging from Doncaster Works in 1935, the first streamlined 'Pacific' – 2509 Silver Link – began hauling the "Silver Jubilee" express (King's Cross – Newcastle) in both directions daily, five days a week for two weeks without respite or relief because a second A4 was not yet ready. This represented two 232 mile non-stop runs each day at an average speed of over 70 mph. At the inaugural run, Silver Link set a record by reaching a top speed of 112.5 mph, an average of 100 mph being maintained continuously for 43 miles. What a pity no one seemingly thought it necessary or appropriate to preserve this historic locomotive as it awaited cutting up at Doncaster – its birthplace - in the winter snows of February, 1963.

Although the obvious literal translation of a "link" is something which joins or connects (in this case, cities) the expression "silver link", as with so many others associated with the names of locomotives and trains in Scotland and the North East Region (e.g. *Abbotsford*, *The Lady of the Lake*, the Fair Maid, the Talisman etc.) originates from the work of *Sir Walter Scott*:

> "It is the secret sympathy
>
> The silver link, the silken tie
>
> Which heart to heart, and mind to mind
>
> In body and in soul can bind"
>
> (The Lay of the Last Minstrel – 1805)

60015 QUICKSILVER

60016 SILVER KING

60017 SILVER FOX

Three further Pacifics turned out in 1935 continued the "silver" theme, painted silver to match the colour of the train. Quicksilver clearly conveys the impression of speed. Silver King offers a reminder, so it has been suggested, that the train was a celebration of the Silver Jubilee of the King's accession to the Throne. Silver Fox, despite the embellishment of a running fox on each side of the boiler casing, has no obvious connection with either speed or royalty (the name being derived from the American red fox in a colour phase in which the fur becomes black with long silver-tipped hairs) although the locomotive did capture and briefly hold the world speed record for steam by attaining 113 mph on 27th August, 1936.

The "Silver Jubilee" service between London and Newcastle ended in 1939; the silver livery had disappeared from the locomotives even earlier.

60026 MILES BEEVOR

No. 4485 Kestrel was one of the Class to lose its bird name and in September, 1947, was renamed Miles Beevor who had succeeded **Sir Charles Newton** to become the last Chief General Manager of the LNER, albeit on an acting basis pending nationalisation of the railways. *Kestrel* later re-appeared on Peppercorn Class A1 Pacific No. 60130.

Miles Beevor (1900-94) was educated at Winchester and at New College, Oxford. Following a brief period of military service in 1918 as a Royal Engineer Officer Cadet, he graduated from Oxford (BA) in 1921 and qualified as a Solicitor in 1925.

A successful legal career as a solicitor in private practice culminated in his appointment as Chief Legal Adviser to the LNER in 1943 and, four years later, as Acting Chief General Manager. Miles Beevor might not have been appointed Chief General Manager but for the imminent retirement of Newton's obvious successor although, given the legal implications of the approaching nationalisation, it was probably thought to be in the best interest of the LNER to appoint a lawyer to the post. As it happened, Beevor was appointed as Chief Secretary and Legal Adviser of the British Transport Commission in October, 1947, (a post he held until 1951) and, of necessity, was obliged to divide his time between managing the LNER and setting up the BTC.

From 1952 to 1956, Miles Beevor was Managing Director of the Brush Electrical Engineering Company.

60027 MERLIN

This locomotive was, of course, named after the member of the falcon family of birds and not the wizard of Arthurian legend. Both Merlin and 60024 **Kingfisher** had plaques depicting the birds fitted to both sides of the boiler casing.

The other members of the class which retained their bird names until withdrawal were 60018 **Sparrow Hawk,** 60019 **Bittern,** 60020

Guillemot, 60021 **Wild Swan**, 60022 **Mallard**, 60023 **Golden Eagle**, 60025 **Falcon**, 60029 **Woodcock**, 60031 **Golden Plover**, 60032 **Gannet** and 60033 **Seagull**.

60028 WALTER K. WHIGHAM

No 4487 *Sea Eagle* was re-named Walter K. Whigham in October, 1947; the original name was subsequently also transferred to a Class A1 'Pacific' (60139).

Walter Kennedy Whigham (1878-1948), a Banker by profession, was Deputy Chairman of the LNER from 1946 (in succession to **Lord Faringdon**) until the year of his death. In common with other Directors of the Company, he had served in the Great War (being mentioned in despatches 3 times), first in the *North Staffordshire Regiment* and afterwards on the staffs of 51st (Highland) Division and 4th Corps.

60030 GOLDEN FLEECE

In October, 1947, the LNER introduced a third streamlined train – given the title of the "West Riding Limited" – to travel between King's Cross and Leeds/Bradford. A4 Pacifics were again rostered for this duty and two of them – 4495 Golden Fleece (originally named Great Snipe) and 4496 Golden Shuttle (subsequently re-named **Dwight D. Eisenhower** in 1948) were given names suggestive of the Yorkshire Woollen Industry.

60034 LORD FARINGDON

The final locomotive in the Class entered service in 1938 as No. 4903 *Peregrine,* the name later carried by Class A1 'Pacific' 60146, and was re-named in March, 1948, after a former Chairman of the Great Central Railway and, following Grouping, Deputy Chairman of the LNER with a special interest in financial matters. (Chairman: Finance Committee)

DAVID H. BALDWIN

Alexander Henderson (1850-1934) entered the City firm of Deloittes (Accountants to GWR) in 1867, when 17 years of age. Shortly afterwards, he moved to a firm of stockbrokers and became a member of the Stock Exchange in 1872. In company with his two younger brothers, he developed business interests in South America, the most profitable of which were in the Buenos Aires and Great Southern Railway.

In 1888, Henderson became a director of the Manchester Ship Canal. He was invited to join the Board of the Manchester, Sheffield and Lincolnshire Railway (subsequently *Great Central* Railway) and formed a syndicate with £4 million capital to underwrite the proposed London extension. He became Chairman of the GCR in 1899.

He was knighted in 1902 and, as Sir Alexander Henderson, entered politics as Liberal-Unionist MP for West Staffordshire (1906-1913). He was briefly MP for St. George's Hanover Square before being raised to the peerage and created 1st Baron Faringdon in 1916.

As Chairman of the GCR, he was involved in the development of Immingham Docks and unsuccessfully pursued merger discussions with both the *Great Northern* and *Great Eastern* Railways.

From 1902 to 1913 the name 'Sir Alexander' was carried on GCR Class D9 locomotive No. 1014. In 1913, the name was transferred (as 'Sir Alexander Henderson') to a Class D10 locomotive which, following his elevation to the peerage, was re-named Sir Douglas Haig (and Prince Henry in 1920). In November, 1917, Class 9P locomotive No. 1169 was named 'Lord Faringdon' a name it carried until withdrawal in December 1947. Three months later, in March, 1948, the name was affixed to Class A4 Pacific No. 4903/60034.

CLASS A3

INTRODUCTION AND GENERAL CHARACTERISTICS

Only a few months before the formation of the L.N.E.R. on 1st January, 1923, the Great Northern Railway (GNR), one of the constituent companies, decided to name its two new "Pacific" locomotives. The names chosen, appropriately enough, were *Great Northern*, which became only the second GNR engine ever to be named, and **Sir Frederick Banbury**, after the last Chairman of the Company.

First introduced by the GNR in 1922 as Class A1, Nigel Gresley's new 3-cylinder 4-6-2 'Pacific' design was intended to haul passenger train loads as heavy as 600 tons. The design was adopted by the LNER following Grouping; its arrival heralded the beginning of a new era of locomotive design and performance on the East Coast Main Line.

The third locomotive to be built entered service in February, 1923. It was subsequently named **Flying Scotsman** and exhibited at the British Empire Exhibition held at Wembley in 1924. Further A1's were built from 1923 onwards, making a total of 52 engines built between April, 1922, and July, 1925.

Following the famous railway trials which resulted from competing claims at the Exhibition and in which the performance of the A1 compared poorly with that of the newly built GWR "Caerphilly Castle", drastic modifications were made to the design of the 'Pacific' with remarkable results. The modified locomotive was classed A3 and from 1927 onwards the remainder of the class were progressively fitted with higher pressure boilers.

Great Northern was subsequently rebuilt as new Class A1/1 in September 1945 and renumbered 60113.

THE NAMES

Horse racing between the Wars was a hugely popular pastime, many of the principal courses being served by the LNER. Few people owned cars, there were no motorways, and travel over any distance was largely by train or charabanc. Little wonder, then, that the LNER, which conveyed legions of punters to and from race meetings in its territory and beyond, should have chosen to adopt the names of well-known racehorses for all but a handful of its new express locomotives.

Some of the horses chosen had "star" quality and would undoubtedly have featured in any list of names drawn up to represent 'classic' racehorses (e.g. **Gladiateur, Pretty Polly, Isinglass, Brown Jack**). Others, with less noteworthy achievements to their names, probably had the good fortune to be "in the right place at the right time" i.e. popular winners in the "public eye" at a time when the LNER had chosen to use racehorses as the basis for naming a class of locomotives.

Although over 50 races are represented in the Class through the names of winning horses, a small number of classic races predominate over others. The names of 43 A3's are included among the 55 LNER 'Pacifics' dedicated to winners of the Derby, including all but one of the consecutive winners of the race between 1917 and 1934.

43 winners of the St. Leger, run at Doncaster since 1776, are commemorated in the names of LNER 'Pacifics'. Of these, no fewer than 33 were represented by A3's, including all consecutive winners for the years 1922 – 34. (The remaining ten are accounted for in 3 x Class A1 'Pacifics' and 7 x Thompson/Peppercorn A2's).

The English Triple Crown comprises the Epsom Derby, named after Lord Derby and run every June since 1789, the St. Leger (referred to above) and the 2000 Guineas, a mile contest at Newmarket in May. The Triple Crown has been won only fifteen times since 1809; the names of eight such winners are commemorated among the A3's, namely **Gladiateur**(1865), **Ormonde** (1886), **Isinglass** (1893), **Galtee More** (1897), **Flying Fox** (1899), **Diamond Jubilee** (1900), **Gay Crusader** (1917), and **Gainsborough** (1918). The other winners, *Pommern* (1915) and *Bahram* (1935) feature elsewhere among the Peppercorn 'Pacifics'.

THE FIELD

78 locomotives numbered 60035 to 60112. All save those marked with an asterisk were named after racehorses.

60035	Windsor Lad	60067	Ladas	60099	Call Boy
60036	Colombo	60068	Sir Visto	60100	Spearmint
60037	Hyperion	60069	Sceptre	60101	Cicero
60038	Firdaussi	60070	Gladiateur	60102*	Sir Frederick Banbury
60039	Sandwich	60071	Tranquil	60103*	Flying Scotsman
60040	Cameronian	60072	Sunstar	60104	Solario
60041	Salmon Trout	60073	St. Gatien	60105	Victor Wild
60042	Singapore	60074	Harvester	60106	Flying Fox
60043	Brown Jack	60075	St. Frusquin	60107	Royal Lancer
60044	Melton	60076	Galopin	60108	Gay Crusader
60045	Lemberg	60077	The White Knight	60109	Hermit
60046	Diamond Jubilee	60078	Night Hawk	60110	Robert the Devil
60047	Donovan	60079	Bayardo	60111	Enterprise
60048	Doncaster	60080	Dick Turpin	60112	St. Simon
60049	Galtee More	60081	Shotover		
60050	Persimmon	60082	Neil Gow		
60051	Blink Bonny	60083	Sir Hugo		
60052	Prince Palatine	60084	Trigo		
60053	Sansovino	60085	Manna		
60054*	Prince of Wales	60086	Gainsborough		
60055	Woolwinder	60087	Blenheim		
60056*	Centenary	60088	Book Law		
60057	Ormonde	60089	Felstead		
60058	Blair Athol	60090	Grand Parade		
60059	Tracery	60091	Captain Cuttle		
60060	The Tetrarch	60092	Fairway		
60061	Pretty Polly	60093	Coronach		
60062	Minoru	60094	Colorado		
60063	Isinglass	60095	Flamingo		
60064	Tagalie	60096	Papyrus		
60065	Knight of Thistle	60097	Humorist		
60066	Merry Hampton	60098	Spion Kop		

DAVID H. BALDWIN

THE FORM

60035 WINDSOR LAD

Winner: 1933   Criterion Stakes
             1934   Chester Vase, Newmarket Stakes, the Derby, Great Yorkshire Stakes, the St. Leger
             1935   Burwell Stakes, Coronation Cup, Rous Memorial, Eclipse Stakes

Windsor Lad was considered the best horse of his age, a fine stayer with a good turn of speed.

After being unplaced in his first two races as a two year old, he won the Criterion Stakes. He then won nine of his next ten races, his only defeat being when he came third in the Eclipse Stakes as a three year old.

Between winning the Derby and the St. Leger in 1934, Windsor Lad was sold by the Maharajah of Rajpipla to the English bookmaker Martin H. Benson with the stipulation that the stallion should never leave England. He thus became the first horse since 1827 to have changed hands after winning the Derby and the only horse to win both events under different ownership. His St. Leger victory was achieved in a time which equalled the record set for the race by **Coronach** in 1926.

60036 COLOMBO

Winner: 1933   Norfolk Stakes, Richmond Stakes
             1934   Craven Stakes, 2000 Guineas

Having won the 2000 Guineas and the oldest of the trial fixtures, the Craven Stakes, Colombo was entered for the 1934 Derby as clear favourite.

Nowhere is superstition more rife than in horse racing, and the Craven Stakes was regarded as being particularly unlucky so far as the Derby was concerned, no winner of the trial fixture having succeeded in the

Derby since 1898. True to tradition (and with the aid of a little "pilot error" on the part of his jockey) Colombo failed as one of the hottest favourites in many years, the race being won by **Windsor Lad.**

60037 HYPERION

Winner:	1932	Dewhurst Stakes, Norfolk Stakes
	1933	Chester Vase, the Derby, the Prince of Wales's Stakes, the St. Leger

Son of **Gainsborough**, Hyperion was one of the most celebrated and revered thoroughbreds in racing history. Following his two classic wins in 1933 (the Derby and the St. Leger), the horse was subsequently England's champion sire five times.

Barely more than 15 hands, and described as a "short-legged, light-boned colt" Hyperion was extremely lazy and had to be worked hard to achieve race fitness. Nevertheless, he achieved 9 wins in 13 starts (with one second and two thirds) before being retired to stud in 1935.

The ease of his Derby victory, in a new record time, made Hyperion something of a public idol. As photographs of the event appear to confirm, the winning margin was at least double the official four lengths; the race judge subsequently confessed to having made "a conservative estimate".

Hyperion's progeny included *Owen Tudor, Sun Chariot, Hycilla, Sun Stream* and *Sun Castle.*

60038 FIRDAUSSI

Winner:	1931	Dewhurst Stakes
	1932	Jockey Club Stakes, Gordon Stakes, the St. Leger

Bred and owned by the Aga Khan, and described as "a big, lusty chestnut", Firdaussi won 8 races from 21 starts.

60039 SANDWICH

Winner: 1931   St. Leger

Born in 1928, Sandwich displayed an ideal mix of speed and stamina. As a three year old, he ran fifth in the Craven Stakes, was almost last in the 2000 Guineas but, six days later, won the Chester Vase.

Despite closing fast in the final stretch, Sandwich came third in the Derby (won by **Cameronian**), went on to win the King Edward VII Stakes and then the St. Leger, by four lengths, coming from behind, as was his style.

He did not produce much of value in the stud.

60040 CAMERONIAN

Winner: 1931   St. James's Palace Stakes, 2000 Guineas, the Derby

This little colt was sired by **Gainsborough** in 1928. As a three year old, he came third in the Craven Stakes, but won the 2000 Guineas, the Derby and St. James's Palace Stakes in quick succession. Sadly, the Triple Crown eluded him when he came last in the St. Leger; he was subsequently found to be unwell.

At stud, Cameronian sired *Scottish Union* and the dam of *Chamossaire*; he was exported to Argentina in 1941.

60041 SALMON TROUT

Winner: 1924   Dewhurst Stakes, the Princess of Wales's Stakes, the St. Leger

Born in 1921, Salmon Trout was the last of the St. Leger winners sired by **The Tetrarch**, his dam being a daughter of **St. Frusquin**.

Purchased as a yearling for 3000 guineas he raced for the Aga Khan. On retirement, he was sent to stud in South Africa.

60042 SINGAPORE

Winner: 1930   St. Leger
               1931   Doncaster Cup

This son of **Gainsborough**, born in 1927, did not race as a two year old. At three, he won just once at Sandown, but then improved steadily throughout the year. With Gordon Richards in the saddle, he started as joint-favourite for the St. Leger, a race which he won easily.

The following season, he was unlucky not to win the Ascot Gold Cup, the winner having barged into him in the final furlong. He ended the season by winning the Jockey Club Stakes and was retired to stud, siring Chulmlegh, also a winner of the St. Leger.

He was sold to Brazil in 1943.

60043 BROWN JACK

Winner: 1928   Champion Hurdle
        1929-34   Queen Alexandra Stakes
           1930   Goodwood Cup, Doncaster Cup
           1931   Chester Cup, Ebor Handicap
           1932   Prince Edward Handicap
           1933   Rosebery Handicap

Brown Jack was one of the 'stars' in the A3 firmament. No flat racer in Britain has ever enjoyed such popularity. Usually ridden by the revered Steve Donoghue, who sent the horse a congratulatory telegram on his 20th birthday, Brown Jack became a national institution. Born in Ireland, the horse first changed hands as a yearling for £110. Reputedly fat, lazy and lethargic, he came last in his first race in 1927. By the end of his career he had run in 55 races and had won no fewer than 25 of them, being placed 12 times.

In his early career, the horse ran in 10 races under National Hunt Rules, winning 7 of them and being placed twice. Following his victory in the Champion Hurdle in 1928, Brown Jack returned to racing on the flat, apparently at Donoghue's suggestion. Appropriately, his true domain was Royal Ascot and his fame in the annals of the Turf is due primarily to his marvellous record in the Queen Alexandra Stakes, which he won six years in succession from 1929 to 1934.

The 1934 event, the moment of his true apotheosis, involved a famous tussle between an ageing Brown Jack and a horse named Solatium, to whom he was conceding 8 lbs and 6 years. The scenes which followed his victory by two lengths were the stuff of horse racing legend as ecstatic racegoers pushed and jostled their way to the unsaddling enclosure to express their idolatry of this great old horse. By all accounts, their hero milked the applause, seemingly pausing at the entrance to the winner's enclosure to ensure that all his admirers were in place before walking in to a great ovation.

60044 MELTON

Winner	1884	Norfolk Stakes, Middle Park Stakes
	1885	The Derby, St. Leger
	1886	July Cup

In May, 1985, the aristocratic owner of Melton received a telegram of congratulation from his friend Oscar Wilde which read:-

"I understand that Milton's 'Paradise Lost' is being revived and will appear in Derby Week and will be published under the title 'Paradox Lost' by Melton."

The horse had just won the 1885 Derby from Paradox through a brilliant piece of riding from the legendary Fred Archer, whose career produced 2,748 winners and 21 Classic victories.

60045 LEMBERG

Winner:	1909	Norfolk Stakes, Middle Park Stakes, Dewhurst Stakes
	1910	Champion Stakes, Jockey Club Stakes, the Derby, St. James's Palace Stakes, Eclipse Stakes (dead heat with **Neil Gow)**
	1911	Champion Stakes, Coronation Cup, Doncaster Cup

(See 60082 **Neil Gow**)

A talented horse, and top two year old, Lemberg was seemingly overshadowed by his marginally more successful half-brother, **Bayardo**.

Retired to the stud in Newmarket, Lemberg was the leading British sire in 1922. He died in 1928 at the age of 21.

60046 DIAMOND JUBILEE

> Winner: 1900   2000 Guineas, the Derby, Eclipse Stakes, St. Leger

One of the eight winners of the Triple Crown celebrated in the names of the A3's, Diamond Jubilee, reputedly a fiery colt and notoriously difficult to ride, was full brother to the 1896 Derby and St. Leger winner **Persimmon**, also owned by the Prince of Wales

60047 DONOVAN

> Winner: 1888   Norfolk Stakes, July Stakes, Middle Park Stakes,
> Dewhurst Stakes
> 1889   The Derby, Prince of Wales's Stakes, St. Leger

A bay colt sired by **Galopin** in 1886, Donovan was undoubtedly one of the best British racehorses of the late nineteenth century, with only three defeats in twenty one starts. He was, however, fated to live in the shadow of his legendary half-brother, **St. Simon**.

Donovan, the dominant two year old of his generation was a firm favourite to win the classic races of 1889. Having won the Prince of Wales's Stakes at Leicester, he shocked the racing world by coming second in the 2000 Guineas to a colt he had soundly beaten in the earlier race. This was all the more regrettable because Donovan easily won that season's Derby and St. Leger.

Having broken down in training, he was retired to the stud where he was not particularly successful. He was shot on 1st February,

1905, having severely injured himself after running into a tree in his paddock.

60048 DONCASTER

Winner:	1873	The Derby
	1874	Goodwood Cup
	1875	Ascot Gold Cup

Given the close association between the LNER and the railway town of Doncaster, one might readily assume that this was one of the four A3's not associated with racehorses. Doncaster was, in fact, the winner of several classic races, including the 1873 Derby at odds of 45-1.

This handsome, blaze-faced, chestnut colt was foaled in 1870. Finishing unplaced in the 2000 Guineas of 1873, Doncaster developed very quickly. He easily won that year's Derby, finished third in the French Grand Prix in Paris and was beaten by a short head in the St. Leger.

Because of his exceptional pedigree and proven form in the classic races, after his 1875 victories in the Ascot Gold Cup and the Alexandra Plate, Doncaster was selected as the cornerstone of the rebuilding of the Duke of Westminster's Eaton stud at Chester. He was eventually sold to the Empress of Austria and died in her ownership in 1892.

The horse was originally named All Heart and No Peel! Its descendants included **Ormonde** and **Flying Fox**, both winners of the coveted English Triple Crown.

60049 GALTEE MORE

Winner:	1896	Molecomb Stakes, Middle Park Stakes
	1897	2000 Guineas, the Derby, St. Leger

Another celebrated winner of the Triple Crown, this big, bay thoroughbred was the first Irish-bred horse to triumph in the Derby at Epsom.

Sired in 1894, Galtee More was named after the highest peak of the Galtee Mountains overlooking the Golden Vale. Following his transfer to Newmarket, the horse emerged as one of the best two year olds of his generation. At three, the year in which he won the Triple Crown, he proved nearly unbeatable.

He was subsequently sold to the Russian government for £21,000 and became a successful sire in Russia and, later, in Germany.

Galtee More died in January, 1917, aged 23 years. While being loaded aboard a train for shipment to a stud at Hoppengarten, the stallion unfortunately slipped and sustained a broken leg.

60050 PERSIMMON

Winner:	1895	Coventry Stakes, Richmond Stakes
	1896	Jockey Club Stakes, the Derby, St. Leger
	1897	Ascot Gold Cup, Eclipse Stakes

Persimmon was the full brother of **Diamond Jubilee** and one of the celebrated trio of Classic winners owned by the future Edward VII (the others being Diamond Jubilee and **Minoru).** The then Prince Edward ploughed the prize money, millions of pounds in today's terms, into the Sandringham Estate, particularly the vast walled gardens. When his guests expressed amazement at the acres of kitchen garden, herbaceous borders, ornamental pergolas and greenhouses full of exotic fruit, he replied simply; "All Persimmon, all Persimmon".

A life-size bronze statue of the Prince of Wales's great champion stands outside the Royal Stud at Sandringham; Persimmon's stuffed head is displayed at the National Horseracing Museum in Newmarket.

60051 BLINK BONNY

Winner:	1855	Gimcrack Stakes
	1857	The Derby, the Oaks

Blink Bonny was one of only 5 fillies to win the Derby, in a record time of 2 min. 45 secs.

Following a tough race in the 1857 Derby she won the Oaks (a race for three year old fillies over 1½ miles) with great ease. She ought to have gone on to win the St. Leger, for which she started odds-on favourite, but was reined back by her jockey, John Charlton, at the instigation of a crooked bookmaker named Jackson.

60052 PRINCE PALATINE

Winner:	1911	The Gordon Stakes, St. Leger
	1912	Jockey Club Stakes, Eclipse Stakes, Doncaster Cup, Ascot Gold Cup
	1913	Coronation Cup, Ascot Gold Cup

Prince Palatine and **Tracery**, the St. Leger winners of 1911 and 1912 respectively, met in opposition for the first time in the race for the 1913 Ascot Gold Cup, with Prince Palatine as odds-on favourite.

Four furlongs from home Tracery was in the lead with Prince Palatine, going along easily, in fourth position about 20 lengths behind. Tracery suddenly disappeared from view. It transpired that a man named Hewitt had rushed onto the course brandishing a suffragist flag in one hand – echoes of the earlier incident resulting in the death of Emily Davison at Tattenham Corner – and a fully loaded revolver in the other. Hewitt was bowled over by Tracery and seriously injured; Tracery fell and Prince Palatine was obliged to jump over him, going on to win the race in a record time.

Sold to stud in both England and France, in 1920 Prince Palatine was sold on to a breeder in Kentucky and shipped to the U.S.A. Four years later, the horse was burned to death in a stable fire.

60053 SANSOVINO

Winner:	1923	Gimcrack Stakes
	1924	The Derby, Prince of Wales' Stakes

One of the unbroken sequence of Derby winners 1917-31 commemorated in the names of the A3's. Sansovino was the sire of

Sandwich, winner of the 1931 St. Leger.

Sansovino's six-length victory in the Derby was in a driving rainstorm on a very heavy course which seems to have suited this big, strong colt better than his competitors.

The following season, he broke down in the Jockey Club Cup, his final start, and was retired to the stud.

60054 PRINCE OF WALES*

One of the four locomotives in the class not associated with racehorses although, as LNER No. 2553, the engine had originally been named **Manna** (see 60085). It was renamed in 1926 following a visit to the Doncaster Works by the Prince of Wales, who had inspected the locomotive during his tour of the workshops and facilities.

60055 WOOLWINDER

Winner: 1907   Sussex Stakes, St. Leger

This bay colt, foaled in 1904, won nine races during his career and was beaten only once as a three year old; unfortunately, that "once" was the Derby, in which he came second.

Woolwinder went on to win the 1907 St. Leger, which he entered as favourite in a field of twelve, in good weather and before a large crowd, which included King Edward VII.

60056 CENTENARY*

Despite the resonance in the name, Centenary was another of the handful of A3's not named after racehorses . The engine was so named because it was the first locomotive built at Doncaster Works in 1925, the year of the railway centenary celebrations.

60057 ORMONDE

Winner:	1885	Dewhurst Stakes
	1886	Champion Stakes, Hardwicke Stakes, 2000 Guineas, the Derby, St. Leger
	1887	Hardwicke Stakes, July Cup

Never beaten in any race, Ormonde won the Triple Crown in 1886 when ridden by Fred Archer.

This bay colt, born in 1883, was said to be the finest racehorse of the nineteenth century, and perhaps of all time.

He won all 15 high-class races he entered in his career, many of them by a distance and giving away weight. Dubbed "The Horse of the Century", Ormonde was the toast of England and of racing society world-wide. After his last race, he was guest of honour at a Mayfair garden party given by his owner, the Duke of Westminster, to celebrate Queen Victoria's Jubilee.

It subsequently came as a shock to many that, after only two seasons at stud in England, he was sold to Argentina. Despite being almost infertile, Ormonde went on to produce foals on three continents and both hemispheres.

In May, 1904, at the age of 21 years, facing increasing difficulty in breathing and a sudden onset of partial paralysis, Ormonde was humanely destroyed and buried in California. He was later exhumed and his bones returned to England.

The skeleton of this classic racehorse resides in the Natural History Museum in London.

60058 BLAIR ATHOL

Winner:	1864	The Derby, Jersey Stakes, St.Leger

This son of **Blink Bonny,** born in 1861, was leading sire in Great Britain and Ireland in 1872, 1873, 1875 and 1877, his progeny winning six of the English classic races.

60059 TRACERY

Winner: 1911   Sussex Stakes
                 1912   St. James's Palace Stakes, St. Leger
                 1913   Eclipse Stakes, Champion Stakes

Although of English pedigree, Tracery was bred in the United States and owned by the President of the New York Jockey Club.

Tracery was the best sire son of the Triple Crown winner, Rock Sand, who had been sold to stud in the USA when his racing days were over. Sent to England, Tracey was unraced as a two year old due to spavins and other problems.

His first race at three was the Derby, in which he was soundly beaten by **Tagalie**. Thereafter, he improved considerably and showed himself to be a plucky and versatile competitor. His winning run was interrupted when, in the Ascot Gold Cup, a mentally unstable man dashed into his path, bringing him down. (See 60052 **Prince Palatine)**

After his 1913 victories, Tracery was retired to the stud (including a spell in Argentina) where he was moderately successful. Following his return to England, he died, in 1924, from complications following colic.

60060 THE TETRARCH

Winner: 1913   Coventry Stakes, Champagne Stakes

Described as "possibly the fastest horse ever seen on the English Turf" Ireland's 'spotted wonder' won the 1913 Coventry Stakes at Ascot by ten lengths.

This big, speckled, black-and-white colt only raced as a two year old, but the impression he left was one of unlimited speed and untested talent. When he first appeared at Newmarket, racegoers made a joke of his resemblance to a child's rocking horse. The joke was on them when, ridden by Steve Donoghue, The Tetrarch (placed third in the betting) "exploded" away from his 22 rivals to win his debut by four lengths 'in a canter'.

He won his next two races with comparative ease, but was almost beaten in the National Breeders' Produce Stakes at Sandown because of a bad start due, apparently, to him becoming entangled in the tapes at the off. He redeemed himself by trouncing his opponents in his next three races, including the Champagne Stakes at Doncaster, acquiring a reputation as probably the greatest two year old of all time and, potentially, the greatest runner ever.

Shortly afterwards, The Tetrarch was injured in training and withdrawn for the remainder of the season, going into winter quarters as the heavy favourite for the Derby. Sadly, his injured leg failed to heal and he was retired to stud in Ireland with an untarnished record of seven wins in seven starts.

He was retired from the stud in 1926, serving as a hack to pick up mail from the local village and run other errands. He died at Ballyfinch Stud in 1935 at the age of 24; his grave is marked by a plaque commemorating his achievements.

The Tetrarch was champion sire in 1919, his progeny having won stakes to the value of nearly £28,000. He was the sire of **Salmon Trout**, winner of the St. Leger in 1924.

60061 PRETTY POLLY

Winner:
1903 Champagne Stakes, Cheveley Park Stakes, Middle Park Stakes
1904 1000 Guineas, the Oaks, Coronation Stakes, Nassau Stakes, Park Hill Stakes, St. Leger
1905 Coronation Cup, Jockey Club Cup, Champion Stakes
1906 Coronation Cup

Indisputably, one of the greatest racemares of all time.

Exceptional from the start of her career, in which she won 22 of 24 races run during the period 1902 to 1906, Pretty Polly won her first race, the British Dominion Plate at Sandown by 10 lengths according to the official record, although the consensus of opinion apparently placed the margin of victory at about 40 lengths. The filly won her eight other races of the 1903 season and seven out of eight in 1904, including the 1000 Guineas at Newmarket and the St. Leger. In 1905, she also won all her races and in 1906, her last year of racing, won two more. Her total winnings exceeded £37,000.

In the 1904 season, Pretty Polly was entered to run (and won) the 1000 Guineas, the Oaks and the St. Leger but not, unfortunately, the 2000 Guineas or the Derby. This is unfortunate, because it was generally considered at the time that the mare would have gone on to win all five Classic races and, in so doing, would have taken the record held by **Sceptre** in winning four of them (losing in only the Derby, in which she came fourth).

Pretty Polly just missed being a contemporary of Sceptre, her senior by two years. Taken together, their careers spanned the period 1901 to 1905 which era witnessed the triumphs – and occasional failures – of two of the greatest mares ever seen on the Turf.

In the 1906 Ascot Gold Cup, Pretty Polly was beaten into second place by *Bachelor's Button*, the winning distance being no more than a length. **Cicero**, the 1905 winner of the Derby, was unplaced. The silence which greeted Pretty Polly when she reached the winning post reflected the crowd's widespread regret at her failure. The winner was denied the cheer he deserved, almost as if the public resented the way he had robbed them of seeing the great mare crown her exceptional career by winning the most highly-prized of the honours to be gained at Ascot. Pretty Polly had no chance to make amends; she suffered a setback in training and retired.

Pretty Polly's only other defeat was in the Autumn of 1904, when she was beaten in the Prix du Conseil Municipal at Longchamp after a long and tiring journey. She had gone to France the unbeaten winner of 15 races, including the 1000 Guineas, the Oaks and the St. Leger; it was so taken for granted that she would return home still unbeaten that the news of her downfall came as a great shock to the racing world.

60062 MINORU

Winner: 1909 Greenham Stakes, 2000 Guineas, the Derby, St. James's
Palace Stakes, Sussex Stakes

This horse was the third of Edward VII's outstanding Classic winners, the others being **Persimmon** and **Diamond Jubilee.**

Minoru was one of four winners of the Epsom Derby sired by the chestnut stallion Cyllene, the others being **Cicero, Lemberg** and the filly **Tagalie.** He was a bay colt of 1906, bred in Ireland and leased to run in the colours of King Edward VII. At first, he showed little promise or potential but, following a successful outing in the Greenham Stakes at Newbury, it was decided to enter him for the 2000 Guineas. He won that race in fine style, beating the favourite **Bayardo,** who was short on training, into fourth place.

Minoru was then entered for the Derby, preferred in the betting to Bayardo, with both colts losing favouritism to the American horse Sir Martin.

During the race, Sir Martin fell and impeded several runners, including Bayardo. Minoru was in the handy position of being in the right place at the right time, avoided the mix-up and went on to win by a head. He entered three more races in the colours of the King, before Edward's death in 1910 ended the lease agreement.

Following the King's death, Minoru was exported to Russia where – so the story goes – he was seized by the Bolsheviks during the revolution and executed (i.e. shot) because of his aristocratic background and associations! Whatever the truth of the matter, it is a fact that both he and *Aboyeur,* who had also been exported to stud, disappeared during the revolution and were never seen again. In direct contrast to their Derby successes, both horses now had the misfortune to be in the wrong place at the wrong time!

60063 ISINGLASS

Winner: 1892 Norfolk Stakes, Middle Park Stakes
1893 2000 Guineas, the Derby, St. Leger

1894   Jockey Club Stakes, Eclipse Stakes,
        Princess of Wales's Stakes
1895   Ascot Gold Cup

Another winner of the Triple Crown (1893). During his racing career, Isinglass earned record winnings for a British horse not surpassed until 1952.

Foaled in 1890, Isinglass was a big, strongly- built colt with an extreme streak of laziness. He would not exert himself, either in training or when racing, but was still exceptional enough to win all three races in which he was entered as a two year old, and, with them, the Triple Crown. In the 2000 Guineas, the indolent Isinglass won by three quarters of a length and went on to win the Derby by a length and a half. Later in the year he won the St. Leger by half a length.

The aura of invincibility which then surrounded Isinglass was dented somewhat when he finished second in his next race, the Lancashire Plate. He was never defeated again. As a four year old, he won all four races in which he was entered in 1894, although he only narrowly avoided defeat in the Princess of Wales's Stakes. The ground was hard, Isinglass had developed the habit of eating his bedding as well as his own droppings, causing digestive upsets, and had to carry a staggering 143 lb against the other highly-fancied horses entered for the race, including the 2000 Guineas and Derby winner **Ladas**. Isinglass won by a head, Ladas coming in third.

On softer ground for the Eclipse Stakes, and again saddled with 142 lb, Isinglass was back to his masterful self and beat Ladas into second place.

Isinglass retired with eleven victories from twelve starts, having repeatedly demonstrated his superiority over his rivals. He proved somewhat disappointing at stud, in that he failed to sire a Derby winner, although he did produce three classic winners plus two sons who went on to become very influential stallions.

60064 TAGALIE

Winner: 1912   1000 Guineas, the Derby

Tagalie holds the unique distinction of being the only grey filly to have won the Derby, beating **Tracery** (winner of the 1912 St. Leger) into third place.

As a juvenile, Tagalie won the Post Stakes and finished third in the Cheveley Park Stakes. In the following Spring, she won the 1000 Guineas at odds of 20-1 and finished a good second in the Newmarket Stakes. After an effortless win in the Derby, she finished unplaced in each of her three remaining races.

Tagalie was a disappointment in the stud, producing only four foals. She died soon after foaling in 1920, at the age of eleven.

This locomotive was originally named *William Whitelaw*, after the Chairman of the LNER. In 1941, the name was transferred to an A4 Class 'Pacific' (formerly Great Snipe).

60065 KNIGHT OF THISTLE

Winner: 1897   Royal Hunt Cup

This locomotive was correctly named Knight of **the** Thistle (after the horse which had won the 1897 Cup) until 1932, when new name plates were fitted, omitting "the".

Some claim that this was merely an error in the casting of new plates which was never subsequently rectified. Others contend that the omission was deliberate, in order to mitigate offence caused to the Order of the Thistle and to Lord Lyon, King of Arms and Secretary of the Order. Quite why the naming of a locomotive after a racehorse should have incurred his displeasure is not clear but, if this was the case, the chosen remedy (i.e. to omit "the") was both inappropriate and meaningless.

An alternative solution would have been the use of a substitute name – a common enough practice – and there was no shortage of suitable contenders whose accomplishments equalled or surpassed those of Knight of the Thistle.

Perhaps the most obvious choice would have been "Rock Sand", winner of the 1903 Triple Crown, whose name had been considered for inclusion in the second batch of A3 names but was not ultimately selected.

60066 MERRY HAMPTON

Winner: 1887   The Derby

Merry Hampton has sometimes been criticised as one of the least capable winners of the Derby, his only victory, although he came close to winning the St. Leger. Although talented, he proved difficult to train and his racing career was cut short because of delicate legs which were prone to injury or damage.

Merry Hampton was also a failure as a sire, producing no runners of note.

60067 LADAS

Winner: 1893   Coventry Stakes, Champagne Stakes, Middle Park
                    Stakes
           1894   2000 Guineas, the Derby

Named after the swiftest of Alexander the Great's runners, Ladas was a prolific winner during 1893/94 but failed to win another race. He was beaten by **Isinglass** in both the Princess of Wales's Stakes at Newmarket and the Eclipse Stakes at Sandown, results which showed that while Ladas was a good horse, his four year old rival was a better one. Ladas was subsequently defeated in both the St. Leger and the Jockey Club Stakes and retired to stud. He became quick tempered and increasingly difficult to handle and was put down in 1914.

60068 SIR VISTO

Winner: 1895   The Derby, St. Leger

As a two year old Sir Visto raced twice. He won the Imperial Produce Stakes at Kempton and was unplaced in the Woodcote Stakes at Epsom.

In the following year (1895), he came third in both the 2000 Guineas and the Newmarket Stakes. It was already evident that the three year olds that season included no horses of exceptional merit and that anything might happen in the Derby. Sir Visto's owner, Lord Rosebery, had as good cause as anybody to be hopeful of victory, if only because his horse was bred to stay. Coming around Tattenham Corner with seven horses ahead of him, Sir Visto's prospects must have seemed almost hopeless but the horse's stamina began to tell and he got up to win the race by ¾ of a length.

After a failure in the Princess of Wales's Stakes a month later, Sir Visto waited for the St. Leger, for which he started favourite, to again win by ¾ of a length. He was then beaten in the Jockey Club Stakes and, as a four year old, ran 5 times, also unsuccessfully.

In retrospect, Sir Visto is viewed as a very moderate performer both on the Turf and, subsequently, at the stud. He was destroyed in 1914, a few months after **Ladas** had been put down.

60069 SCEPTRE

Winner: 1901   July Stakes
            1902   1000 Guineas, 2000 Guineas, the Oaks, St. James's Palace Stakes, Nassau Stakes, St. Leger
            1903   Jockey Club Stakes, Hardwicke Stakes, Champion Stakes

Sceptre, a bay filly sired in 1899 by **Persimmon**, was destined to become a racing legend in her own lifetime.

In 1902, as a three year old, she became the only horse in history to win four English Classics and went on to achieve the second-highest total ever of classic wins.

Despite her undoubted prowess, Sceptre's offspring were largely disappointing racehorses. She died in 1926 at the age of 27.

(See 60061 **Pretty Polly** for information regarding these two legendary fillies)

60070 GLADIATEUR

Winner: 1865   2000 Guineas, the Derby, St. Leger
              1866   Ascot Gold Cup

Winner of the 1865 Triple Crown (as part of a nine race winning sequence) when the French-bred colt's victory shook the foundations of the British racing establishment, much to the obvious delight of an ecstatic Parisian press which dubbed Gladiateur "the avenger of Waterloo". The horse had little difficulty in successfully challenging the supremacy of English thoroughbreds despite having a grossly enlarged joint on his foreleg as a result of being trodden on when a foal.

Following his death, Gladiateur's tail, which now resides in the National Horseracing Museum at Newmarket, was presented by the French jockey club to their English counterparts, with the proud boast that this was the only part of the colt's anatomy that English racehorses ever saw!

60071 TRANQUIL

Winner: 1923   1000 Guineas, St. Leger, Jockey Club Cup

Foaled in 1920 and bred by Lord Derby, Tranquil had a successful season as a three year old in 1923 (beating **Papyrus** in the St. Leger) but was not a good broodmare.

60072 SUNSTAR

Winner: 1911   2000 Guineas, the Derby

Sunstar's two classic wins came as a three year old. Having won the 2000 Guineas, he entered the Derby as favourite, although the odds might have been different had it been widely known that he was nursing an injury sustained in training. As it was, he won convincingly, despite breaking down short of the wire, as his trainer had correctly predicted.

Sunstar was a great success as a sire and as a broodmare sire. **Book Law**, winner of the 1927 St. Leger, was one of his sons.

60073 ST. GATIEN

Winner: 1884   The Derby (dead heat with **Harvester**), the Queen's Vase, Jockey Club Cup, Cesarewitch Handicap
            1885   Ascot Gold Cup, Jockey Club Cup
            1886   Jockey Club Cup

60074 HARVESTER

Winner: 1884   The Derby (dead heat with **St. Gatien**)

Harvester was a bay colt foaled in 1881. Following two good wins as a juvenile, at age three he won the Payne Stakes at Newmarket, came third in the 2000 Guineas and shared honours with St. Gatien in the Epsom Derby.

He had only moderate influence as a sire.

60075 ST. FRUSQUIN

Winner: 1895   Middle Park Stakes, Dewhurst Stakes
            1896   2000 Guineas, Eclipse Stakes, Princess of Wales's Stakes

One of the most celebrated racing rivalries of the nineteenth century was between two outstanding sons of leading sire **St. Simon**:

St. Frusquin and **Persimmon**. They met three times, St. Fruquin wining twice.

Although lacking the sleekness and elegance of Persimmon, and suffering from rheumatism throughout his racing career, St. Frusquin, bred and raced by Leopold de Rothschild, was defeated only twice in eleven starts, coming second on both occasions.

He enjoyed a long and successful career at the stud. He was leading sire twice, compared to Persimmon's four times, but did produce six classic winners, compared to Persimmon's five.

St. Frusquin was put down at the age of 21 in 1914, having outlived Persimmon by six years.

60076 GALOPIN

| Winner: | 1874 | Norfolk Stakes |
| | 1875 | The Derby |

Although never really tested, Galopin was brilliant and versatile as a racer (winning all five of his starts at age three) and very successful at the stud.

He was the sire of **Donovan** and **St. Simon**; his grandsons included **St. Frusquin**.

He died in June, 1899, at the ripe old age of 27.

60077 THE WHITE KNIGHT

Winner:	1906	Queen's Vase, Newbury Autumn Cup
	1907	Ascot Gold Cup, Coronation Cup, Goodwood Cup
	1908	Ascot Gold Cup, Coronation Cup

Bred in Ireland, The White Knight was the outstanding stayer of his generation and the only colt ever to have won the Coronation Cup at Epsom twice (in 1907 and 1908).

60078 NIGHT HAWK

Winner: 1913   St. Leger

After an indifferent career as a three year old, Night Hawk entered the St. Leger at odds of 100-1 in a not particularly exciting field, many of the best competitors having either been sold abroad or broken down. He won by two lengths in a field of ten other horses, this being his only ever win.

He was subsequently sold to Australia, where he was equally unimpressive as a stallion.

60079 BAYARDO

Winner: 1908   Hardwicke Stakes, Richmond Stakes, Middle Park
                          Stakes, Dewhurst Stakes, New Stakes
               1909   Prince of Wales's Stakes, Eclipse Stakes, St. Leger,
                          Champion Stakes
               1910   Chester Vase, Ascot Gold Cup

When Bayardo died prematurely from thrombosis in 1917, aged eleven, his son **Gay Crusader** had won only the first of the three races which gave him that year's Triple Crown. Another son, **Gainsborough**, who was to capture the Triple Crown of 1918, had yet to make his appearance as a two year old.

Bayardo made his first public appearance at Ascot in 1908 where he won the New Stakes easily. This was the first of seven races he won that season, in which he was unbeaten.

In 1909 Bayardo came a poor fifth in the Derby (won by **Minoru**) and fourth in the 2000 Guineas (also won by **Minoru**). Following these failures, he took every opportunity to demonstrate the outstanding qualities with which he had been blessed and, from Derby Day 1909 to August of the following year, carried everything before him.

As a three year old, Bayardo won eleven races, including the Eclipse Stakes and the St. Leger. The following season he won the Ascot Gold Cup and three other races. Of all the previous Ascot Cup winners, only *Batchelor's Button* had covered the 2½ miles in faster time (by just one fifth of a second) no doubt due to being pressed towards the finish by **Pretty Polly.**

In 1910, Bayardo was defeated in the Goodwood Cup, possibly because he had been given a task – in terms of weight and age conceded – which was beyond even his capabilities. This was his last appearance on a racecourse and in 1911 he was retired to the stud.

60080 DICK TURPIN

> Winner: 1933   Chester Cup

Although it is not clear why this particular racehorse was included in the class – it can hardly have been on the basis of its track record or the number of classic wins - the name "Dick Turpin" will have been associated in the minds of some racegoers with equestrian exploits of quite a different nature although, sadly, the truth of the matter bears only passing resemblance to the legend.

The popular image of Dick Turpin is derived almost entirely from Harrison Ainsworth's novel "Rookwood" (1834) which romanticised his escapades as a highwayman. It was this book that introduced Turpin's most famous exploit: his ride from London to York on the horse Black Bess. It is, however, more likely that the ride was made almost two hundred years earlier by another highwayman, "Swift John" Nevison, who had robbed and killed a sailor at Gadshill at 4.00 am but established an alibi by arriving in York at 7.45 pm on the same day.

Ironically, Turpin does have indirect associations with the Turf. In 1739 he was arrested in York for horse stealing and hanged on the present-day site of York Race Course.

60081 SHOTOVER

> Winner: 1882   2000 Guineas, the Derby, King Edward VII Stakes,
> Jersey Stakes, Park Hill Stakes

This chestnut filly, foaled in 1879, came only third in the 1882 St. Leger and thereby failed in her attempt to carry off the Triple Crown.

60082 NEIL GOW

Winner: 1909   Champagne Stakes, Prince of Wales's Stakes, Imperial Produce Stakes
           1910   Craven Stakes, 2000 Guineas, Eclipse Stakes (dead heat with **Lemberg**)

In 1909, as a two year old and after two failures, Neil Gow won the National Breeders Produce Stakes, the Prince of Wales's Stakes at Goodwood, the Champagne Stakes at Doncaster and the Imperial Produce Stakes at Kempton.

His performance in this last race was one of the most extraordinary ever seen. In going described as "dreadfully heavy", Neil Gow had only two opponents. At the off, when the barrier was raised, the horse whipped round and began to race in the opposite direction. By the time the jockey had checked him and turned him round, his two opponents were nearly a furlong away. To everyone's surprise, Neil Gow and his jockey set off in pursuit and, no doubt because of the very heavy going, gradually closed the gap to win by a head.

In the 2000 Guineas the following year, there was a memorable duel between Neil Gow and **Lemberg**. For two furlongs they raced side by side with never more than a head between them. Neil Gow eventually won by a short head.

In the Derby, won by **Lemberg**, Neil Gow finished fourth. He and **Lemberg** met again in the Eclipse Stakes to repeat their earlier thrilling tussle in the 2000 Guineas. This time, they ran a dead heat.

A few weeks later, Neil Gow broke down with irreparable trouble in one of his hocks and began his stud career the following season. He did not achieve distinction as a sire.

For the uninitiated, and those interested in the name within a name,

Neil Gow (1727-1807) was by far the best known of the Scots fiddle composers, from whose dance tunes *Robert Burns* drew many of the airs for his songs. Gow is regarded as the father of Strathspey and Reel music, composing over 200 Scottish airs. Successive Dukes of Athol became his patron. Along with his brother and sons, Neil Gow formed an ensemble which played at Highland weddings and balls in the great houses of Scotland.

60083 SIR HUGO

Winner:　　1892　　The Derby

Sir Hugo won the Derby as a rank outsider, beating the much-fancied La Fleche, a winning daughter of **St. Simon**.

60084 TRIGO

Winner:　　1929　　The Derby, St. Leger

Trigo, foaled in 1926, was a successful juvenile in Ireland and went on to win six races in England and Ireland at two and three years.

He failed to match expectations in the 2000 Guineas and was entered in the Derby as his stable's second string. On a rain-swept day, he won the race by half a length at odds of 33/1. He won his next start, the St. Leger, and scraped home in the Irish St. Leger a week later.

At the end of 1929, Trigo was retired to the stud, where he failed to impress.

60085 MANNA

Winner:　　1924　　Richmond Stakes
　　　　　　1925　　2000 Guineas, the Derby

Manna easily won the 1925 2000 Guineas and the Derby (the latter by eight lengths) but, despite being the odds-on favourite for the

45

race, could only manage tenth place in the St. Leger. At the end of the race, he came off the track lame, his Triple Crown hopes having been dashed by a knee sprain, possibly sustained en route to the start line.

At stud, Manna sired **Colombo**, himself a 2000 Guineas winner.

60086 GAINSBOROUGH

Winner: 1918   200 Guineas, the Derby, Ascot Gold Cup, St. Leger

The thirteenth winner of the English Triple Crown, Gainsborough was the first horse to win a classic race in the racing colours of a woman owner – Lady James Douglas.

His 1918 feat (including victory in the 2000 Guineas by no fewer than 112 lengths) was not repeated until 1934 by *Bahram* and, subsequently, by Nijinsky II in 1970.

Gainsborough was the son of **Bayardo** and the sire of **Hyperion** and **Solario**. His bloodlines remain influential today.

Despite the romantic association in the name, Gainsborough was not named after the famous portrait painter but as a result of searches by his owner through the then current railway guide. After turning page after page she eventually alighted upon Gainsborough which she selected as "sounding well and having a good masculine ring about it."

60087 BLENHEIM

Winner: 1929   Norfolk Stakes
            1930   The Derby

Blenheim's victory in the 1930 Derby represented one of the most memorable runnings of this historic race – particularly over the last two furlongs – when the Aga Kahn's 18/1 outsider, almost unobserved, made a sustained run well away from the rails to collar and beat the leading two horses by one and two lengths respectively.

Contemporary reports refer to "a stunned silence that could almost be felt" as Blenheim, ridden by the celebrated Harry Wragg, swooped down to snatch victory almost on the post.

60088 BOOK LAW

Winner: 1926 Queen Mary Stakes
1927 Jockey Club Stakes, Coronation Stakes, Nassau Stakes, St. Leger

Book Law, foaled in 1924, was a staying filly of the highest quality, but she was also versatile. In addition to her four wins as a three year old, she finished second in both the 1000 Guineas and the Oaks. At four, she finished third in both the Coronation Cup and the Eclipse Stakes, in the latter to Lord Derby's colt **Fairway**.

At stud, she produced Eclipse Stakes winner Rhodes Scholar and Archive, a non-winning son, who went on to sire the champion jumper Arkle.

60089 FELSTEAD

Winner: 1928 The Derby

Felstead was a bay colt foaled in 1925. His sire was **Spion Kop** and his Dam Sire **Lemberg.**

He entered the Derby with no real prospect of winning after achieving only one moderate second place in four outings as a juvenile. He improved dramatically as a three year old, winning his maiden at Newbury with ease, finishing fourth in the 2000 Guineas and running second over 7 furlongs at Epsom, a distance much too short for him.

This was the Derby in which the favourite, **Fairway**, was unsettled by the unruly behaviour of elements of the crowd; Felstead's superior stamina told in the race and, ridden by Harry Wragg, he won by one and a half lengths.

He had to be withdrawn from the St. Leger because of injury.

At stud, Felstead produced two classic-winning fillies, Rockfel and *Steady Aim.*

60090 GRAND PARADE

Winner: 1919   St. James's Palace Stakes, the Derby

Grand Parade was a black horse, foaled in Ireland in 1910 from a mare reputed to have pulled a cart (but with the impressive name of Grand Geraldine.)

He showed promise as an early two year old, winning in Ireland and England, but was considered to be some way short of the best of his generation. His development continued in the following season but, because of a trace of lameness, he took his place in the Derby field as very much his owner's second string. He came in at 33/1 after a brave run on his first start as a three year old.

After winning a two-horse race at Ascot, Grand Parade went to stud in 1920. He was not a spectacular sire, most of his stock lacking his stamina.

The LNER's worst rail accident occurred near Falkirk in December, 1937. Thirty five people were killed when, in heavy snow and conditions of poor visibility, an express from Edinburgh ran into a stationary train at 60 mph after overrunning signals. The locomotive, a Pacific named "Grand Parade" was irreparably damaged and subsequently scrapped, a replacement being built at Doncaster bearing the same name and number.

60091 CAPTAIN CUTTLE

Winner: 1922   St. James's Palace Stakes, the Derby

WHAT'S IN A NAME

Captain Cuttle, "the best looking horse seen on the British Turf in generations", was born in 1919. A backward colt, he had only one outing at age two, coming second in the Rous Plate at Doncaster.

Having easily won his first race as a three year old, he ran in only third in the 2000 Guineas. Rumours that he lacked stamina were dispelled by his victory in the Derby, which he won by four lengths and in a record time of two-and-half minutes. Following his victory in the St. James's Palace Stakes, he developed tendon trouble and was withdrawn from the St. Leger. At four, he easily won the Prince of Wales's Stakes at Kempton, following which his tendon trouble re-surfaced and he was retired to stud.

60092 FAIRWAY

Winner: 1927 Coventry Stakes, July Stakes, Champagne Stakes
         1928 Eclipse Stakes, Champion Stakes, St. Leger

         1929 Princess of Wales's Stakes, Jockey Club Cup, Champion
               Stakes

Temperamentally, Fairway, the winner of twelve races, was "highly strung" and could get nervous to the point of distraction: he was robbed of probable victory in the 1927 Derby by the behaviour of unruly elements in the crowd who yanked handfuls of hair from his tail as he made his way to the start.

Retired to the stud in 1931, Fairway was the leading sire in 1936, 1939, 1943 and 1944. His progeny included *Blue Peter, Watling Street* and *Honeyway*.

60093 CORONACH

Winner: 1925 Champagne Stakes
         1926 Eclipse Stakes, St. James's Palace Stakes,
               the Derby, St. Leger
         1927 Hardwicke Stakes, Coronation Cup

A big, handsome chestnut, born in 1923. Coronach was the co-champion two year old in England with three wins from four races entered. Having easily won his first race at age three, he was beaten into second place in the 2000 Guineas by **Colorado**. He entered the Derby under a cloud of suspicion about his ability to stay the course, but won easily by five lengths, beating Colorado and 17 others on a soggy track with poor visibility due to constant drizzling rain.

Like **Captain Cuttle**, he went on to win the St. James's Palace Stakes at Ascot. He triumphed in the Eclipse Stakes by six lengths and, finally, in the St. Leger, beating a field of 12 by two lengths.

At age four, despite signs of respiratory problems, he went on to win the Coronation Cup and Hardwicke Stakes. His condition worsened and he was again beaten by Colorado in his last two races.

He was retired to the stud, where he proved to be a disappointment.

60094 COLORADO

Winner: 1925 Coventry Stakes
1926 2000 Guineas
1927 Eclipse Stakes, Princess of Wales's Stakes

The winner of nine races, Colorado was retired to the stud in 1928 and died the following year. He was second leading sire in 1932 and 1933.

(See 60093 **Coronach**)

60095 FLAMINGO

Winner: 1928 2000 Guineas

Sired by *Flamboyant*, Flamingo narrowly won the 2000 Guineas from the much bigger and more imposing grey, Royal Minstrel.

He then entered the Derby as second favourite to **Fairway** (who was unsettled by the behaviour of supposed "admirers" in the crowd), and might have gone on to win, but for some apparent private duel between his jockey and Gordon Richards on Sunny Trace at a pace which neither horse could sustain. **Felstead** came up to win by a length, and Flamingo had to be content with second place.

Flamingo was not particularly successful as a sire.

60096 PAPYRUS

> Winner: 1923   Chester Vase, the Derby

Sired by **Tracery** in 1920, Papyrus won the Epsom Derby in 1923 and came second in the St. Leger.

Following his victory at Epsom, Papyrus was matched in a race against a horse named Zev, that year's winner of the Kentucky Derby. An estimated 60,000 people were in attendance at the Belmont Park Course (U.S.A.) to see the American horse win easily by 5 lengths on a circuit which was described as bearing a close resemblance to a mud bath.

Descendants from Papyrus include the legendary Shergar.

The high speed exploits of this locomotive on the London-Newcastle run are referred to elsewhere (see Class A4). Papyrus was the last A3 to haul the up "Flying Scotsman" before the service was taken over completely by the A4 Pacifics in August, 1937.

60097 HUMORIST

> Winner: 1921   The Derby

A colt of exceptional ability, Humorist was plagued by illness and intermittent bouts of coughing, which led to his withdrawal from a number of races. Stable staff were at a loss to understand why he could be perfectly well one day and listless the next.

His condition seemed to improve and he went into winter quarters as the clear favourite for the 1921 classic races. He looked to have the 2000 Guineas easily won, but faltered on the rising ground in the finishing straight, to come in an exhausted third.

In the Derby, ridden by Steve Donoghue, Humorist put in a brave performance to win by a neck, but the race left him so weak and exhausted that he was visibly trembling in the winner's enclosure.

Two weeks after winning the 1921 Classic, Humorist died from a tubercular lung condition. Sic transit gloria mundi!

60098 SPION KOP

Winner: 1920   The Derby

Foaled in 1917 by **Spearmint**, Spion Kop was a handsome bay colt with a blaze and four white feet. He came second in five of the six races in which he was entered as a two year old, and it was believed that he would mature sufficiently to become a classic contender at three.

When he easily won his first race at Ripon, the stable became convinced that he could do well in the Derby, a conviction not, however, shared by the bookmakers. Despite the long odds against him, Spion Kop won the race convincingly in a new record time.

The Derby proved to be the pinnacle of Spion Kop's career; he failed to win any of his next six races, including the St. Leger and the Ascot Gold Cup.

His performance at the stud was respectable: he sired **Felstead,** a Derby winner, and *Bongrace*, a winner of the Doncaster Cup.

The horse derived its name from the Boer War battle (Spioenkop, 1900) on a small rocky hill west of Ladysmith which resulted in an ignominious and unnecessary British defeat. The topography of the battlefield has resulted in the name "kop" – commonly a prominent isolated hill – being permanently associated with a part of many English soccer league grounds.

60099 CALL BOY

Winner: 1926 Middle Park Stakes
1927 The Derby

Born in 1924, Call Boy was only a moderate performer as a two year old, and his prospects at three were deemed good, but not great. Despite this, he entered his first race, the 2000 Guineas, as favourite; he was beaten in the last stride by a short head, although many observers considered the result to have been a dead-heat.

He easily won his next race against a moderate field and went on to win the Derby, for the most part leading the race from start to finish in yet another moderate field of 23 horses.

Shortly after Call Boy's Derby victory, the first to be broadcast by BBC Radio, his owner, Lord Curzon, died of a heart attack, which voided the horse's further engagements, including the St. Leger. He never ran again.

In the stud, Call Boy proved to be almost sterile.

60100 SPEARMINT

Winner: 1906 The Derby

Spearmint's early racing career gave no hint that he was a potential Derby winner. One of his stable companions, a filly named Flair, was much fancied for the race but badly lacerated a leg in an accident about three weeks before the event. The stable now had to fall back on Spearmint, who seemed to thrive on the additional hard work and exercise.

A few days before the Derby, a gallop with **Pretty Polly**, who was approaching the end of her racing career, revealed Spearmint in a very different light and as a formidable candidate for Derby honours. He won the race by a length and a half and shortly afterwards went over to Paris where he duly won the Grand Prix. Unfortunately, he then developed leg trouble and was turned out to stud.

60101 CICERO

Winner:	1904	Coventry Stakes, July Stakes
	1905	Newmarket Stakes, the Derby

Cicero was unbeaten as a two year old, winning five races including the prestigious Coventry Stakes at Ascot. As a three year old he easily won the Newmarket Stakes and started as odds-on favourite for the Derby. He won the race by one-third of a length, although his key rival that day was not in perfect health, having come from a stable in which there was an epidemic of coughing and fever.

Seven weeks later, Cicero started as odds-on favourite for the Eclipse Stakes but was beaten by ½ length. He went lame just before the St. Leger, which he was expected to win, and did not race again until the following year when he won a Biennial at Newmarket. His next – and final – outing was the Ascot Cup (the race in which *Bachelor's Button* defeated **Pretty Polly**) in which Cicero put in an indifferent performance owing to lack of training and leg trouble.

60102 SIR FREDERICK BANBURY*

See preamble "Introduction and General Characteristics".

Sir Frederic Banbury was the last Chairman of the GNR and sometime Conservative Member of Parliament for the City of London. Firmly opposed to the proposed Grouping, he vigorously led Parliamentary opposition to the proposal in the House, which nevertheless became law in the Railways Act, 1921.

60103 FLYING SCOTSMAN*

The third locomotive to enter service, **Flying Scotsman** was so named prior to exhibition at Wembley in 1924.

The name "Flying Scotsman" has long been associated with the North Eastern Railway. It is not certain when the world-famous title was formally adopted, but the 10.00 am King's Cross –

Edinburgh express, inaugurated in June 1862, and a corresponding return service were popularly known as the *Flying Scotsman* well before 1900. The name was also fittingly bestowed upon one of the locomotives (the sole survivor of the A3's) built to haul this train during its steam-age heyday in the 1920's and 30's. **Flying Scotsman** became the first locomotive to achieve a non-stop run from London to Edinburgh on 1st May, 1928. Four years later, on 30th November, 1934, this celebrated engine powered the first steam-hauled train to achieve an authenticated 100 mph.

60104 SOLARIO

Winner: 1925 Princess of Wales's Stakes, St. Leger
1926 Coronation Cup, Ascot Gold Cup

Solario, a strong, well-made and handsome colt, sired by **Gainsborough**, won only one of his three starts as a juvenile. However, he really came into his own at three, finishing fourth in the season's first two classics. This late developer then won at Ascot and Newmarket before cantering home in the St. Leger. As a four year old, he took the Coronation Cup by a staggering 15 lengths and then the Gold Cup at Royal Ascot.

After the death of his owner in 1932, Solario fetched 47,000 guineas at public auction, a record for those times.

Solario was the sire of the Derby winners Midday Sun and *Straight Deal* as well as Exhibitionist, who took the 1000 Guineas and the Oaks in 1937.

The locomotive was the first A3 to be withdrawn, in 1959.

60105 VICTOR WILD

Winner: 1894 Royal Hunt Cup

60106 FLYING FOX

Winner: 1898   Criterion Stakes
1899   2000 Guineas, Jockey Club Stakes, the Derby, Eclipse Stakes, Princess of Wales's Stakes, St. Leger

The 1899 winner of the Triple Crown.

Flying Fox was an extremely talented, if highly strung, bay colt. As a juvenile, he won three of his starts, and provided plenty of evidence that he was going to be an exceptional classic contender.

As a three year old, he easily won the 2000 Guineas, then went on to win the Derby after his closest rival, the French colt Holocauste, accidentally shattered his leg during the course of the race, and fell. Flying Fox won the Princess of Wales's Stakes and the Eclipse Stakes at Sandown , followed by the St. Leger.

When Flying Fox won the Eclipse Stakes at Sandown Park his owner, the Duke of Westminster, gave the whole of the Stake, amounting to £9,285, to the Royal Alexandra Hospital, Rhyl. That gift was commemorated by the presentation of a weathervane in the form of a fox.

His victory at Doncaster made him the second winner of the Triple Crown bred by the Duke of Westminster, the first being Flying Fox's grandsire, **Ormonde**.

The Duke died shortly afterwards and Flying Fox went to the stud in France, where he enjoyed considerable success.

He died in March, 1911, at the age of 15.

60107 ROYAL LANCER

Foaled in 1919 by **Spearmint**, Royal Lancer captured both the English and the Irish St.Leger.

This is one of those instances, however, where the owner was better known, and certainly more popular, than the horse.

Royal Lancer was owned by the 6th Earl of Lonsdale, an eccentric, flamboyant and extremely rich "dandy" whose yellow coach and yellow-liveried footmen were greeted with rapturous applause when they appeared at race meetings. He became the best-known figure on the racecourse after the Prince of Wales.

The Earl had been an outstanding sportsman in his youth, and is best-known for the respectability he brought to boxing through the creation and award of the Lonsdale belts.

As a stallion, Royal Lancer was sold to stud in South Africa.

60108 GAY CRUSADER

> Winner: 1917   2000 Guineas, Ascot Gold Cup, the Derby, Champion Stakes, St. Leger

Another winner of the Triple Crown.

Sired by **Bayardo**, Gay Crusader was a light-framed bay with a doubtful temperament which became increasingly more difficult as he grew older.

As a juvenile, he entered two races, winning one and being unplaced in the other. At three he won the 2000 Guineas without difficulty. His classic season might well have ended there because of Government concerns about the continuation of racing during the war, given the large quantities of feed being consumed by racehorses at a time of national food shortages. In the event, the Board of Trade allowed racing to continue on a restricted basis and conducted at Newmarket: consequently, the Derby, won by Gay Crusader, was not run until July, and at Newmarket not Epsom.

The wartime substitute St. Leger was also run at Newmarket, as the September Stakes. Gay Crusader won easily, and went on to add more victories to his tally, all at Newmarket.

Tendon injury forced Gay Crusader's retirement to the stud, where he enjoyed only moderate success. He died in 1932, aged 18.

60109 HERMIT

Winner: 1867   The Derby, St. James's Palace Stakes

Hermit won the 1867 Derby in a snowstorm at odds of 66 to 1. In so doing, he gave his owner, Henry Chaplin, sweet revenge over the Marquis of Hastings, who had eloped a few years earlier with Chaplin's fiancée and who lost his £100,000 wager against Hermit's win.

At stud, Hermit became one of the most popular and fashionable stallions of his time. He was leading sire in Britain seven years in succession, 1880 to 1886. His daughter, **Shotover**, who captured the 2000 Guineas and the Derby and came third in the St. Leger, was one of the five classic winners sired by him.

60110 ROBERT THE DEVIL

Winner: 1880   Cesarewitch Handicap, Champion Stakes, St. Leger
           1881   Ascot Gold Cup

Robert the Devil's racing career is mostly remembered for the intense and, at times, unpleasant rivalry which grew up between him and the Duke of Westminster's Bend Or, a son of **Doncaster** from the mare Rouge Rose and, in his turn, sire of **Ormonde**.

In the 1880 Epsom Derby, Bend Or came from behind to beat Robert the Devil by a head. Robert the Devil's jockey, leading by four lengths, was seemingly slow to respond as Bend Or gained steadily upon him, probably because he had not anticipated a serious challenge from his rival, Fred Archer, who was handicapped by having an injured arm in a heavy brace and was, in effect, riding one-handed and without the aid of a whip.

After the race, the owners of Robert the Devil lodged a challenge to Bend Or's pedigree, based upon rumours started or spread by a disaffected former groom at the Duke of Westminster's stables, that Bend Or and another colt by Doncaster had been erroneously switched as yearlings and that Bend Or was not, in fact, the son of Rouge Rose. A protracted Steward's Inquiry eventually dismissed the challenge, but the controversy rumbled on for some considerable time.

An injury sustained in Bend Or's Derby win affected him for the remainder of the year, and was evident in his first loss when he ran in the St. Leger in heavy rain and finished fifth behind Robert the Devil. He was defeated twice more by his adversary before the end of the year, coming second to him in both the Great Foal Stakes and the Champion Stakes.

Returning to the track at age four, Bend Or avenged his previous year's losses, beating Robert the Devil by a head in the Epsom Gold Cup.

60111 ENTERPRISE

Winner: 1886   July Stakes
            1887   2000 Guineas

60112 ST. SIMON

Winner: 1884   Ascot Gold Cup, Goodwood Cup

Last, but by no means least.

It is generally accepted that the unbeaten St. Simon, the "prototype" of the present day thoroughbred, was the most influential sire of the nineteenth century. Although never really tested in his racing career St. Simon, a bay son of **Galopin,** was unrivalled as a racehorse and considered superior to another unbeaten wonder horse, **Ormonde.**

St. Simon was purchased unraced as a two year old by the Duke of Portland. His finest performance came in the 1884 Ascot Gold

Cup when he beat the previous year's winner by a staggering 20 lengths. He won the 1884 Goodwood Cup by a similar margin as the climax of an eleven race career and retired unbeaten.

St. Simon was equally unrivalled in his stud career and was champion sire nine times, seven in succession. He sired the winners of 17 classic races between 1890 and 1900 and, overall, his progeny, which included the Derby winners **Persimmon** and **Diamond Jubilee** won 571 races worth £553,158.

Aged 27, St. Simon died from an apparent heart attack on 2nd April, 1908, shortly after his morning exercise: his memory is perpetuated in the St. Simon Stakes, run at Newbury since 1969.

The horse's hide was preserved and for some time was on display in a glass case in the entrance hall at Welbeck Abbey Stud. His skeleton was given to the Natural History Museum in London, but is no longer on display. A gold mounted hoof is exhibited at the Jockey Club in Newmarket and another pair are in the Racing Museum at York.

CLASS A1

INTRODUCTION AND GENERAL CHARACTERISTICS

In September, 1945, *Edward Thompson*, then Chief Mechanical Engineer of the LNER, rebuilt the pioneer Pacific **Great Northern** (see Class A3: Introduction and General Characteristics) to produce a somewhat ungainly locomotive whose subsequent performance invariably found it relegated to secondary duties because of its unreliability.

It is widely held that this was an intentionally vindictive act on Thompson's part, his way of showing that the Gresley era had finally come to an end, even though he himself had little time left in which to make any significant and lasting contribution.

Whatever Thompson's intentions might have been, there was no further rebuilding of Gresley locomotives and it is quite possible that the staff in the drawing office at Doncaster deliberately dragged their feet over the design of Thompson's intended new Pacific in view of his imminent retirement. This allowed time for his successor *A. H. Peppercorn* to make significant changes to Thompson's A1 design, although by no means all of it was discarded.

The result was a superb locomotive which, not surprisingly, closely resembled its predecessor, Peppercorn's A2 Pacific (1947). Although the driving wheel diameter on the A1, at 6' 8", was 6" greater than the A2, the arrangement of cylinders and valve gear was the same and the boilers were interchangeable.

In January, 1947 **Great Northern** was reclassified A1/1 to make way for the Peppercorn Pacifics which comprised the remainder of the A1 Class. This locomotive was withdrawn from service in November, 1962.

The A1's were renowned for their reliability and exceptionally high mileage between works overhauls. Some of the Class had the reputation of being rough riders but they were generally strong and dependable engines, popular with their crews.

The first A1 entered traffic in August, 1948. Withdrawal commenced towards the end of 1962 and, by the Summer of 1966, all 49 had gone.

THE NAMES

It had not originally been intended to name the A1's and only the first locomotive in the Class – 60114 – was named shortly after entering traffic. The remainder did, however, gradually acquire a miscellany of names between April, 1950 and July, 1952.

Other than those locomotives which, taken together, had associations with **Sir Walter Scott** and/or Scotland, the largest single group of names (13) was of winning racehorses, thereby continuing a well-established tradition with the A3's and A2's. It has to be said, however, that with the notable exception of 60133 **Pommern** – the sole winner of the Triple Crown included among the A1's – very few horses of "star" quality appear in the Class, compared with the A3's, or even the Peppercorn A2's, which had already "bagged" the names of the Classic winners of the 1940's, including the immediate post-war years. The names selected for the A1's fall into no particular shape or pattern, other than the fact that they do include 8 winners of the Doncaster Cup. Interestingly, of all the LNER Pacifics (all Classes) named after racehorses, no fewer than 16 were, inter alia, winners of this, the oldest of the three major Cup races.

Reference has already been made to the "Scottish" connection. Six locomotives were given names formerly carried on "Scott" Class engines of the **North British** Railway and commemorated some of the Waverley novels of Sir Walter Scott and/or characters who appear in them. A further ten A1's inherited names once allocated to NBR "H" Class locomotives and associated with Scottish history, folk-lore or legend. Whether directly or indirectly, these names were also associated with some of the principal towns and cities served by the North British Railway. Inevitably, associations with Scott are also never very far away.

Of the remainder, four A1's were given the names (and badges) of the principal constituent railway companies of the LNER, six commemorated the achievements of the locomotive engineers of the **Great Northern** and **North Eastern** Railways and a further six carried bird names (four of them displaced from the A4's).

THE CLASS

A total of 50 locomotives (including A1/1) numbered 60113 to 60162

60113	Great Northern	60139	Sea Eagle
60114	W. P. Allen	60140	Balmoral
60115	Meg Merrilies	60141	Abbotsford
60116	Hal o' the Wynd	60142	Edward Fletcher
60117	Bois Roussel	60143	Sir Walter Scott
60118	Archibald Sturrock	60144	King's Courier
60119	Partrick Stirling	60145	Saint Mungo
60120	Kittiwake	60146	Peregrine
60121	Silurian	60147	North Eastern
60122	Curlew	60148	Aboyeur
60123	H. A. Ivatt	60149	Amadis
60124	Kenilworth	60150	Willbrook
60125	Scottish Union	60151	Midlothian
60126	Sir Vincent Raven	60152	Holyrood
60127	Wilson Worsdell	60153	Flamboyant
60128	Bongrace	60154	Bon Accord
60129	Guy Mannering	60155	Borderer
60130	Kestrel	60156	Great Central
60131	Osprey	60157	Great Eastern
60132	Marmion	60158	Aberdonian
60133	Pommern	60159	Bonnie Dundee
60134	Foxhunter	60160	Auld Reekie
60135	Madge Wildfire	60161	North British
60136	Alcazar	60162	Saint Johnstoun
60137	Redgauntlet		
60138	Boswell		

DAVID H. BALDWIN

"(NOT) ONLY FOWLS AND HORSES ....."

60113 Great Northern

One of the two new 'Pacific' locomotives named by the Great Northern Railway (the other being *Sir Frederick Banbury)* prior to Grouping on 1st January, 1923.

Plans to build a railway connecting London and York were first mooted as early as 1827, but construction work did not begin until 1846 following enactment of the necessary legislation. Although the ultimate objective of the Great Northern Railway Company, under its Chairman Edward Denison, was to provide a direct link from London to York via Peterborough, with branches to Sheffield and Wakefield, progress initially was low. The first section of the line, Louth to New Holland, for Grimsby and Hull, was opened on 1st March, 1848. The following year services were operating between Peterborough and Doncaster. In August, 1850, the line was extended southwards from Peterborough to a temporary station close by the site of the present King's Cross. Trains could now be operated from London to York via Peterborough, Boston, Lincoln and Retford.

The London terminus at King's Cross was completed in 1852. The following year the GNR had access to Bradford, Cambridge, Leicester and Manchester. An extensive network of branch lines enabled the Company to reach all the principal towns in West Yorkshire by 1860, from which date its passenger income was supplemented by substantial revenues from the transport of coal.

Although not the oldest or the largest of the 7 major constituent companies which came together on 1st August, 1923, the GNR came to dominate the association, largely because Nigel Gresley, who had formerly been its Locomotive Engineer, became Chief Mechanical Engineer of the newly formed LNER.

60114 W.P. Allen

This locomotive was named in August, 1948, to celebrate the

achievement of a railwayman who successfully made the transition from footplate to board room.

William Philip Allen CBE (1888 – 1958) was an engine driver on the **Great Northern** and, subsequently, General Secretary of the Associated Society of Locomotive Engineers and Firemen (ASLEF) during the period 1940 – 1947. In 1948, he became a member of the newly-formed Railway Executive and remained in that office until 1953, when he became Chief of Establishment and Staff for the British Transport Commission (and Manpower Adviser from 1955).

The naming ceremony was carried out at King's Cross Station on 28th October, 1948, by *Sir Eustace Missenden*, Chairman of the Railway Executive, whose own name was being carried on an S.R. "Battle of Britain" Class Pacific.

60115 MEG MERRILIES

This engine was one of six A1's which inherited names formerly carried by "Scott" class locomotives of the North British Railway, introduced in 1909 for express workings between Edinburgh and Perth.

Meg Merrilies is the old gypsy woman in Sir Walter Scott's "**Guy Mannering**" (see 60129). She is portrayed as "the exact impression of an ancient sibyl" (witch, fortune teller or sorceress) being six feet tall with long and tangled black hair. She:-

"wore a man's great coat over the rest of her dress, had in her hand a godly sloe-thorn cudgel, and in all points of equipment, except her petticoats, seemed rather masculine than feminine. Her dark elf-locks shot out like the snakes of the gorgon, between an old fashioned bonnet called a bongrace, heightening the singular effect of her strong weather beaten features, which they partly shadowed, while her eye had a wild roll that indicated something like real or affected insanity. Her attitude was that of a sibyl in frenzy."

The connection between Meg's headgear and another member of the A1 Class (see 60128) is, of course, purely fortuitous.

Of incidental note, Meg Merrilies also features in Keats' poem

> "Old Meg she was a gypsy,
>
> She lived upon the moors......"

which, predictably, has spawned a number of saucy rhyming parodies.

60116 HAL O'THE WYND

A name also formerly carried on a "Scott" Class locomotive of the NBR, Hal o'the Wynd (also known as Henry Wynd/Gow/Smith) is the blacksmith/armourer hero in Sir Walter Scott's "The Fair Maid of Perth". He is described as "diminutive and crooked, but fierce" and "a man of most unusual share of strength".

The novel is set in Scotland in the fourteenth century. Henry, a renowned swordsman, forcibly thwarts an attempt by the King's profligate son and his henchman to abduct Catherine, daughter of *Simon Glover*. Despite his intervention on her behalf, his passion for combat makes him unattractive as a suitor to the gentle Catherine, despite her father's approval of him.

Later, Henry takes part in a battle between the champions of two feuding clans, at the end of which, with most of the sixty combatants either dead or wounded, he confronts the son of the opposing clan chief, with whom he has developed a bitter rivalry. His opponent loses his nerve, runs away and, later, ashamed of his cowardice, commits suicide. Henry, weary of battle and sickened by the carnage, declares that, henceforth, he will renounce arms and fight only in the service of his country. His reward, finally, is acceptance by Catherine Glover.

Scott's novel is based upon and closely parallels a famous battle between 30 champions of two clans (thought most likely to have been Clan Chattan and Clan Cameron, although Davidson, Kay and MacPherson are also considered possibles) which took place on the North Inch at Perth in 1396. Before the battle commenced it was discovered that Clan Chattan was a man short; a bandy-legged local blacksmith known as Hal o' the Wynd/Henry Wynd volunteered to take his place.

The story goes that the battle was fought with such ferocity that there was only one survivor on the losing side. Clan Chattan had eleven survivors, of whom only Hal o' the Wynd was unwounded; their victory was due largely to his phenomenal strength and courage and the skill with which he wielded his broadsword. The descendants of the blacksmith, were referred to in Gaelic as "the race of the bent smith" and the Smiths to this day are a branch (sept) of the Clan Chattan.

The name Gow is derived from the Gaelic word "Gobba", meaning a blacksmith or armourer, but it may also be a shortening of the Gaelic term meaning "son of the smith". The Gows made their homes chiefly in Perthshire and Inverness and included *Neil Gow*, the most celebrated of Scottish fiddlers and composer of many popular reels and strathspeys.

60117 Bois Roussel

Racehorse
Winner: 1938 The Derby

The first of 13 racehorses to be celebrated among the names of the A1's, Bois Roussel won the first televised Derby in 1938.

This French-bred brown colt (1935) was sired by Vatout from Plucky Liege, a daughter of *Spearmint* and one of the most important broodmares of the last century. He was named after the Haras du Bois Roussel stud farm in France.

In 1938, Bois Roussel, owned by the son of the late Admiral Lord *Beatty*, was entered for the Epsom Derby as a 30/1 outsider, his only previous win being the Prix de Juigne at Longchamp in the Spring. From the start, Pasch was in the lead, and looked as if he might be the sixth favourite to win the Derby in the inter-war years, but Bois Roussel suddenly came from nowhere to storm past both Pasch and **Scottish Union** and win by four lengths. He completed his season by coming third in the Grand Prix de Paris.

At stud, Bois Roussel was the sire of classic winners in England, Ireland and France, including *Tehran* (St. Leger). His progeny were noted for their stamina and staying power.

60118 ARCHIBALD STURROCK

One of Nigel Gresley's predecessors, Archibald Sturrock was appointed Locomotive Superintendent to the Great Northern Railway, just before the opening of the company's main line from London to York and held the post from 1850 to 1866.

Born into a prosperous Dundee family in September, 1876, and to his banker father's apparent astonishment and disdain, Sturrock's connection with steam locomotives began at the age of 16, when he was apprenticed to a foundry which was constructing an engine for the Dundee and Newtyle Railway. By 1840, he had been appointed principal assistant/works manager to Daniel Gooch at Swindon.

He remained with the Great Western until 1850 when, on Brunel's recommendation, he was appointed Locomotive Superintendent to the **Great Northern**. When asked by the directors if he could recommend a good Carriage and Wagon Superintendent, the resourceful Sturrock promptly proposed himself, thereby securing an immediate increase of 50 per cent in salary.

He was inventive as well as resourceful and, in 1863, invented the steam tender, an auxiliary engine designed to give extra power on starting or at low speeds. They made it possible for heavy trains to be hauled up gradients as steep as 1 in 178 but were heavy on steam and hard work for the enginemen.

At the age of 50, possibly because of a costly failure in the further development of the steam tender, Sturrock retired to a life of country pursuits, (a retirement that was to last no fewer than 43 years), and was succeeded by his cousin, **Patrick Stirling.** He died in London on 1st January, 1909, aged 92 years.

60119 PATRICK STIRLING

Patrick Stirling (1820 – 95) was the most eminent of a remarkable family of locomotive engineers that included his cousin **Archibald Sturrock**, whom he succeeded as Locomotive Superintendent to the GNR in 1866.

Born at Kilmarnock in 1820, Stirling served his apprenticeship at the Dundee foundry where his cousin had also served his time, became foreman of Neilson's Locomotive Works in Glasgow and eventually, in 1853, Locomotive Superintendent of the Glasgow and South Western Railway, a post he held until his move to the GNR in 1866. He remained in Doncaster until his death in office in 1895.

Patrick Stirling built his engines for speed and power, particularly on the London-Manchester and London-York expresses and to compete against the Midland Railway and L&NWR in the famous "Races to the North". The locomotive for which he is best known – the 8ft. diameter driving wheel 4-2-2 'Stirling Single' – first appeared in 1870. Stirling Single No.1 is preserved in the National Collection at York.

Stirling could be inflexible and dogmatic in his beliefs. He disliked the concept of compound engines and abhorred domed boilers, likening them to "chamberpots".

He was, however, much loved and respected by the railwaymen of the GNR who, on the occasion of his 70th birthday, erected a fountain in his honour in Doncaster. Over 3000 GNR men accompanied his funeral procession in pouring rain when he died in 1895.

60120 Kittiwake

The practice of naming locomotives after British birds that were noted for being "swift or strong of flight", originally adopted for the Gresley A4's, was continued in the A1's although of the six engines so affected, only Kittiwake and 60122 **Curlew** carried bird names which had not previously been displaced from the streamlined 'Pacifics'.

60121 Silurian

Racehorse
Winner: 1923 Doncaster Cup

One of the 8 winners of the Doncaster Cup included among the 13 A1's which carried the names of racehorses.

Born in 1919, Lord Derby's Silurian was another good stayer, a necessary quality in the Doncaster Cup. His dam sire was *St Simon*.

In addition to his victory at Doncaster, Silurian also won the Queen's Handicap and came second, by a head, in the Ascot Gold Cup.

He was sent to stud in Argentina, where he was leading sire in 1930, 1931, and 1934.

60122 Curlew

See 60120 **Kittiwake**

60123 H.A. Ivatt

Henry Alfred Ivatt (1851 – 1923) succeeded **Patrick Stirling** as Locomotive Engineer of the GNR in 1896. On Ivatt's retirement he was, in turn, succeeded by Nigel Gresley.

Ivatt was educated at Liverpool College and then entered the L&NWR Locomotive Works at Crewe as an apprentice. Having gained practical experience as a fireman on express engines working out of Crewe, he was eventually (1874) given control of the Holyhead Locomotive Depot, before being promoted to the Chester District. Ivatt then joined the Great Southern and Western Railway, Ireland, at Inchicore works, where he became locomotive engineer in 1886. In 1895, he returned to England to become the Chief Locomotive Superintendent of the GNR.

With the GNR, Ivatt set about designing replacements for Stirling's locomotives, which were no longer powerful enough for the heavier express trains. The larger versions of his designs appeared from 1902 onwards and, once superheated, became outstanding performers well into the 1930's. He introduced the first 4-4-2 "Atlantic" locomotive in Great Britain, named "Henry Oakley" after the General Manager of the GNR.

Ivatt retired in 1911 and died in 1923. He was the father-in-law of O.V. Bulleid of Southern Region fame, and for so long Gresley's right-hand man. His son, H.G. Ivatt, was the last Chief Mechanical Engineer of the LMS.

60124 KENILWORTH

Kenilworth is another name first carried on a "Scott" class locomotive of the NBR and is the title of a novel by Sir Walter Scott, published in 1821. Interestingly, both the original bearer of the name (Class D30 No. 62431) and the A1 which carried it from March, 1949, were briefly in service with British Railways at the same time.

60125 SCOTTISH UNION

Racehorse
Winner: 1937   Middle Park Stakes
            1938   St. James's Palace Stakes, St. Leger
            1939   Coronation Cup

Foaled in 1935, Scottish Union was a son of *Cameronian*, winner of the 1931 Derby and 2000 Guineas.

A good runner, he won the Rous Memorial Stakes and Middle Park Stakes as a two year old and, at three, took the St. Leger and St. James's Palace Stakes, coming second in both the 2000 Guineas and the Derby. At four, he went on to win the Coronation Cup and came second to *Blue Peter* in the Eclipse Stakes.

He was not a successful sire.

60126 SIR VINCENT RAVEN

Having commemorated the influential locomotive engineers of the Great Northern Railway, those responsible for naming the A1's turned their attention to the most prominent designers and engineers of the **North Eastern** Railway.

Vincent Litchfield Raven was born on 3rd December, 1859, at Great Fransham in Norfolk, where his father was Rector. He was educated at Aldenham School in Hertfordshire. In 1876, he entered the service of the NER as a pupil of **Edward Fletcher**. He became an Assistant Mechanical Engineer in 1893, and Chief Mechanical Engineer in 1910, a post he held until the end of 1922.

Raven's designs continued NER traditions, but he was also the innovative designer of numerous classes of locomotive including the B16 and Q7 engines and the A2 Pacific (an unsuccessful competitor to the Gresley A1).

In 1915, Vincent Raven became Superintendent of the Woolwich Royal Arsenal and was knighted in 1917. When the LNER was formed in 1923, he was appointed as Technical Adviser (Nigel Gresley being preferred as CME), but resigned this position in the following year.

He died on 14th February, 1934.

Sir Vincent Raven was the father-in-law of *Edward Thompson*, CME of the LNER (in succession to *Sir Nigel Gresley*) from 1941-46. The locomotive which bore his name received its nameplates at a ceremony in Darlington on 3rd August, 1950.

60127 WILSON WORSDELL

Wilson Worsdell (1850-1920) was a member of a Quaker engineering dynasty which included his father, Nathaniel, who designed the first railway passenger vehicle for Stephenson, and his elder brother Thomas, who became Locomotive Superintendent of the Great Eastern Railway and, subsequently, of the North Eastern Railway.

Both brothers spent time at Crewe and with the Pennsylvania Railroad in the USA. Following his return to England in 1870, Wilson Worsdell worked for the London and North Western Railway before becoming Assistant Locomotive Superintendent of the North Eastern Railway in 1883. He succeeded his brother as Superintendent (the forerunner of the post of CME) in 1890 and, over the next 20 years, produced a series of progressive designs, influenced by his spell in America, notably express 4-4-0's and "Atlantics".

The naming ceremony for the locomotive which carried his name took place at Newcastle Central Station on 30th October, 1950.

60128 BONGRACE

Racehorse
Winner: 1926   Jockey Club Cup, Doncaster Cup

Sired by *Spion Kop* and owned by Lord Rosebery, Bongrace was considered talented but lazy. Needing an occasional "reminder" from the whip to keep her interested, she failed to win The Oaks, despite being much fancied, because her jockey had the misfortune to drop his whip some way from home.

Nevertheless, Bongrace did win 5 races as a three year old in addition to those referred to above.

60129 GUY MANNERING

The third locomotive to bear the name, including an earlier "Scott" class engine of the North British Railway.

Sir Walter Scott's novel "Guy Mannering", set in the eighteenth century, tells the story of Harry Bertram, son of the laird of Ellangowan and his struggles to regain his rightful inheritance following his kidnapping and abduction as a child.

The novel includes the notable characters of **Meg Merrilies**, who assists Harry at the cost of her own life, and *Dominie Sampson* (see Class D30), the young Harry's uncouth and simple-minded tutor.

60130 KESTREL

The name of this British bird of prey was originally carried on Class A4 Pacific No. 4485, which entered service in February, 1937.

In September 1947, the locomotive was re-named *Miles Beevor*; the bird name thus displaced later re-appeared on Class A1 Pacific No. 60130, introduced in September 1948.

60131 OSPREY

Similarly, Class A4 Pacific No. 4494 was named Osprey until July, 1942, when it was re-named *Andrew K. McCosh*.

The bird name was subsequently re-allocated to Class A1 Pacific No. 60131, which entered service in October, 1948.

60132 MARMION

Although the name has obvious associations with Sir Walter Scott, and had previously been carried on four (predominantly nineteenth century) locomotives of the LNWR/LSWR, 'Marmion' was not a name inherited from either the "Scott" or "H" Classes of the NBR and thus had the distinction of being newly introduced into Class A1 in 1948.

"Marmion: A Tale of Flodden Field", is a poem by Sir Walter Scott, set in the time of King Henry VIII and published in 1808.

60133 POMMERN

Racehorse
Winner: 1914   Richmond Stakes
              1915   2000 Guineas, The Derby, St. Leger
              1916   Coronation Cup

Although 8 winners of the English Triple Crown (comprising the Epsom Derby, the St. Leger and the 2000 Guineas) are commemorated among the names of the Gresley Class A3 Pacifics, only one such winner – Pommern – is included among the 13 racehorses incorporated in the names of the Peppercorn A1's

It has to be said, however, that his success in winning the wartime Triple Crown (comprising the 2000 Guineas, the New Derby and the re-styled September Stakes, all run at Newmarket), has never attracted much praise or appreciation, possibly because Pommern was regarded as the best of a somewhat moderate bunch.

Jockey Steve Donoghue's 1915 Derby win, in a fast time, was the first of six successes eventually registered by him in this, the world's most prestigious classic race, including a hat-trick of wins on *Humourist* (1921), *Captain Cuttle* (1922) and *Papyrus* (1923). Had he captured the Derby in 1924, (won by *Sansovino* with Tommy Weston on board), he could have made it five wins in a row, coming in first on *Manna* in 1925.

60134 FOXHUNTER

Racehorse
Winner: 1932   Doncaster Cup
              1933   Ascot Gold Cup

Sired by Foxlaw, himself a winner of the Ascot Gold Cup in 1927, Foxhunter enjoyed a successful stud career, first in Britain, then in Argentina, when his racing days were over. His progeny had a reputation for stamina.

His mother, Trimestral, had the rare distinction of being the dam of the winner of the Ascot Gold Cup three years in a row, Foxhunter taking the race in 1933 and his half-brother, Trimdon, winning in 1931 and 1932.

60135 MADGE WILDFIRE

Another name formerly carried on a "Scott" class locomotive of the North British Railway.

'Madge Wildfire' is the nickname of Magdalen Murdockson, daughter of Meg, characters in Scott's "The Heart of Midlothian". She is portrayed as a beautiful but somewhat scatterbrained girl, driven insane by seduction and the murder of her infant child.

60136 ALCAZAR

Racehorse
Winner: 1934   Ebor Handicap, Doncaster Cup

60137 REDGAUNTLET

The name 'Redgauntlet' was formerly carried by "Scott" class locomotive No. 897, which entered service in September, 1909.

Scott's historical novel, published in 1824, takes the form of a series of letters and centres around a further abortive attempt on the throne by the Young Pretender after the failure of the '45 rebellion.

Sir Edward Redgauntlet is a fanatical Jacobite and supporter of 'Bonnie Prince Charlie'. As part of his plan for helping the Pretender he kidnaps Sir Arthur Darsie Redgauntlet, his nephew and the head of the family. Alan Fairford sets out to rescue his friend Darsie, and their adventures form the substance of the novel. In the end, Sir Edward is forced to flee abroad and Prince Charles Edward's hopes again come to nothing.

A famous feature of the book is "*Wandering Willie's* Tale", a classic ghost story.

60138 BOSWELL

Racehorse
Winner: 1936 St. Leger
         1937 Eclipse Stakes

60139 SEA EAGLE

Another of the four A1 bird names originally allocated to Class A4 Pacifics, No. 4487 Sea Eagle was re-named *Water K. Whigham* in October, 1947.

60140 BALMORAL

Continues the association of the A1 Class with things Scottish, but only indirectly with Sir Walter Scott, the name 'Balmoral' – as with 60132 **Marmion** – being newly introduced (to the Eastern Region) in December 1948.

Balmoral Castle was acquired for Queen Victoria by Prince Albert in 1852 and has been the Scottish home of the Royal Family since that date. The original castle was demolished in 1853; a larger replacement commissioned by the Prince Consort was completed in 1856.

When Queen Victoria died in 1901 Balmoral Estates passed, under the terms of her will, to King Edward VII, and from him to the line of succession. It has been suggested that, but for the popularity of **Sir Walter Scott**, whose historical novels ranked in the top three in the stocks of most Victorian lending libraries even in the final decade of the nineteenth century, Queen Victoria might not have established Balmoral as a highland retreat.

60141 ABBOTSFORD

Closely associated with Sir Walter Scott is 'Abbotsford', his home near Melrose on the Tweed.

In 1812, Scott purchased and then demolished a small farmstead named Cartley Hole Farm in order to commence building his own grand "mediaeval" mansion – named Abbotsford – which was eventually ready for occupation in 1824. The "romantic historic" style of the house, which has become one of Scotland's national monuments, reflected Scott's literary style; in its final state Abbotsford has been described as a state-of –the-art modern house in the guise of an antiquated baronial hall.

The name 'Abbotsford' was formerly carried on an "H" Class locomotive of the NBR, introduced in 1906 for the Waverley Route between Edinburgh and Carlisle. When superheated they became Class I (and C11 under the LNER).

60142 EDWARD FLETCHER

Edward Fletcher was born in Northumberland in 1807. He was apprenticed to George Stephenson in 1825 and was involved with the construction of the *Rocket* and with the opening of the Canterbury and Whitstable Railway.

After a year at Canterbury, he returned north. Initially, he was with the York, Newcastle and Berwick Railway and, in 1854, became locomotive superintendent for the newly-formed **North Eastern**.

Fletcher's "big engine" policy produced some notable designs for both freight and passenger locomotives which were considered to be ahead of their time in regard to both size and performance. No.

910, one of the 55 engines of the '901' class built between 1872 and 1882, is preserved in the National Collection.

The rugged, "no nonsense" locomotives of his '708' class proved popular with enginemen and were built in large numbers; around 100 passed into LNER ownership in 1923.

Edward Fletcher retired in 1882 and died at Newcastle in 1889.

60143 SIR WALTER SCOTT

Sir Walter Scott was born in Edinburgh on 15th August, 1771. At the age of 18 months he contracted polio, which left him permanently lame in his right leg. He was sent to recuperate with his grandfather in the Borders, where he first started to hear the history and legends of the area which were the source of much of his literary inspirations.

Scott was educated at Edinburgh High School and University and became an apprentice at his father's legal practice in 1786. He was called to the Bar in 1792, around which time he started collecting the ballads of the Borders area which he later published.

In 1813, Scott refused the offer of the laureateship and instead recommended Southey for the honour. Eclipsed to some extent by *Byron* as a poet in spite of the great popularity of his romantic verses, he turned his attention to the historical novel. He succeeded in re-creating periods of history through accurate description and skilful characterisation.

The first of Scott's novels, 'Waverley', dealt with the Jacobite rebellion of 1745; published anonymously in 1814, it was hugely successful. During the 15 years that followed, Scott, who became a Baronet in 1820, produced a succession of popular novels. They were written anonymously, appearing variously as "by the writer of Waverley" and by the fictitious Jedediah Cleishbotham. They became known collectively as the Waverley novels, although they had many different subjects, characters and settings.

Although little read now, Scott's influence as a novelist was considerable; he was read avidly throughout the nineteenth century, after which his popularity and reputation gradually declined.

He died in 1832.

60144 KING'S COURIER

Racehorse
Winner:　　1900　Doncaster Cup
　　　　　　　1901　Jockey Club Cup

Bred in the United States, King's Courier was sired by the American horse Kingston, son of an imported English mare. Astonishingly, Kingston lost only twice in 35 races and, on both occasions, came second!

The winner of races in the USA at two, King's Courier was sent to England where, in the colours of Lord Ellesmere, he won the Doncaster Cup and Jockey Club Cup.

60145 SAINT MUNGO

Another of the ten A1's which inherited names previously carried on "H" class locomotives of the North British Railway.

Saint Mungo (meaning 'dearest' or 'dear one') is an alternative name for St. Kentigern, the patron saint of Glasgow and traditional founder of Glasgow Cathedral.

He is represented with his episcopal cross in one hand and a salmon and ring in the other. This alludes to the popular legend in which King Roderich had surreptitiously thrown into the River Clyde a ring which he had once given to his wife, Queen Longuoreth, and had subsequently discovered on the finger of a sleeping Knight. The queen, being unable to produce the ring when asked to do so by her husband, had been thrown into jail on suspicion of adultery. Pleading her innocence, she sent a messenger to Saint Mungo and begged him to help her. Saint Mungo instructed the queen's messenger to go out and fish in the river. The messenger returned with a salmon whose stomach, when cut open, was found to contain the ring. Having been re-united with it, the queen was able to "prove" her innocence.

The coat of arms of the City of Glasgow includes the salmon with the ring in its mouth.

60146 PEREGRINE

The fourth of the A1 bird names previously allocated to an A4 Pacific had been carried by the final locomotive in that class from July, 1938, to March, 1948, when it was re-named *Lord Faringdon* after the first Deputy Chairman of the LNER.

60147 NORTH EASTERN

One of the constituent companies of the LNER (1923).

In 1854 , three companies, York & North Midland, Leeds Northern and the York, Newcastle & Berwick amalgamated to form the North Eastern Railway. The amalgamation produced a system 700 miles long, with administrative headquarters at York. The North Eastern Railway continued to expand and gradually other companies were taken over. This included South Durham and Lancashire (1862), Stockton and Darlington (1863) and the West Hartlepool Railway (1865).

The North Eastern Railway now had a virtual monopoly of rail transport in the north-east, but relied heavily for its income on the movement of coal and other raw materials associated with the staple industries of that region. This trade declined significantly in the 1870's and the company increasingly promoted passenger travel.

60148 ABOYEUR

Racehorse
Winner: 1913   The Derby

Favourite to win the 1913 Derby was a horse named Craganour, at odds of 6-4 on. Aboyeur, one of four horses at 100-1, was generally considered something of a forlorn hope in this great classic race; he had won only one of three races as a 2 year old and had been unplaced at Kempton on his only previous outing at 3 years. To all appearances, therefore, Aboyeur was a "no hoper" and Craganour a racing certainty in a field which also included a horse named Anmer, owned by King George V, at odds of 50-1.

At Tattenham Corner, a suffragette named Emily Davison waited until the leading batch of horses, including Aboyeur (then 3 lengths ahead of Craganour) had thundered past, squeezed through the rails and seemingly made a grab for Anmer's reins, bringing down the King's horse and fatally injuring herself in the process.

The race between Aboyeur and Craganour, neither of which had been affected or checked by the incident, developed into a "bumping and barging" match. As the two went past the post, Craganour led by a head. However, the Stewards disqualified the winner on a charge of jostling the second horse, Aboyeur, and awarded the race to him, even though the scrimmaging had clearly been caused by both parties.

Aboyeur ran in two further races, was beaten on both occasions, and was then sold to the Imperial Racing Club of St. Petersburg for 13,000 guineas.

60149 AMADIS

> Racehorse
> Winner: 1909   Doncaster Cup, Jockey Club Cup, Queen's Vase

60150 WILLBROOK

> Racehorse
> Winner: 1914   Doncaster Cup

Following Willbrook's victory, the Doncaster Cup was suspended for the duration of the war and the race was not re-instated until 1919.

60151 MIDLOTHIAN

Another name formerly carried on an "H" class locomotive of the North British Railway.

Midlothian is a land-locked region bounded on the north and west by Edinburgh and the Pentland Hills, on the north and east by East Lothian, and on the South by the Scottish Borders and the Moorfoot Hills. Prior to 1975, Midlothian was often referred to as "Edinburghshire" and included Edinburgh, parts of the Borders and East and West Lothian. Boundary changes then made the area one of four districts in the Lothian Region. In 1996 it became a unitary authority.

The site of the "Heart of Midlothian", the fifteenth Century Tolbooth, can today be seen clearly marked out in stone setts in the cobblestones of Edinburgh's High Street. The Tolbooth, demolished in 1817, was the administrative centre of the town, prison and one of several sites of public execution. It features in Sir Walter Scott's novel, also titled 'The Heart of Midlothian', published in 1818.

Former connections between Edinburgh and Midlothian are commemorated in a variety of other ways, including the name of the football club 'Heart of Midlothian' (or 'Hearts') based at Tynecastle Stadium.

60152 HOLYROOD

A name formerly allocated to an "I" Class (Superheated "H") locomotive of the NBR.

Founded as a monastery in 1128, the Palace of Holyrood House in Edinburgh is the official Scottish residence of the British Royal Family. Situated at the lower end of the Royal Mile, Holyrood is closely associated with key incidents and events in Scotland's sometimes turbulent past, including the murder of David Rizzio, Secretary to Mary, Queen of Scots (who lived there between 1561 and 1567).

Holyrood House was begun in 1498 by the Scottish King James IV, but the greater portion of it was built in the time of Charles II.

60153 FLAMBOYANT

> Racehorse
> Winner: 1921   Doncaster Cup
>   1922   Goodwood Cup

Flamboyant was sired in 1918 by *Tracery* from Simonath, daughter of *St Simon* and granddam of *Papyrus*.

He, in turn, was the sire of the 2000 Guineas winner *Flamingo* and, later, leading sire in Germany in 1936.

60154 BON ACCORD

Not a racehorse, but a name (formerly carried on an "H" class locomotive of the NBR) used to refer to the northern Scottish city of Aberdeen, having supposedly been conferred upon it by Robert the Bruce.

Tradition has it that the citizens of Aberdeen aided 'the Bruce' in 1306 by attacking the English garrison at the castle and killing the defenders. The password on the night the castle was taken was, apparently, 'Bon Accord', subsequently adopted as the city's motto at the instigation of Robert I.

60155 BORDERER

First bestowed upon NBR "H" class locomotive No. 881 in August, 1906, the name 'Borderer' – used to refer to an inhabitant of the culturally and historically important Borders region of Scotland – was "inherited" by Class A1 Pacific No. 60155 in September, 1949.

60156 GREAT CENTRAL

The nucleus of the Great Central Railway (which formed part of the LNER in 1923) was the Sheffield, Ashton-under-Lyne and Manchester Railway, incorporated in 1837. The first section of this line (from Manchester to Godley) was opened to passenger traffic in 1841; within 5 years, following the construction of the Woodhead Tunnel (3 miles long) the line was opened throughout, linking both sides of the Pennines.

In 1847, the Grimsby docks and other lines were amalgamated with the original company under the title of the Manchester, Sheffield and Lincolnshire Railway. Thus the M.S.L. was essentially a provincial system linking Lancashire with the East Coast. Several attempts were made to obtain powers to construct a new main line to London, in order to overcome the problems associated with being dependent upon the company's commercial rivals for access to London termini.

In 1892, permission was obtained for what was known as the 'London Extension', which stretched from Annesley to Marylebone via Nottingham, Leicester, Rugby and Aylesbury. The line was opened for goods traffic in July, 1898, and for passenger services in March, 1899. Two years previously, the MSL had taken over further lines and had adopted the title of Great Central Railway on 1st August, 1897.

The London Extension, with its terminus at Marylebone, led to the introduction of express passenger services from London to the North and the Midlands by an alternative route.

60157 GREAT EASTERN

The opening in 1839 of a short line linking the east of London with Romford marked the beginning of the Eastern Counties Railway. Towards the end of 1848, further railways were started in various parts of East Anglia; from such fragmented beginnings ultimately sprang the Great Eastern Railway.

A new London terminus at Liverpool Street was opened to local traffic in February, 1874, and for all traffic in November, 1875. The construction of Liverpool Street gave rise to the development of the most intensive network of steam-hauled suburban services in the world and the introduction of main line express trains connecting with Cambridge, King's Lynn and Hunstanton, Norwich and Cromer and Colchester, Ipswich, Yarmouth and Lowestoft. Ultimately, the railway fed steamship services to the Hook of Holland, Antwerp and *Zeebrugge*.

The introduction of day excursion trips to East Anglia led to the rapid development of a chain of seaside resorts served by the railway. Apart from these services, the Great Eastern extended its activities northwards to connect with Spalding, Sleaford, Doncaster and York, and an alternative route was thereby introduced between London and the North of England.

The Great Eastern also became part of the LNER in 1923.

60158 ABERDONIAN

Another name formerly carried by an "H" Class locomotive of the NBR and by LNER No. 9903 which, until May, 1934, had been named *Cock o'the North* but was renamed 'Aberdonian' to free up the name for Gresley's P2 Class No. 2001 (the original "H" class 'Abderdonian' had already been scrapped).

(See also 60154 **Bon Accord**)

60159 BONNIE DUNDEE

John Graham, Earl of *Claverhouse*, Viscount Dundee, became better known as "Bonnie Dundee".

His fame is celebrated in the lyrics of the song "The Bonnets o' Bonnie Dundee", based on a poem by **Sir Walter Scott** (and parodied by Lewis Carroll in 'Through the Looking Glass' and by

Rudyard Kipling in the 'Jungle Book')

Claverhouse was the elder son of Royalists, a Protestant by religion and a firm believer in the "divine right" of Kings to rule without challenge or question.

A soldier by profession, Claverhouse earned the nickname "Bloody Clavers" because of his brutal suppression of the Covenanters (Presbyterian rebels who opposed Anglicanism) who had vowed to overthrow James VII (James II of England) because of his failure to fulfil a promise to accept and promote the Protestant religion.

In 1688, when William of Orange invaded the country, James II made Claverhouse second-in-command of the Scottish army and, before fleeing abroad, bestowed upon him the title of Viscount Dundee.

In James's absence, Claverhouse raised the king's standard outside the city of Dundee and, with a force of 2,500 men, set out to confront General Hugh Mackay who had been sent with 4,000 troops to crush the Scottish rebellion.

Despite its numerical superiority, Mackay's force was ambushed and overwhelmed at the Battle of Killicranky Pass and retreated in disarray with only 800 survivors. However, Claverhouse himself had been mortally wounded in the battle, shot in the chest as he charged at the head of his cavalry. He died shortly afterwards, and was buried in the churchyard at Blair Atholl.

The Jacobite forces, with no leader as capable as Dundee to replace him, were defeated in battle by veterans of the Covenanters uprising and the rebellion came to an end in May, 1690.

Claverhouse's exploits had been commemorated in 1906 by the North British Railway which named an "H" class locomotive "Bonnie Dundee".

60160 AULD REEKIE

The name 'Auld Reekie', previously carried by 'H' class locomotive No. 872, referred to Edinburgh old town. It was so called because it generally appeared to be capped by a cloud of 'reek' or smoke and was described by Scott (in **Marmion**) as being, despite its beauty, "an odorous, inconvenient, old-fashioned town of about 70,000 inhabitants".

60161 NORTH BRITISH

The North British Railway was proposed as a separate entity by the Edinburgh and Glasgow railway, which did not want to risk the construction of a branch line extending from Edinburgh and Berwick. It was heavily supported by George Hudson, the "Railway King", who was promoting an East Coast alliance of companies with lines extending down the east coast of Britain through York.

The NBR originally ran from North Bridge station in Edinburgh (where it did not at first connect to any other lines) to Berwick station (where it was similarly isolated and disconnected as the Tweed had not yet been bridged). Along the course of its route the NBR did, however, have a branch to Haddington and connections to the Edinburgh and Dalkeith Railway.

Following a major building and acquisition programme, which provided connections to Glasgow, Stirling, Dundee, Hamilton, Peebles, Galashiels, Aberdeen, St. Andrews, Carlisle and a large number of other locations, the company was nearly bankrupted and even lost control of its original mainline when the **North Eastern** Railway gained permission to run express services between Berwick and Edinburgh. After recovery, the NBR grew to have the largest track mileage of any of the Scottish railway companies. It became part of the LNER in 1923.

60162 SAINT JOHNSTOUN

With its origins dating back to Roman times, Perth acquired the status of a burgh in the early twelfth century and became the capital city of Scotland until the middle of the fifteenth century.

In 1126, following construction of the Kirk of St. John the Baptist, Perth became known by the alternative name of Saint Johnstoun ("St. John's town") and continued to be referred to in this way until the seventeenth century.

Saint Johnstoun is the origin of the name of Perth's professional football club – St. Johnstone.

The name "Saint Johnstoun" was originally carried on an "I" class (superheated "H") locomotive of the North British Railway.

CLASS A2

INTRODUCTION AND GENERAL CHARACTERISTICS

In reality, Class A2 comprised four classes in one; none of them could be described as an unqualified success story overall. The Thompson designs in particular had a chequered and somewhat controversial history compared with those introduced by Peppercorn, which were generally more successful.

60501 – 60506 (6)

Class A2/2. In 1943, Gresley's magnificent Class P2 2-8-2's, introduced in 1934 for working over the difficult line between Edinburgh and Aberdeen, were extensively rebuilt as 'Pacifics' by **Edward Thompson** and re-classified.

The Class A2/2's were probably the least successful of Thompson's 'Pacific' designs and were progressively withdrawn between 1959 and 1961 after a somewhat undistinguished career, during which they were frequently consigned to freight and parcels traffic.

60507 – 60510 (4)

Class A2/1. The final four Gresley V2's under construction were also turned out as 'Pacifics' by Thompson in 1944, but retained their smaller V2 boilers. The resulting power classification (6MT) was less than that given to the remainder of the "Class" (7MT).

All four locomotives were often relegated to secondary duties. They, too, suffered early withdrawal, the last one disappearing from service in February, 1961.

60500
60511 – 60524 (15)

Class A2/3. These brand new 'Pacifics' were introduced by Thompson in 1946 as a development from Class A2/2.

In the immediate post war period many of the older Pacifics were in a somewhat run down and dilapidated condition with the result that the A2/3's played a major part in mainline duties and continued to do so until the advent of dieselisation, although they were progressively replaced on the top diagrams by the Peppercorn A1's. Withdrawal commenced towards the end of 1962 and all had gone by mid-1965.

60525 – 60539 (15)

Class A2. In 1947, the new Chief Mechanical Engineer, **A. H. Peppercorn**, re-designed the intended second batch of A2/3's with 6' 2" driving wheels but with a shorter wheelbase. The A2's were a far more attractive design than Thompson's variant, having the outside cylinders astride the front bogie. The modernity of the design included a self-cleaning smokebox and electric lighting.

Of the 15 locomotives built, all but one (No. 525) were completed and entered service after Nationalisation of the railways on 1st January, 1948.

The decision to fit single chimneys to such an enterprising and otherwise innovative design is surprising and resulted in a tendency to heavy coal consumption and poor steaming. The performance of six of the A2's was enhanced by the fitting of Kylchap double blast pipes and chimneys. In 1961, one of the six – 60526 **Sugar Palm** – attained a speed record for the Class of 101 mph on Stoke Bank (location of *Mallard*'s 1938 world speed record run); ironically, the first A2 was scrapped one year later in 1962 and all except 60532 **Blue Peter** (now preserved) had been withdrawn from service by 1966.

THE NAMES

For his Class P2 locomotives Gresley had revived heroic Scottish names previously associated with the North British H and I Classes, supplemented by others chosen from suggestions put forward by schoolboy readers of the "Boys' Own Paper". The Thompson A2/1's (built 1944/45) received Scottish names with similar heroic or romantic associations, affixed to the larger smoke deflectors with which the four locomotives were provided between October, 1946, and April, 1948.

With the exception of 60500 and 60525, which were named in recognition of the two CME's whose designs comprised the A2's, the remainder of the "Class" were named after racehorses, thereby continuing a long established LNER tradition.

The 28 racehorses thus commemorated in the names of the A2's included one winner of the English Triple Crown (**Barham**) and two others (**Airborne** and **Blue Peter**) which came close to achieving that distinction.

Most of the horses whose names were selected to adorn the A2's achieved their successes during the period 1941 – 1947. All the winners of the Derby and the St. Leger during those years were included.

Five of the final 6 names in the Class relate to an earlier period of time (1905-1919) and include two quite prolific winners in **Hornet's Beauty** and **Bachelor's Button**, although neither won any of the great Classic races. In the case of the final four locomotives, the Doncaster Cup achieved a prominence which was perpetuated in the later naming of the Peppercorn Class A1's.

DAVID H. BALDWIN

THE CLASS

A total of 40 Locomotives numbered 60500 to 60539

60500	Edward Thompson	60520	Owen Tudor
60501	Cock o' the North	60521	Watling Street
60502	Earl Marischal	60522	Straight Deal
60503	Lord President	60523	Sun Castle
60504	Mons Meg	60524	Herringbone
60505	Thane of Fife	60525	A. H. Peppercorn
60506	Wolf of Badenoch	60526	Sugar Palm
60507	Highland Chieftain	60527	Sun Chariot
60508	Duke of Rothesay	60528	Tudor Minstrel
60509	Waverley	60529	Pearl Diver
60510	Robert the Bruce	60530	Sayajirao
60511	Airborne	60531	Bahram
60512	Steady Aim	60532	Blue Peter
60513	Dante	60533	Happy Knight
60514	Chamossaire	60534	Irish Elegance
60515	Sun Stream	60535	Hornet's Beauty
60516	Hycilla	60536	Trimbush
60517	Ocean Swell	60637	Bachelor's Button
60518	Tehran	60538	Velocity
60519	Honeyway	60539	Bronzino

"WHEELS FARRAGO"

60500 EDWARD THOMPSON

Having graduated in Mechanical Sciences from Pembroke College, Cambridge, Edward Thompson worked both in industry and for the railways before being appointed Carriage and Wagon Superintendent of the GNR in 1912 and, subsequently, Workshop Manager of the Stratford Works.

When, in 1941, Thompson unexpectedly succeeded *Sir Nigel Gresley* as Chief Mechanical Engineer of the LNER, he was a man in a hurry. As Gresley's former Deputy, with particular responsibilities for

94

locomotive maintenance, Thompson was only too well aware of the shortcomings in the Gresley creations. He was also confronted by an immediate need to standardise designs and simplify maintenance procedures because of the constraints then imposed by wartime conditions.

With so little time to go before his own retirement in June, 1946, Thompson had much to do to introduce what he considered to be the necessary modifications to existing designs and, in particular, eliminate the weak feature of the Gresley 'Pacifics' i.e. the conjugated valve gear, which resulted in at least one dozen of the locomotives fitted with it being under repair at any one time.

It is said that Thompson's programme of work (see Introduction and General Characteristics) demonstrated a disdain for Gresley's engineering abilities. It is no secret that both men disagreed with each other on a number of fundamental issues and this animosity has been interpreted as a continuation of old rivalries between the NER (Thompson) and the GNR (Gresley). It has even been suggested that Thompson bore a grudge against his predecessor because Gresley had been preferred as CME of the LNER over *Sir Vincent Raven*, who was Thompson's father-in-law.

Whatever the truth of the matter, the verdict of history has not been particularly kind to Edward Thompson, whose critics generally regarded the changes introduced by him as being so radical that he succeeded only in "throwing the baby out with the bath water". In Thompson's defence, it has to be said that his B1 and L7 designs were well proportioned, readily maintained and easy to build in a country short of resources.

Outwardly, taciturn and aloof, Thompson would probably have attracted greater sympathy and support had his approach to his subordinates been less cavalier and his communication skills better developed.

Some believe that the LNER Board had **A. H. Peppercorn** in mind as Gresley's eventual successor and were placed in a dilemma by Sir Nigel's unexpected death in 1941. Thompson was then the most senior serving engineer, having received regular promotions until he was Mechanical Engineer, Doncaster, the next most important post to the CME himself.

Thompson explained after his retirement that he believed that the LNER's locomotive fleet desperately needed standardisation and that he intended to embark on a programme to reduce the number of types in service. *Sir Ronald Matthews* vetoed the introduction of new designs in wartime but, after obtaining an independent report from Stanier, agreed to the rebuilding of some existing Gresley-types.

Thompson's rebuilding of the Gresley P2's (problems with the conjugated gear, tyre wear and poor performance) was at first opposed by *Andrew K. McCosh*, Chairman of the Locomotive Committee, although McCosh became an enthusiastic convert to Thompson's rebuilding of all six in the light of favourable reports received from drivers of the rebuilt **Cock o' the North.**

This locomotive was named on the eve of Thompson's retirement at a ceremony held at Marylebone Station on 31st May, 1946.

60501 Cock o' the North

Reference has already been made to the fact that Gresley had revived heroic Scottish names carried by the North British 'H' and 'I' Classes for his P2's. The name 'Cock o' the North' had formerly graced "I" Class No. 903, introduced in August, 1911.

The Clan Gordon, one of the great families and major landowners of northwest Scotland, has played a prominent part in Scottish history and in the service of the Scottish Crown.

The third Earl of Huntly, (a title assumed by the Gordons in the fifteenth century), commanded one wing of the Scots army at Flodden and survived to tell the tale. When he died in 1523, he was succeeded by his grandson, George, who was made Lieutenant of the North. Whilst visiting George at Huntly Castle, the Queen

Regent, Mary of Guise, referred to him as 'Cock o' the North', a term which thenceforth was used to refer to all Gordon chiefs in succession.

A monument erected at Fochabers in Morayshire in honour of George, 5th Duke of Gordon, who raised the 92nd (Gordon) Highlanders in 1795, refers to him in this way. (Of incidental note, it will be recalled that the 92nd and other Highlanders achieved immortality by their famous charge at Waterloo, reputedly hanging on to the stirrups of the Scots Greys for greater momentum.)

The dukedom of Gordon became extinct in 1836; the rank of Marquis of Huntly, together with the chieftainship of the Clan Gordon, passed to the Earls of Aboyne.

60502 EARL MARISCHAL

The title of Great Marischal (pronounced "Marshall") originates from the French word 'marechal'. In addition to exercising the military (or martial) responsibilities associated with the title, the holder became custodian of the Scottish royal regalia, protector of the King at Parliament and, when necessary and appropriate, his diplomatic representative.

The title was first conferred by Malcolm II upon a warrior who killed his adversary the King of Denmark at the Battle of Barrie in 1010. The recipient was also made custodian for the King of the lands of Keth (origin of "Keith") in Midlothian. Although the line of succession is not always easy to follow, the title of Great Marischal then remained hereditary for over 700 years. In 1324 **Robert the Bruce** specifically made the office hereditary to the Keiths in recognition of the service given by Sir Robert de Keth, his commander of cavalry at the Battle of Bannockburn.

Around 1380, Sir Edward Keith-Marischal became Lord Keith, which title continued until 1458 when William Keith, 4th Lord Marischal, was made an Earl. A further ten Keiths then held the title of Earl Marischal until the failure of the Jacobite risings in

1715, when George Keith, the tenth and last Earl Marischal – a supporter of the Stewart cause – had to flee to the continent where he subsequently entered the service of Tsar Frederick the Great. George, who died childless in 1778, was stripped of his title by writ of attainder following the failure of the rebellion, and the Keith family also forfeited their lands.

60503 LORD PRESIDENT

The prominent Scottish family of Dalrymple originates from the parish of Stair, in Kyle, mid-Ayrshire. James Dalrymple of Stair (1619 – 1695) was to become one of the most eminent lawyers and statesmen of his day, eventually being elevated to the peerage as Viscount Stair. Stair's "Institutions of the Law of Scotland", first published in 1681, was the foundation of modern Scots law.

James Dalrymple graduated in Arts from Glasgow University in 1637. In 1638 he commanded a company in the Earl of Glencairns' regiment. In 1641, while still in uniform, he became a Professor of Philosophy at Glasgow, a post he held until 1647. In the following year he was called to the Scottish Bar, becoming an advocate. He was sent to Breda to invite Charles II to return to Scotland and assume his father's throne.

At the Restoration, Dalrymple was made one of the Lords of Session by Charles II and Knighted. In 1671, he became **Lord President** of the Court of Session, the highest judicial post in Scotland.

When he offended the future James VII by refusing to take the Test Oath (the purpose of which was to assert royal supremacy over the Church), he resigned his high office and fled to Holland. He returned with William of Orange following the 'Glorious Revolution' of 1689, was reappointed Lord President and, in due course, became the 1st Viscount Stair.

Lord Stair was also the father of Janet Dalrymple, whose tale was immortalised by *Sir Walter Scott* in "The Bride of Lammermoor".

60504 MONS MEG

In 1457, King James II of Scotland was presented with a pair of massive siege guns ('bombards') by his uncle the Duke of Burgundy. The sole surviving gun, known as "Mons Meg" is today displayed in Edinburgh Castle.

Made at Mons in Flanders, the cannon fired gunstones weighing 330 lbs/150 kg over a distance of two and half miles. In 1497, it saw action against the English at the siege of Norham Castle on the river Tweed but, because its great weight (over six tons) meant that it could only be moved at the rate of three miles a day (needing more than 100 men to manoeuvre it), by the middle of the sixteenth century it was retired from military service and restricted to the firing of salutes at important state ceremonies.

Mons Meg is known to have been fired in 1558 to celebrate the marriage of the infant Mary Queen of Scots to the Dauphin of France. When it was fired in 1681 to celebrate the birthday of the Duke of Albany (later King James VII) the barrel burst and had to be repaired. The gun was never fired again and left to rust.

Mons Meg was taken to England in 1754 and stored in the Royal Armouries in the Tower of London, along with other obsolete guns and weapons confiscated from the recently defeated Jacobite army. Following a campaign led by Sir Walter Scott and the Society of Antiquaries of Scotland, the gun was returned to Edinburgh Castle in March, 1829, having been escorted through the City from the Port of Leith by three troops of cavalry and the 78th Highlanders. The Royal Standard was hoisted, the bells rang out in St. Giles' Cathedral, and the bands played to cheering crowds

After 20 years in the prison vaults at Edinburgh Castle, to which the gun had been removed in 1980 because of concern over its conservation, Mons Meg reappeared on the ramparts of the castle in July, 2001, and there remains on display.

According to some authorities, "Meg" is derived from the Greek word *megas*, meaning 'great'. Others contend that "Meg" in Scotland is one of the short forms of "Margaret".

'You pays your money ......'

60505 THANE OF FIFE

"The Thane of Fife had a wife; where is she now?"

(Lady Macbeth)

For those familiar with 'the Scottish play', the above quotation from the famous sleepwalking scene will readily identify the Thane of Fife as Macduff, slayer of the "tyrannical" Macbeth.

Macbeth was immortalised by Shakespeare as the epitome of evil, a scheming murderer who usurped power illegitimately and who met a thoroughly deserved death at the hands of his enemies. In view of this reputation, which was entirely the creation of chroniclers whose stories Shakespeare embellished, it is important to recognise that Macbeth was regarded by all his contemporaries as a legitimate Scottish King. Although he did gain power by killing King Duncan I in 1040, this needs to be seen as the result of the kind of feud which was typical of early mediaeval Europe. Macbeth was the first Scottish King ever to make a pilgrimage to Rome and appears to have been a successful and effective monarch during his 17-year reign, which was ended by further "power play".

Macduff plays an important part in Shakespeare's drama, but the historical links between Macbeth and the Thane of Fife are somewhat more tenuous than portrayed by the bard. Macduff had been a supporter of King Duncan and may well have chosen to follow Malcolm on his flight into Northumbria, but there is no evidence that his wife and children were harmed in any way by Macbeth.

Contrary to the Shakespearean version of events, which culminated in Macduff bearing Macbeth's severed head to Malcolm, the battle of Dunsinnan (Dunsinane) near Perth, was indecisive, although it did result in Macbeth losing control of significant parts of the Kingdom. Malcolm launched another attack in 1057, as a result of which Macbeth was killed at Lumphanan near Aberdeen. It is possible that Macduff was present at both battles, but not in the dramatically decisive way portrayed by Shakespeare.

The name 'Thane of Fife' was formerly carried on an 'H' class locomotive of the NBR which entered service in July, 1906.

60506 WOLF OF BADENOCH

Alexander Stewart, son of the Scottish King Robert II, was not so much a 'hero' as a villainous creature of legend, notably barbarous even by the standards which prevailed in the middle of the fourteenth century.

Known as the Wolf of Badenock, Alexander ruled over the lands in his possession with cruelty and oppression, evicting or dispossessing those who crossed or displeased him.

Such was his rage when the Bishop of Moray took the side of his deserted wife, the Countess of Ross, that he ransacked and burned the Bishop's ecclesiastical centre of Elgin, forcing the terrified inhabitants to flee with their families into the surrounding countryside.

In 1390, the Wolf set fire to Elgin Cathedral, destroying many of its irreplaceable records and possessions. His father demanded that he do penance for this outrage under the watchful eye of the nobility and church dignitaries. He was subsequently pardoned and received back into the Church, although it appears from his behaviour that his repentance was superficial and short-lived.

Legend has it that Wolf of Badenoch died around 1400 AD after playing a game of chess with the Devil (which, presumably, he lost). In keeping with the best traditions which surround such matters, the night was racked by violent storms, with thunder, lightning and hailstones. When dawn broke and the storm abated, the Wolf's dead body was found in the banqueting hall of his castle. Although he appeared to have suffered no bodily injury, the nails in his boots had all been torn out. His men were discovered outside the castle walls, dead and blackened as if struck by lightning.

DAVID H. BALDWIN

The Wolf of Badenoch was buried in Dunkeld Cathedral.

60507 HIGHLAND CHIEFTAIN

The names 'Highland Chief' and 'Highland Chieftain' had formerly been carried on locomotives of the NBR (1911) and the LNER (1929) prior to the entry into service of Class A2/1 No. 507 in September, 1944.

Even today, the expression 'Highland Chieftain' conjures up romantic images of a tartan-clad Braveheart, the "noble savage" so beloved of the late eighteenth century Romantic movement in Art and Literature. Such heroic images have parallels in most other minority cultures (Indian brave or Zulu warrior, for example), where they serve as a rose-tinted reminder of better days – assuming, of course, that such days ever existed.

By the thirteenth century, the clan system was well established in the Scottish Highlands. The clan was a tribal organisation, a social grouping based on kinship. At its head was a Chief, who was also the owner of its lands. A large clan might have branches or septs, headed by Chieftains, who originally would be related to, or approved by, the Chief. ('Chief' and 'Chieftain' are taken here as being synonymous).

Between the Chief and the clansmen were the tacksmen who rented from him large tracts of land which they, in turn, sub-let for a profit. They were responsible for rent collecting and also for mobilising the men of the clan when the Chief wished to go to war.

Clans played a major part in the Jacobite rebellions of 1715 and 1745, after which their individual tartan Highland dress was banned. But by 1745 the system was already changing. Some Chiefs were becoming more interested in money than men, giving consideration to the possibilities for agriculture and forestry and dispensing with the tacksmen as costly intermediaries.

By the eighteenth century, with agricultural improvements spreading from the Lowlands and some road-building (and, hence, improved communications) taking place, clans and their Chiefs were being brought more and more into contact with "southern" ways. To what would have been a gradual social change the battle of Culloden gave brutal impetus, but even without the violent reaction of the Lowland authorities (the banning of tartan, the forfeiture of estates etc.) the old clan system was gradually being absorbed into a more modern economic society.

The fact that the Highland tradition did not die completely was due to a number of influences, including the Romantic movement referred to earlier. The great upsurge of interest in Highland dress came in 1822, after the celebrated visit to Edinburgh of King George IV, an event master-minded by Sir Walter Scott, whose novels had seized the public imagination. Not only the king, but also the Lord Mayor of London appeared in the kilt, as did Scott himself. Soon every well-known family in Scotland, Highland and Lowland, had its own tartan and within 75 years of its having been proscribed, the kilt had become Scotland's national dress.

In addition, Queen Victoria's love of the Highlands and *Balmoral*, together with her patronage of the Braemar Highland Gathering, helped sustain the fashion and the genuine interest in Scotland's Highland heritage.

60508 DUKE OF ROTHESAY

Rothesay is the chief town of the county and island of Bute. The village which grew up around Rothesay Castle was made a royal burgh by Robert III who, in 1398, created his eldest son David, Duke of Rothesay, which ultimately became the highest Scottish title of the heir apparent to the throne of the United Kingdom.

The present Prince of Wales holds several Scottish titles, including Duke of Rothesay, all of which were vested in the heir to the throne of Scotland by an Act of the Scottish Parliament in 1469.

The name 'Duke of Rothesay' was carried by an 'H' class locomotive of the North British Railway which entered traffic in June, 1921.

DAVID H. BALDWIN

60509 WAVERLEY

In addition to the Class A1/1 Pacific constructed in November, 1944, no fewer than seven standard gauge locomotives have carried the name 'Waverley', in recognition of the popularity and significance of the series of books by Sir Walter Scott which followed the publication of his first novel in 1814. Three of these seven locomotives, representing the London and North Western, Great Western and North British Railways, entered service more or less simultaneously in 1905/06.

Further, 'Waverley' has also been commemorated in a variety of other ways, including the name of Edinburgh's principal railway terminus; the NBR route across the Scottish Borders connecting Edinburgh and Carlisle; a steam-hauled express service on the London Midland Region route from St. Pancras to Edinburgh; and a River Clyde paddle steamer.

Sir Walter Scott's first novel was an immediate success. There followed the "Waverley novels" – romances of Scottish life that reveal Scott's great gift as a storyteller and his talent for vivid characterisation. The most successful of those works, like 'Waverley' itself, dealt with the two Jacobite rebellions of 1715 and 1745 against the new Hanoverian Kings of Great Britain, while others were concerned with earlier historical periods such as the Scottish religious wars and with the history of Edinburgh. They include *Guy Mannering* (1815), The Antiquary (1816), The Heart of Midlothian (1818), The Bride of Lammermoor (1819) and The Legend of Montrose (1819).

(See also Class A1 No. 60143)

60510 ROBERT THE BRUCE

Robert the Bruce (1274 – 1329), despite being portrayed in some quarters as a self-seeking opportunist, is probably Scotland's greatest national hero, even in comparison to his contemporary William Wallace. He was distantly related to the Scottish royal family but also owned lands in England, thereby owing allegiance to King Edward I.

Robert first joined the Scottish resistance movement around 1297, shortly after the defeated and humiliated John Balliol had surrendered his crown to Edward. To all outward appearances, however, he remained loyal to the English monarch during a period when Scottish independence had increasingly become a lost cause.

In 1298, the Bruce took over the guardianship of Scotland jointly with John Comyn of Badenoch, Balliol's nephew. On 13th February, 1306, he murdered Comyn in a Dumfries church, a deed for which he was outlawed by Edward I and excommunicated by the Pope.

Six weeks later, in a symbolic act of defiance, Robert the Bruce was crowned King of Scotland at Scone, from which location Edward had previously removed the Stone of Destiny and taken it to England. The Scots were routed at the battle of Methven by the enraged Edward, "the Hammer of the Scots", and a succession of further defeats led to the Bruce seeking refuge in the remote Scottish islands in the legendary world of caves and an inspirational spider.

He returned to the Scottish mainland in 1307, shortly before the death of Edward I and the succession of the ineffective Edward II. Robert waged a highly successful guerrilla war against the English occupiers culminating, in 1314, in the emphatic defeat of the numerically superior English army at Bannockburn.

A series of successful attacks across the Border finally brought recognition of the Bruce's kingship from an enfeebled English government. The Treaty of Northampton (1328) marked the re-establishment of an independent Scotland, Edward II's incompetence and Scottish patriotic fervour having been brilliantly exploited by Robert's active and shrewd leadership.

When Robert the Bruce died in 1329, his body was buried at Dunfermline but, in compliance with his last request, his heart was removed and taken on the Crusades by James "Black" Douglas who, just before he was killed in Moorish Spain, had apparently brandished and hurled it at the enemy. Happily, this once vital organ was recovered and subsequently buried at Melrose Abbey.

60511 AIRBORNE

Winner: 1946   The Derby, the Princess of Wales's Stakes, the St.Leger

On an overcast, drizzly day in June, 1946, and on going described as "heavy", Airborne, ridden by Tommy Lowrey, became the most recent of four grey horses to win the Derby.

Although he went on to win a total of five races in his career, including the 1946 St. Leger at Doncaster, his form prior to the Derby had been unremarkable, and he entered the race as a rank outsider in a field of 17 runners.

It must have seemed to the bookmaking fraternity, however, that virtually everyone who had served in or been associated with someone who had served in the RAF or the First Airborne Division had betted on Airborne, because the size of the pay-out when he came in at odds of 50/1 apparently bankrupted a number of bookmakers on the basis of that one result, a situation not repeated since.

At the stud, Airborne proved to be a better sire of jumpers than flat racers, although he did produce Silken Glider, winner of the 1957 Irish Oaks.

60512 STEADY AIM

Winner: 1946   The Oaks

Steady Aim, sired by *Felstead*, (a son of *Spion Kop* by *Spearmint*) won the 1946 Oaks, a flat race over a mile and a half for three year old thoroughbred fillies, run at Epsom Downs in early June.

She was ridden in the race by Harry Wragg, who had steered **Sun Stream** to victory in The Oaks in the previous year.

Wragg had a career as a jockey spanning 27 years, during which time he won 13 classic races, (including the 1928 Derby on Felstead, Steady Aim's sire). Because he could time his challenge in a race to perfection, he had acquired the nickname "the Head Waiter".

He became a trainer in 1947.

60513 DANTE

Winner:	1944	Coventry Stakes, Middle Park Stakes
	1945	The Derby

Dante became the last Yorkshire-trained winner of the Derby.

His Newmarket victory, by two lengths over Lord Rosebery's Midas, and witnessed by a crowd of over 50,000 people, including King George VI and Queen Elizabeth, was his eighth victory in nine starts, his only defeat being in the 2000 Guineas, when he came second, by a neck.

Dante's Derby win, at odds of 100/30, was to be his last race because, tragically, he became almost blind by the time of the St. Leger (won by **Chamossaire**) and had to be withdrawn.

His memory is perpetuated in the Dante Stakes, inaugurated in 1958, a flat-race for three year old thoroughbreds run at York in May, and considered the premier Derby trial.

60514 CHAMOSSAIRE

Winner:	1945	St. Leger

Chamossaire, a son of Precipitation, who had also sired **Airborne**, winner of the 1946 Derby, won the 1945 substitute St. Leger held at York racecourse. Ridden by Tommy Lowrey in a field of ten, and at odds of 11/2, Chamossaire beat the King's horse, Rising Light, into second place by two lengths. The favourite, **Dante**, had been withdrawn.

Coming only a couple of weeks after V-J Day, the York meeting was the first in peacetime and quite a celebration; 200,000 people were at the Knavesmire for the St. Leger alone, making this the largest number of people ever assembled to watch this classic race, many of them making the trip as their V-J holiday.

People started trekking to the course at 6 am and vast crowds arrived at York station in special trains. Among the early arrivals were charabanc loads of 'Geordies' and pitmen from the Durham area.

As part of the response to the logistical problems arising from this 'invasion', German prisoners-of-war were marshalled to clear a large area of the Knavesmire for a car-park. Coincidentally, workmen were, at the same time, busily filling in a tunnel discovered under the stand in the ten shilling ring by which previous German inmates had hoped to escape during the war.

Following his retirement, Chamossaire became a leading sire in England, producing 3 winners of the Irish Derby, (including his top earner, Santa Claus, which also won the Epsom Derby) and one St. Leger winner.

60515 Sun Stream

Winner:	1944	Queen Mary Stakes
	1945	1,000 Guineas, The Oaks

Sun Stream, a daughter of *Hyperion*, was foaled in 1942 and bred by Lord Derby. She won the Queen Mary Stakes at two and, at three, with Harry Wragg on board, became one of 46 fillies to win both the 1000 Guineas and The Oaks.

As a broodmare, Sun Stream produced 4 winners.

60516 HYCILLA

Winner:	1944	Champion Stakes, The Oaks

Foaled in 1941 by *Hyperion* out of Priscilla Carter, Hycilla was the champion three year old filly in England. She won The Oaks and the Champion Stakes in 1944, but was unplaced in the St. Leger.

Hycilla was retired to the stud in America, producing four minor winners.

60517 OCEAN SWELL

Winner: 1944   The Derby, Jockey Club Cup
           1945   Ascot Gold Cup

Ocean Swell, a good stayer who won six races, was sired by **Blue Peter**. Owned by Lord Rosebery, he was ridden to victory in the 1944 Derby by Billy Nevett, who also rode **Dante** to success in 1945. The race was held at Newmarket under wartime restrictions, and the 10,000 crowd was only a fraction of the number in attendance at the last peacetime race in 1939.

Ocean Swell went on to win the Ascot Gold Cup when the race returned from its temporary home at Newmarket in 1945.

He disappointed at the stud, and died relatively early at the age of 13.

60518 TEHRAN

Winner: 1944   St. Leger

Ridden by Gordon Richards, Tehran, a son of *Bois Roussel*, won the 1944 St. Leger, on the July Course at Newmarket.

Tehran's owner, the 67 year old Aga Khan, "celebrated" his win by buying several horses at the Newmarket Sales, and by publishing the banns for his fourth marriage, his intended being a former "Miss France" thirty years his junior.

He was leading sire of 1952 (Tehran, that is) producing Tulyar, winner of the 1952 Eclipse Stakes and King George VI & Queen Elizabeth Diamond Stakes, plus the winners of the 1951 Eclipse Stakes and the 1958 Irish Oaks.

60519 HONEYWAY

Winner: 1946   Champion Stakes, King George V Stakes

On of *Fairway*'s most important sire sons, and a brilliant sprinter, Honeyway won the July Cup at four and, at five, the Cork and Orrery Stakes, Victoria Cup, King George V Stakes and the Champion Stakes. His best distance was six furlongs but, in this latter race, he stretched to ten furlongs, beating Gulf Stream.

Also in 1946, he won the Emirates (Airline) Champion Stakes which, by 2004, had become Newmarket's most valuable race of the season.

Retired to the stud, Honeyway proved infertile, and so was put back in training at six, where he won the Coombe Stakes plus two other races and finished third in the July Cup.

Returned to the stud, his fertility problems were resolved and he proved a successful stallion. His progeny included Great Nephew, sire of Shergar.

60520 OWEN TUDOR

Winner: 1941   The Derby
            1942   Ascot Gold Cup

Owen Tudor was a son of *Hyperion*, foaled in 1938. He had 6 wins in 13 starts.

At two, he was rated among the top 8 juveniles of the year, winning the Salisbury Stakes on his first outing, and coming second in the Boscawen Stakes.

At three, ridden by Billy Nevett, he won the wartime substitute Derby at Newmarket at odds of 25/1 and went on to win the Column Stakes.

At four, he won the Ascot Gold Cup, also run at Newmarket because of wartime restrictions. Gordon Richards' win on Owen Tudor was the first of a hat-trick of Gold Cups for the champion jockey.

Owen Tudor's record as a sire was impressive, his sons including the brilliant miler **Tudor Minstrel** and the grey Abernant, winner of 14 of his 17 races.

60521 WATLING STREET

Winner: 1942   The Derby

Watling Street, another son of *Fairway*, was bred by Lord Derby at the Thornton Stud, near Thirsk.

Aged two, he won the Chesterfield Stakes and took second place in the Coventry Stakes. At three, he won the Shelford Stakes, then came second in the 2000 Guineas.

Ridden by Harry Wragg, Watling Street won the 1942 wartime Derby by a neck, at odds of 6/1, in a field of 13 runners. He then came second in the St. Leger, beaten by the filly star and season champion, **Sun Chariot**.

Watling Street went to stud at four, but sired only a few stakes winners, with no top class runners. Sent to the USA in 1952, he died in the following year.

60522 STRAIGHT DEAL

Winner: 1943   The Derby

Winner of a wartime substitute Derby in 1943, Straight Deal, son of *Solario*, was owned by Dorothy Paget, daughter of Lord Queensborough and an American heiress mother, who had registered her colours in 1930. Winner of five races, including the Derby, Straight Deal was ridden by Tommy Carey, and came in at odds of 100/6.

The rich and eccentric Dorothy Paget, who had rather more money than sense, owned a stable of thoroughbreds as well as the stud farm in Ireland where Arkle was foaled. Her horses won over 1500 races in both flat and hurdling. She owned seven Cheltenham Gold Cup winners, including Golden Miller five times, 1932-36 inclusive. Although she spent today's equivalent of many millions of pounds on bloodstock, Straight Deal was home bred and sire of the Champion Hurdle winner of 1957.

Dorothy Paget thought nothing of betting £10,000 on one of her horses(or of losing at least £20,000 in one day, which she did often), usually dressed in the same shapeless coat and French beret superstition dictated she wore year after year. Despite the number of winners, her returns from racing were far below her outlay; she blamed her trainers and changed them frequently. She could be demanding and difficult and was well-known for telephoning trainers in the middle of the night; at least one trainer (Walter Nightingale, trainer of Straight Deal, whose win gave Miss Paget her only classic success in 30 years of flat racing), rebelled against her unreasonable behaviour, threatening to turn her horses loose on Epsom High Street if she did not take them away from his yard within 24 hours.

When she was driving one day to the races her Rolls Royce broke down. Seeing the local butcher's Baby Austin, she instructed her secretary to commandeer it, offering £200. When it was refused, because the owner was about to take his mother for a drive, she raised the offer to £300, plus a trip to the races with her – without the mother. The offer was quickly accepted. (Her secretary routinely carried up to £5,000 for such miscellaneous expenses). After this little contretemps, Dorothy Paget always took two Rolls Royces to race meetings, to avoid any mechanical embarrassment.

Perhaps not surprisingly, she was only 54 when she died of heart failure in 1960.

60523 SUN CASTLE

Winner: 1941   St. Leger

A son of *Hyperion*, foaled in 1938, Sun Castle came third in the 2000

Guineas of 1941, was unplaced in the Derby, and won the wartime substitute St. Leger, run at Manchester, in which he defeated **Owen Tudor**.

Kept in training, he developed tetanus and was humanely destroyed.

60524 HERRINGBONE

Winner: 1943   St. Leger, 1000 Guineas

Herringbone was sired by King Salmon, (a son of *Salmon Trout*), who had enjoyed racing success as a winner of the Eclipse Stakes and the Coronation Cup, and as a runner-up in the Derby and the 2000 Guineas.

Owned by Lord Derby, and ridden by Harry Wragg, Herringbone won the 1943 St. Leger at odds of 100/6, and went on to capture the 1000 Guineas, both run as wartime substitute races at Newmarket.

The 1000 Guineas is the fillies' equivalent of the 2000 Guineas, run over the same course and distance as the early-May meeting. The youngest of the five classics, it was inaugurated as recently as 1814!

60525 A. H. PEPPERCORN

Arthur H. Peppercorn was born in Leominster on 29th January, 1889, and apprenticed to the Great Northern Railway in 1905. He became the last Chief Mechanical Engineer of the LNER on 1st July, 1946, in succession to **Edward Thompson**.

During his brief spell in office (18 months) he ceased production of Thompson's A2/2 Pacific but persisted with the Thompson rebuild of the Gresley K4 (now reclassified K1) of which he ordered 70. He also continued production of the Thompson B1's and L1's.

Peppercorn is best known for his Class A1 and A2 Pacifics. The former, in particular, acquired a reputation as being among the best steaming locomotives ever to run in Britain.

Peppercorn retired from British Railways in 1949 after only 2 years with the new regime. He died on 3rd March, 1951.

(See also Classes A1 and A2 – Introduction and General Characteristics)

60526 SUGAR PALM

Winner:	1942	Steward's Cup
	1943	Steward's Cup
	1944	Nunthorpe Stakes

At stud in Newmarket, the stallion Sir Cosmo produced a bloodline of crack sprinters, including Sugar Palm. A great public favourite, he was successful in 21 races, none of them the major classics.

The Steward's Cup, won in consecutive years by Sugar Palm, is a race for three year old thoroughbreds held at Goodwood. The Nunthorpe Stakes, normally run at York during the Ebor Festival meeting in August, was held at Newmarket in 1944.

60527 SUN CHARIOT

Winner:	1941	Middle Park Stakes, Queen Mary Stakes
	1942	St. Leger, 1000 Guineas, The Oaks

All three races won by Sun Chariot in 1942 were held at Newmarket that year and made a major contribution towards a record quartet of classic victories for King George VI (the fourth race being the 2000 Guineas won by Big Game). Despite her fiery temperament, which gave Gordon Richards one or two problems, Sun Chariot was considered one of the finest fillies ever to race and worthy of inclusion in the "hall of fame" alongside the likes of *Sceptre* and *Pretty Polly*.

Sired by *Hyperion*, Sun Chariot was bred in Ireland by the National Stud and leased to King George VI for racing. A brilliant, but moody, sometimes erratic filly, she showed little early potential and was nearly retired unraced but, just in time, sorted herself out and never looked back.

Undefeated in 4 starts, including the Queen Mary and Middle Park Stakes, Sun Chariot emerged as champion two year old over stablemate Big Game and **Watling Street**.

At three, she was third in her debut race, her only career loss in 9 starts, and then won the Sarum Stakes, plus her three classic successes with Gordon Richards. In The Oaks, she caused three false starts then, at the final break, bolted in the wrong direction but still managed to win the race by a length.

As a broodmare, she produced four stakes winners from eleven foals before her death in 1963.

Considering her contribution to the King's record of four classic winners it is, perhaps, surprising that a race – the Sun Chariot Stakes – was not named after the filly until 1966.

60528 TUDOR MINSTREL

Winner: 1946   Coventry Stakes
            1947   2000 Guineas, St. James's Palace Stakes

Tudor Minstrel was sired by **Owen Tudor** from Sansonnet, a daughter of *Sansovino*.

Ridden by Gordon Richards, Tudor Minstrel had won all 6 races entered as a three year old. When he finished fourth to the French-trained **Pearl Diver** in the 1947 Derby, some newspapers described his defeat as a national tragedy. He had won the 2000 Guineas in a canter by a record eight lengths, and providing Gordon Richards with a first Derby win was supposed to be a formality. He started at 4/7 at Epsom, but refused to settle, fought for his head from the start, and was beaten early in the straight. Afterwards, he proved to be an exceptional miler, easily winning the St. James's Palace Stakes.

It took Gordon Richards 28 attempts to win the Derby, which he finally did, on Pinza, in 1953 at the age of 49 and in the week in which he received a Knighthood from the newly-crowned Queen Elizabeth II.

60529 PEARL DIVER

Winner: 1947 The Derby

This tall, French-trained horse, whose dam was the first mare to win the Prix de L'Arc de Triomphe, shocked the racing world by winning the 1947 Epsom Derby at odds of 40/1, his only English victory.

(See 60528 **Tudor Minstrel**)

60530 SAYAJIRAO

Winner: 1947   Lingfield Derby Trial, Irish Derby, St. Leger
           1948   Hardwicke Stakes

Sayajirao was sired by Nearco from Rosy Legend (also the dam of **Dante**, winner of the 1945 Derby).

Bred in Middleham at the Manor House Stud, Sayajirao set a European Yearling Auction record of 28,000 Guineas, unbeaten until 1966. He proved to be well worth the money. Owned by the Maharajah of Baroda he came third in the 2000 Guineas and the Derby, before winning the 1947 Irish Derby and the St. Leger at Doncaster.

At stud, he sired winners of the Irish Oaks and the Irish 1000 Guineas, the Cesarewitch, the Ascot Gold Cup and the Goodwood Cup.

60531 BAHRAM

Winner: 1934 Middle Park Stakes, Gimcrack Stakes
1935 St. Leger, The Derby, 2000 Guineas, St. James's Palace Stakes

The Shining Star in the A2 firmament, the Aga Khan's Bahram entered the 1935 St. Leger unbeaten in 8 races and came out of it unbeaten in 9, including that year's "Triple Crown". It was to be another 35 years before Nijinsky won the three classic races in 1970.

This was the third time that the Aga Khan's colours had been successful in the St. Leger, the previous two occasions being when they were placed first by *Salmon Trout* in 1924 and by *Firdaussi* in 1932.

Bahram won the Derby and St. Leger so easily as to invite speculation that he might have been the best horse seen for many years; others were not so sure, pointing to the relative inferiority of the horses he beat. As it was, neither point of view was ever tested because the St. Leger was Bahram's last race. He went to stud with a reputation so great that, at a fee of 500 guineas, his 'book' was full for three years immediately after, if not before, he won the Doncaster Classic.

In 1940, Bahram was sold to the US by the Aga Khan for £40,000. His record as a sire in the States was comparatively palid and he was subsequently sold on to South America where his progeny was equally undistinguished.

60532 BLUE PETER

Winner: 1939 2000 Guineas, The Derby, Eclipse Stakes

In 1939, Lord Rosebery's Blue Peter, a son of *Fairway*, won the 2000 Guineas before proving a dominant winner of the Derby and then adding the Eclipse Stakes. The opportunity to win the St. Leger (and thereby settle the question of supremacy in Europe over the French horse Pharis, which had won the French Derby and the Grand Prix de Paris) was denied him by the outbreak of war in September. But for that occurrence Blue Peter's name may well have joined the illustrious list of winners of the English Triple Crown.

Blue Peter was the sire of **Ocean Swell**, a later Derby hero and winner of the Ascot Gold Cup (see 60517) but otherwise produced only one other Classic winner.

This locomotive is the only A2 to have been preserved following withdrawal.

60533 HAPPY KNIGHT

Winner: 1946 2000 Guineas

Happy Knight, a son of *Colombo*, won the 1946 classic by four lengths. His jockey was Tommy Weston who, 20 years previously, had ridden *Colorado* to victory in the same race.

60534 IRISH ELEGANCE

Winner: 1918 July Cup
1919 Royal Hunt Cup, Portland Handicap

Named after a rose, Irish Elegance was a magnificent, weight - carrying chestnut who won 8 of his 16 races and, like **Sugar Palm**, was adored by the racing public. He is still rated as the second best sprinter of the last century.

Irish Elegance ran third in the Cambridgeshire in 1918, and in 1919 won the Salford Borough Handicap at Manchester, four days before his great victory in the Royal Hunt Cup, carrying 26 pounds more than the second place runner and completing the race in the fastest time recorded to that date.

60535 HORNET'S BEAUTY

Winner: 1911 The King's Stand Stakes, Queen Ann Stakes
1912 Challenge Stakes
1913 The Cork and Orrery Stakes, The King's Stand Stakes, Portland Handicap, King George V Stakes
1914 Challenge Stakes, the Cork and Orrery Stakes

This tough and long-running bay gelding, who won 31 of his 55 starts over 6 seasons, is another horse which caught the public imagination and is widely regarded as the best gelding to race in England in the last century.

60536 TRIMBUSH

Winner: 1947 Doncaster Cup

The Doncaster Cup, once known as the Doncaster Gold Cup, is a flat race for thoroughbreds of three years and over, run during the St. Leger meeting in September. First run in 1766, together with the Goodwood Cup and Ascot Gold Cup it is part of the British Stayers' Triple Crown for horses capable of running longer distances.

60537 BACHELOR'S BUTTON

Winner: 1904 Champion Stakes, the Queen's Vase
         1905 Queen's Vase, Hardwicke Stakes, Doncaster Cup
         1906 Jockey Club Cup, Ascot Gold Cup

(See Class A3 No. 60061 *Pretty Polly*)

Bachelor's Button won 16 of over 40 races in his career, the highlight being his defeat of the wonder mare *Pretty Polly* in the Ascot Gold Cup of 1906, her final race. He was bred in Ireland from a mare costing 45 guineas, whose only success had been a minor race over hurdles at Wye in Kent. He was extremely tough, a dour stayer who could stand any amount of work. Several stable companions were broken down in trials with him.

In the Gold Cup, Bachelor's Button, ridden by American jockey "Danny" Maher, won by a length at odds of 7-1 against. In a field of five, he and Pretty Polly fought it out to the finish, stride by stride. The mare seemed to be unsettled by the sweltering conditions and by having had a wart on her belly lanced in the racecourse stables; whatever the reason, she was beaten by the better horse on the day.

Bachelor's Button failed to get the applause he deserved. It is beyond dispute that, assisted by St. Denis as peacemaker, he had run a brilliant race, but was still viewed as something of a villain. Danny Maher, defiant and triumphant, declared that his assessment of Pretty Polly as a non-stayer had been proved correct.

Bachelor's Button was a failure at stud and died in France in 1916.

60538 VELOCITY

Winner: 1905   Cambridgeshire Handicap
           1906   Doncaster Cup
           1907   Doncaster Cup

60539 BRONZINO

Winner: 1910   Greenham Stakes, Doncaster Cup

Bronzino, whose dam was a daughter of *Galopin*, was a golden chestnut colt, foaled in 1907.

Owned by James de Rothschild, he first raced at age three, winning the Greenham Stakes at the Newbury Spring Meeting. He was unplaced in the 2000 Guineas then ran third in the Grand Prix de Paris, beating Derby winner *Lemberg*. Back in England, he ran second, by a head, in the Doncaster St. Leger, Lemberg finishing third; this was the fastest St. Leger at that time. Two days later, he won the Doncaster Cup. He ran fourth in the Cesarewitch, having bruised his heel a few days before the race.

At age four, he was third in the City and Suburban and second in the Derby Gold Cup. Next season, he ran second for the Manchester Cup, conceding 38 pounds to the winner! He broke down during preparation for the Ascot Gold Cup, and was retired.

Bronzino was shipped to Australia in August, 1912, to begin his stud career and there sired several stakes winners.

CLASS V2

INTRODUCTION AND GENERAL CHARACTERISTICS

The first of the Gresley V2's appeared in June, 1936. A total of 184 were built, numbered 60800 to 60983.

The choice of a "Prairie" 2-6-2 tender locomotive was certainly unusual, if not unique, in this country. The original specification appears to have been for an 'improved' enlarged K3, with larger driving wheels, capable of much heavier mixed traffic haulage at greater speed. In fact, with their large taper boilers and wide fireboxes, the V2's were really smaller "Pacifics" and their proven capabilities eventually resulted in their use on exactly the same diagrams as their larger A3 cousins.

Originally intended for fast freight services, they handled all types of main line traffic and even proved themselves equal to the task of deputising – albeit infrequently – for a failed A4 Pacific.

Although claimed to be mixed traffic types, their great weight made them suitable only for RA9 routes (Class One main lines) unlike the other ubiquitous types on other railways. With an axle loading of 22 tons, the V2's were restricted to 40 per cent of the LNER's route miles. They were barred from **all** of the ex-Great Eastern main lines.

That said, they took all types of traffic over the whole length of the ECML as far north as Aberdeen. Their strength gave a good showing on the difficult Waverley route between Carlisle and Edinburgh and their ability to start heavy loads and accelerate quickly made them preferred to A3's on the Great Central section.

The V2's will be particularly remembered for their Herculean feats during World War II when they were frequently at the head of trains of more than 20 coaches, loaded to 700 tons. On at least one occasion a single V2 hauled no fewer than 26 coaches from Peterborough to London!

Ultimately, but really far too late, the Kylchap double exhaust was fitted to six of the class, enabling what many consider to have been Gresley's true masterpiece to show its real potential, with at least one of the converted locomotives achieving a three figure speed.

V2 withdrawals took place steadily from 1962 and the last one was taken out of service in December, 1966. Only **Green Arrow** has been preserved.

THE NAMES

Only eight of the class were named, possibly because of the difficulty of finding "themed" names for all 184 locomotives although, to begin with, they would have been far better suited to the names of the fleet-footed antelopes inappropriately chosen for 40 of the Thompson B1's.

Of the eight locomotives, seven were named between 1936 and 1939 and one in 1958. The prototype **Green Arrow**, which took its name from the fast freight service introduced by the LNER at that time, was the only one to have its nameplates displayed on the smokebox.

The other 'namers' reverted to the curved dummy splasher-fixed style and comprised famous regiments and a couple of schools. Noticeably, all had connections with Yorkshire or with the North East of England. The regimental titles were in full, resulting in two names of rather absurd length.

60800	Green Arrow
60809	The Snapper, The East Yorkshire Regiment, The Duke of York's own
60835	The Green Howard, Alexandra, Princess of Wales's Own Yorkshire Regiment
60847	St. Peter's School, York, A.D. 627
60860	Durham School
60872	King's Own Yorkshire Light Infantry
60873	Coldstreamer
60964	Durham Light Infantry

V2 "ROCKETS" – THE NAMED LOCOMOTIVES

60800 GREEN ARROW

Faced with growing competition from road transport, the LNER introduced in 1936 a fast overnight Anglo-Scottish rail freight service that could handle anything from parcels to bulk loads. In many respects the forerunner of today's container train, the LNER's publicity Department settled on the name "Green Arrow" for the new service.

Initially, Doncaster built only five V2's, headed by the now preserved No. 4771 (BR No. 60800), which was promptly named 'Green Arrow' after the fast freight service for which it had been designed and constructed.

60809 THE SNAPPER, THE EAST YORKSHIRE REGIMENT, THE DUKE OF YORK'S OWN

This locomotive was officially named (as LNER No. 4780) at Paragon Station, Hull, on 11th September, 1937.

The East Yorkshire Regiment was raised at Nottingham in June, 1685, as Sir William Clifton's Regiment of Foot. It was subsequently named after successive Colonels of the Regiment until 1751, when it became the 15th Regiment of Foot.

In 1702, the Regiment formed part of Marlborough's Army and took part in the battles of Blenheim, Ramillies, Malplaquet and Oudenarde. The 15th served in the West Indies and, after a brief return to England, played a major part in the defeat of the French in the struggle for supremacy in Canada. In memory of General Wolfe's death in the battle for the Heights of Abraham, the Officers took to wearing a black line in their gold lace. In later years, a black backing was incorporated into the Regimental Badge and the action was commemorated every September 13th.

The 15th Foot fought in the war of American Independence from

123

1776 to 1778. At the Battle of Brandywine in 1777, the Regiment ran short of ball ammunition and all but the best shots were ordered to fire small powder charges only ("snapping"), the equivalent of today's "blanks". The bluff succeeded, the enemy attack was not pressed home and the Regiment gained the nickname "The Snappers".

In 1770, the Regiment – now titled the 15th (The Yorkshire East Riding) Regiment of Foot – deployed to the West Indies for another six years. In 1809, it returned to expel the French from Martinique and Guadeloupe. More than sixty years then passed before the 15th saw action again in the Afghan War (1879 – 80). Service in the Boer War (1900 – 02) – by which time the 15th had become The East Yorkshire Regiment – produced many casualties, commemorated in the south aisle of Beverley Minster.

In the First World War, the Regiment grew rapidly to 21 battalions and took part in all the major engagements on the Western Front, including the Somme and Passchendaele, winning four Victoria Crosses among a considerable number of decorations for gallantry.

Following the Armistice of 1918, battalions of the Regiment served in Iraq, India and North China. In 1935 the Regiment was granted the title "The Duke of York's Own".

In 1939, the 2nd, 4th and 5th Battalions, (the latter two being Territorial Units), were sent to France. Following this, battalions of the Regiment served in the Middle East and Sicily. The 2nd and 5th were in the initial assault on the Normandy beaches in 1944, while the 1st was in the final advance in Burma prior to the Japanese surrender in August, 1945.

In 1958, the Regiment was amalgamated with the West Yorkshire Regiment (Prince of Wales's Own) to form the Prince of Wales's Own Regiment of Yorkshire.

60835 THE GREEN HOWARD, ALEXANDRA, PRINCESS OF WALES'S OWN YORKSHIRE REGIMENT

The Regiment was first raised in November, 1688, by Colonel Francis Luttrell at Dunster Castle in Somerset for service under William, Prince of Orange, following his landing at Torbay. (The event is depicted in a painting by the celebrated railway artist Terence Cuneo).

The Regiment first became known as 'The Green Howards' in 1744 – at a time when regiments traditionally took the name of their Colonel – in order to distinguish it from another regiment whose Colonel was also named Howard. As one Regiment wore green facings to its uniform it became known as "The Green Howards". The other regiment wore buff facings and became known as "The Buff Howards" (later 'The Buffs').

The nickname "Green Howards" stuck, and survived until 1920 when it became the official title of the Regiment.

The Regiment first became associated with, and affiliated to, the North Riding of Yorkshire in 1782 when it was granted the title of "The 19th (First Yorkshire North Riding) Regiment of Foot", although it was not until 1873 that Richmond in Yorkshire became the Regiment's home town.

In 1875, Queen Alexandra, then Princess of Wales, presented the Regiment with new colours to replace those which had been carried throughout the Crimean War. The Regiment was granted the title "The Princess of Wales's Own".

In 1881, the name of the regiment was again altered to become "The Princess of Wales's Own Yorkshire Regiment; the name 'Alexandra' was added after the Boer War.

Finally, in 1920, the title of the Regiment became "The Green Howards (Alexandra, Princess of Wales's Own Yorkshire Regiment)".

The Regiment first saw active service in Ireland and was present at the Battle of the Boyne in July, 1690. It served with Marlborough in

Flanders (1707 – 1714) and, like the East Yorkshire Regiment, (then the 15th Foot), took part in the Battle of Malplaquet. Between 1761 and 1854 the Regiment was actively involved in many campaigns, including the American War of Independence.

During the Crimean War (1854 – 56), the 19th Foot played a distinguished part in the Battles of the Alma and Inkerman and in the Siege of Sebastapol, winning two Victoria Crosses in the process.

The period between 1857 and 1897 saw service in India (twice) and in the Sudan. A third Victoria Cross was awarded after the Battle of Paardeberg in the South African (Boer) War (1899 – 1902).

Twenty four battalions were raised during the First World War, when the Regiment was involved in most of the principal battles and campaigns. A further twelve Victoria Crosses were included among numerous awards for gallantry.

Between 1918 and 1939, the Regiment took part in the Third Afghan War of 1919, operations in Palestine during 1938 and many internal security deployments overseas, including those in Shanghai between 1927 and 1930.

In the Second World War, twelve battalions of the Regiment were raised. The Regiment fought in Norway, the Western Desert, Sicily, Italy, Burma, France, Holland and Germany. Two battalions were among the first to land in the assault on D-Day, 1944, where CSM Stan Hollis, 6th Battalion, received the only Victoria Cross to be awarded for bravery on 6th June. Two other Victoria Crosses were won in the Western Desert and Burma.

This locomotive was ceremonially named at Richmond Station, Yorkshire, on 24th September, 1938, (as LNER No. 4806) "to commemorate the 250th year of the raising of the Regiment 1688 – 1938". The chosen name and style (including the singular 'Howard') distinguishes the V2 from LMS 'Royal Scot' Class locomotive No. 46133 *The Green Howards*, which had received its name in May, 1936.

60847 St. Peter's School, York, AD 627

As LNER No. 4818, this locomotive was officially named at York Station on 3rd April, 1939.

The history of St. Peter's School in York spans over 1300 years. Although the exact origins of the school are unknown, the favoured date for the founding of St. Peter's is AD 627, which was the year when the first wooden church of St. Peter was built on the site of the present York Minister and the city became the headquarters of the Roman Mission in Northumbria.

The driving force behind the establishment of the new church was St. Paulinus, a Christian Missionary from Rome and the first Archbishop of York. There is evidence that a song school was built next to the wooden church during Paulinus's reign (AD 627 – 633) and it is most likely that a grammar school co-existed with the song school, as was the case in Canterbury, Rochester and London.

Christianity certainly brought learning to York. In the eight century, the renowned scholar, Alcuin, was Master of the School of St. Peter which received students from all over Europe. By the time he left Britain, York was the most important centre of learning in this part of the country.

The city of York was much changed by the Viking invasion of AD 867, but St. Peter's was by then sufficiently well established to both survive and prosper under the new regime.

Following the Norman Conquest, the modernising tendencies of William the Conqueror and his ministers proved to be beneficial for the school. William's Chaplain established a Chancellor at York Minster, one of whose duties was to act as schoolmaster for St. Peter's.

In 1289, the nave of York Minister was widened and the school was forced to move to a new home on its south side. Borders were housed at nearby St. Mary's Abbey, and continued to be so until the abbey was destroyed during the Reformation in the 16th Century.

Following the destruction of St. Mary's Abbey, an old hospital outside Bootham Bar was converted into a new school called "the School of the Cathedral Church of St. Peter of York". Its first headmaster was appointed in 1575 and St. Peter's entered a new era.

Although the new school site was badly damaged during the Civil War siege of York in 1644, and had to move to Bedern, it continued to flourish and provide a first-class education for its scholars. The school petitioned to establish a University here, but without success.

In 1833, the school moved again – this time to new buildings in the Minister Yard on the site of the Old Deanery. This was short-lived. Just eleven years later, in 1844, St. Peter's moved to its present site in the centre of York.

Famous "old boys" of the School include Guy Fawkes of gunpowder plot fame (or infamy), Oscar- winning musician John Barry and former Yorkshire cricket captains Norman Yardley and Brian Sellers.

60860 DURHAM SCHOOL

The naming ceremony (of LNER No. 4831) took place at Elvet Station, Durham, on 15th June, 1939.

Durham School is one of the most ancient schools in Great Britain. It has a history and tradition that stretches back centuries, possibly as far back as the monastic settlement on Lindisfarne which came to Durham some nine hundred years ago, and may have been moved to Durham City to escape marauding Vikings.

As the Bishop's School, it was reorganised and endowed by Cardinal Langley in 1414 and was re-founded in 1541 by King Henry VIII under the control of the Dean and Chapter of Durham Cathedral. It moved to its present site in the heart of this historic city in 1844.

Durham School Rugby Football Club, founded in 1850, is among the oldest in the world and has produced many international players and also British Lions.

60872 KING'S OWN YORKSHIRE LIGHT INFANTRY

The 51st Regiment of Foot was raised in Leeds in 1755. On 1st August, 1759, the 51st took part in the Battle of Minden and, together with five other British regiments, beat off and drove back three waves of attacking French cavalry.

The 51st was part of Wellington's Peninsula army during the Napoleonic wars and was present at the Battle of Waterloo (1815). It is claimed that the first shots of the battle were fired by the Regiment from its position close to Hougoumont Farm.

In the nineteenth century, the 51st served mainly in India, on the North West Frontier and in Burma. In the army reforms of 1881, the Regiment was paired with the 105th Madras European Light Infantry to form the 1st and 2nd Battalions, respectively, of the King's Own Light Infantry (South Yorkshire Regiment). In 1888, this name was changed to the King's Own Yorkshire Light Infantry (KOYLI).

The 2nd Battalion KOYLI was involved in the Boer War at the turn of the Century. The Regiment raised twenty six Battalions for service in the First World War and saw action on the Western Front, Italy, Salonika and Egypt, winning six Victoria Crosses and almost 1400 other awards for gallantry.

(Of incidental note, *Sir Ronald Matthews*, Chairman of the LNER, saw service in the Great War as an officer in the KOYLI.)

In 1927, the then Duchess of York (subsequently Queen Elizabeth and Queen Mother), was appointed Colonel-in-Chief of the Regiment.

On the outbreak of the Second World War, the 1st KOYLI went

to France, while the 2nd Battalion was in Burma. The territorial battalions served with distinction in North Africa, Italy and North-West Europe. Other battalions of the Regiment were converted to regiments of the Royal Artillery, while the 7th became a regiment of the Royal Armoured Corps and fought at Kohima and Imphal in 1944.

At the end of the war, the KOYLI, whose recruiting area was mainly the industrial West Riding, South and North Yorkshire, was reduced to one regular battalion. Further reforms in 1968 saw the amalgamation of all light infantry regiments into the Light Infantry, the KOYLI forming its second battalion. Distinctions of dress served as an ever-present reminder of the constituent regiments; in the case of the KOYLI, the wearing of white roses on Minden Day.

The nameplates on this locomotive (as LNER No. 4843) were unveiled in Doncaster Works Yard on 20th May, 1939.

60873 COLDSTREAMER

This locomotive was named at King's Cross Station (as LNER No. 4844) on 20th June, 1939. The chosen name distinguishes it from LMS 'Royal Scot' Class locomotive No. (4)6114 *Coldstream Guardsman*, which had entered service in September, 1927.

During the Irish campaign which followed his success in the English Civil War, *Oliver Cromwell* became impressed by the military capabilities of a certain Colonel George Monck and, in August, 1650, created for him a new regiment which he named "Monck's Regiment of Foot". The present-day Coldstream Guards is directly descended from Monck's Regiment and can therefore claim to be the oldest Regiment in continuous service within the British Army.

In September, 1650, Charles Stuart, on his return from exile, seized the offer of a Scottish army to help reclaim the throne of England. Cromwell, with the assistance of Monck's Regiment, decisively defeated Charles's army at the Battle of Dunbar.

After Cromwell's death in 1658, Charles saw again his opportunity to reclaim the throne. Monck's response on this occasion was to assemble his soldiers in the little town of Coldstream on the Scottish border, and march them to London in support of Charles's cause. Despite some opposition, Monck succeeded in breaking the army's domination of government and brought about the election of a free parliament, one of whose first acts was to vote for the Restoration of the Monarchy. On 25th May, 1660, the King landed at Dover, where he was welcomed by General Monck.

In August, 1660, Parliament ordered the disbandment of the entire New Model Army (raised by Cromwell during the Civil War); no exceptions, including Monck's Regiment, were allowed, although it was conceded that they should be the last to be disbanded.

Two days before this disbandment was due to take place, an armed revolt occurred against the Monarch, forcing an alarmed Parliament to somewhat reluctantly call upon Monck's Regiment of Foot for assistance. Monck's men swiftly put down the rebellion and ended the rioting. A now grateful Parliament repealed the order for their disbandment. On 14th February, 1661, Monck's Regiment paraded at Tower Hill. The men symbolically laid down their weapons and, with them, their association with the New Model Army. They were immediately ordered to take them up again as Royal troops in the New Standing Army, receiving the title of "The Lord General's Regiment of Foot Guards".

In 1661, a Royal Commission designated the Regiment "The Second Guards", (the "First Guards" being –post Waterloo- the Grenadiers). To make clear its displeasure at the injustice of this decision, the Regiment took as its motto the phrase "Nulli Secundus" (Second to None) and never accepted that it should be referred to as "The Second Guards". Monck died in 1670, and the Lord General's Regiment became officially known from this time on as the "Coldstream Regiment of Foot Guards".

The Regiment saw much active service throughout the remaining decades of the seventeenth century, gaining its first two Battle Honours at Tangier (1680) and Namur (1695).

The Regiment took part in the Battles of Oudenarde (1708) and Malplaquet (1709) following which, from 1715 to 1742, it enjoyed a largely unbroken spell of peace. In 1745, it played a distinguished part in the Battle of Fontenoy at which the Brigade of Guards marched for half a mile under heavy fire to halt thirty yards from the French Guards. The French fired first, doing little damage; the British response was devastating.

In 1776, following the outbreak of the American War of Independence two Coldstream battalions were in action throughout the conflict and returned home only after Cornwallis had surrendered at Yorktown.

Following the French Revolution in 1793, Britain joined the confederacy against the Republican Government. The Guards Brigade, including the 1st Coldstreams, distinguished itself in several engagements, including the sieges of Valenciennes and Lincelles. The 1st Battalion subsequently sailed to join the Army in Egypt, where a series of operations ended with the surrender of the French Army of Occupation in Cairo. The Regiment was awarded the distinctive badge of the Sphinx, superscribed 'Egypt' for its conspicuous service in the campaign that blighted Napoleon's dream of world conquest.

When Napoleon escaped to France from Elba, the 2nd Battalion of the Coldstreams joined the 2nd Guards Brigade and moved with it towards Waterloo. A defining moment – perhaps **the** defining moment – in the history of this illustrious Regiment was its role in the defence of Hougoumont Chateau, which Wellington had identified as a key position in his defensive line. When the Nassauers were abandoning the Chateau, he ordered in the Guards. "In with you, my lads, and don't let me see you again".

The French first attacked Hougoumont at 11.00 am on 18th June, 1815, and continued to do so for the next eight hours, creating a "battle within a battle". At one desperate moment, a small French detachment succeeded in entering the courtyard but were repulsed by a handful of Coldstreamers , led by Lieutenant Colonel Macdonnell and Sergeant Graham who, with the assistance of men from the 3rd (Scots) Guards, forced back the great doors of the courtyard and held them shut against repeated attempts by the enemy to break through.

The defenders of the Chateau acted as a thorn in the side of Napoleon's left flank throughout the day by causing delay and diversion of forces. "The success of Waterloo", said Wellington afterwards, "depended on the closing of the gates of Hougoumont."

Sergeant Graham received a special medal for brave conduct and shared with Colonel Macdonnell the sum of £500 left in the will of a patriotic clergyman for "the bravest man in England."

The 1st Battalion embarked for the Crimea in 1854 and played an important part in the Battles of the Alma, Inkerman and Sebastapol.

Four Coldstreamers received the Victoria Cross (which had been instituted in early 1856) on their return to England.

The 1st and 2nd Battalions of the Regiment both saw service in the Boer War (1899-1902).

With the outbreak of War in 1914, all three Coldstream Battalions moved to France immediately. The regiment suffered heavily throughout the war, taking part in many significant engagements including the Retreat from Mons, the Battles of the Marne, Aisne and Ypres during 1914-15 and those at Loos, the Somme, Ginchy and 3rd Ypres (Passchendaele) in the War's later stages. A total of seven Victoria Crosses were awarded to Coldstreamers for acts of conspicuous bravery during this war.

In World War II, the Coldstream Guards served throughout Europe and North Africa (France 1939-40, Egypt 1939-42, North Africa 1942, Italy 1943-45, Normandy to the Baltic 1944-45), both as dismounted Infantry and Armoured Battalions.

60964 Durham Light Infantry

This locomotive was named as late as 29th April, 1958, in celebration of the Regiment's bi-centenary 1758-1958.

By the way of background, perhaps it would be helpful to say something at this point about the origins of 'Light Infantry' (applicable equally to 60872 **King's Own Yorkshire Light Infantry**).

Although there had been 'light troops' in the British Army in the 1740's, it was the North American Colonial War between Britain and France in the 1750's which established the concept of 'Light Infantry'.

In this conflict, the heavy equipment, conspicuous red and white uniforms and close formation fighting of the British Army proved to be wholly unsuitable when operating in close country against Indians and French colonists, who had highly developed field craft and marksmanship skills. In consequence, a small corps of 'Light' troops was formed in 1755, consisting of specially trained men able to scout and skirmish, and concentrate and disperse with great stealth and speed.

So effective were these 'Light' troops that steps were taken to increase the number available. Regiments formed 'Light Companies' of soldiers specially selected for their toughness, intelligence, military skills and ability to act on their own initiative. The bugle horn, which subsequently became the emblem of Light troops (and was incorporated within the locomotive nameplate of **Durham Light Infantry)** replaced the drum as the means of communication for the often widely dispersed Light Companies.

The invasion of Spain by Napoleon in 1802 accelerated the development of the Light Infantry concept under the leadership and training of *Sir John Moore* who had joined the 51st Regiment of Foot, later to become **The King's Own Yorkshire Light Infantry**, as an Ensign at the age of fifteen. In 1790, at the age of thirty, he was appointed to command the 51st in Ireland, Gibraltar and Corsica and did so until 1796, when he assumed command of a Brigade.

He became a Major General in 1797 and began to develop further his ideas for the training of infantrymen, grouping regiments to fight together as Light Infantry and eventually forming the Light Division which fought with such distinction in the Peninsula War and took part in every engagement against the French.

The story of the Durham Light Infantry (DLI) began in 1758, when General John Lambton of County Durham first raised the 68th Regiment of Foot as part of the British Army. (See also Class B17 No 61623 *Lambton Castle*) Fifty years later, in 1808, the 68th Foot had the honour of being converted to a Light Infantry regiment and was sent to fight with Wellington's Army in Portugal and Spain, where it won its first Battle Honours. Subsequent service in the Crimea and in New Zealand resulted in the award of three Victoria Crosses to members of the Regiment.

In 1881, the Durham Light Infantry was formed by the merger of the 68th (Durham) Regiment of Foot (Light Infantry) and the 106th Regiment of Foot (Bombay Light Infantry), which became its 1st and 2nd Battalions, respectively. The DLI soon saw service in Egypt and, later, against the Boers in South Africa, where it was involved in the Relief of Ladysmith.

During the First World War, thousands of volunteers from the mines, shipyards, farms, shops, schools, offices and industries of County Durham joined the DLI. By 1918, the Durhams had raised 43 Battalions, with 22 seeing active service overseas – on the Western Front, in Egypt, Italy, Salonika and India.

The DLI fought in every major battle of the Great War – at Ypres, Loos, Arras, Messines, Cambrai, on the Somme and in the mud of Passchendaele. Some 13,000 Durhams died on these battlefields with thousands more wounded, gassed or taken prisoner. Six Victoria Crosses were awarded to members of the Regiment during this conflict.

During the Second World War, 9 Battalions of the DLI fought with distinction in every major theatre – from Dunkirk in 1940, to North Africa (including Tobruk and El Alamein), Malta, Sicily, Italy, Burma and in Europe, from D-Day to the final defeat of Nazi Germany in 1945. Casualties during this war were far fewer than in the Great War, but in several fierce engagements at Arras, Mareth, Primosole Bridge and Kohima, the Durhams suffered heavy losses.

In Belgium, in May 1940, Richard Annand of the 2nd Battalion, DLI, became the first soldier of the Second World War to win the Victoria Cross. In June, 1942, in North Africa, Adam Wakenshaw of Newcastle-upon-Tyne was awarded a posthumous V.C. fighting with the 9th Battalion DLI.

After 1945, the DLI was reduced in size until only the 1st Battalion remained. In 1952-53, the Battalion fought as part of the United Nations forces in Korea, and later served in Cyprus and as part of the Berlin Garrison. In 1966, the Durhams fought their last campaign in the jungles and mountains of Borneo.

Finally, in the Army reforms of 1968, the Regiment was merged with The Somerset and Cornwall Light Infantry, **The King's Own Yorkshire Light Infantry**, and the King's Shropshire Light Infantry to form a new regiment, The Light Infantry, becoming its 4th Battalion. The Regiment has the distinction of not being required to drink the Loyal Toast; a privilege which had formerly been granted to the DLI.

CLASS B1

INTRODUCTION AND GENERAL CHARACTERISTICS

The Thompson B1 mixed-traffic locomotive was a simple, rugged, all-purpose machine with wide route availability, built for secondary passenger and fast freight duties. It is generally considered to be *Edward Thompson's* most useful addition to LNER locomotive stock.

The B1 was the first 2-cylinder main-line locomotive constructed for the LNER since its formation in 1923, such had been Gresley's believe in the 3-cylinder design. With cost savings a wartime priority, Thompson's draughtsmen re-used existing patterns, jigs and tools to economise on materials and labour. Extensive use was made of welding instead of steel castings.

The prototype entered service on 12th December, 1942. Wartime constraints on production meant that the first 10 engines were not completed until 1944. Although only 24 locomotives had been built by the time of Thompson's retirement in June, 1946, a further 300 were on order. Production continued under *A. H. Peppercorn* and, post-nationalisation, under British Railways whose stipulated priority was one of simplicity in building and service. A total of 410 machines had been built by the time construction was ended in April, 1952, preference then being given to BR Standard equivalents.

As befits "go anywhere" locomotives, the B1's operated throughout LNER territory and proved to be generally popular with their crews. They regularly worked named trains including 'The Master Cutler', 'The South Yorkshireman', the 'East Anglian' and, in Scotland, 'The Queen of Scots'.

One locomotive was scrapped following a collision in 1950. Withdrawal of the remainder commenced in 1961 and all had gone by September, 1967.

Two of the Class have been preserved.

THE NAMES

As previously indicated, the prototype entered service in December, 1942. This coincided with a wartime visit to Great Britain by Field Marshal Jan Smuts, Prime Minister of South Africa, in whose honour the locomotive was named **Springbok.**

It was then decided that the first 10 locomotives built at Darlington from 1942, and the second batch of 30, constructed from November 1946 to December 1947, should carry the names of antelopes. This is not generally regarded as a particularly appropriate or inspired choice for the ubiquitous B1's, and there are those who contend that the names of such agile and fleet-footed animals would have been better suited to the V2's. It has to be said, however, that with Thompson as Chief Mechanical Engineer, it was unlikely that there would have been any further naming of Gresley locomotives.

The sixth engine to be built was named **Bongo,** which spawned the risible nickname thenceforth commonly used to refer to members of the Class ("Bongos").

Some antelope names were duplicated, perhaps unwittingly due to the wide variety of African languages and dialects, or perhaps because the lexicon of names soon became exhausted.

During December, 1947 – the last month of the Company's existence – the names of recent or serving LNER Directors not already carried on the A4 'Pacifics' were affixed to 18 engines of the B1 Class then in traffic. The locomotives selected for this purpose worked in the Area of the Company with which each Director was associated (Southern; North Eastern; Scottish).

Keen spotters in the 1950's will have noted from their Ian Allan ABC's that what would have been an unbroken run of 15 Directors (LNER Nos. 1237 to 1251) was interrupted by the absence of any name associated with No. 1239. It had apparently been intended that this locomotive should bear the name of North Eastern Area Director Rupert E. Beckett, one of only five who had served on the Board for the full twenty five years of its existence. In the event, it appears that he declined to have it so applied, and was the only member of the final Board of LNER Directors whose name was not carried on a locomotive.

Space limitations apart – the B1's had to use smaller lettering for the longer plates – it is interesting to note that, perhaps fittingly for a Class which represented utility and simplicity, a more "familiar" style was preferred in the presentation of Directors' names e.g. **Leslie Runciman** and **Geoffrey Gibbs**. This "common touch" tended to conceal some quite distinguished lineages and a wide range of significant achievements; to borrow a phrase from the world of politics, this Board truly was an assembly ' of all the talents'.

Finally, British Railways' sole contribution to the naming of members of the Class came on 13th July, 1951, when No. 61379 was named Mayflower at the request of the Pilgrim Fathers Association.

61000	Springbok	61020	Gemsbok	61040	Roedeer
61001	Eland	61021	Reitbok	61189	Sir William Gray
61002	Impala	61022	Sassaby	61215	William Henton Carver
61003	Gazelle	61023	Hirola	61221	Sir Alexander Erskine-Hill
61004	Oryx	61024	Addax	61237	Geoffrey H. Kitson
61005	Bongo	61025	Pallah	61238	Leslie Runciman
61006	Blackbuck	61026	Ourebi	61240	Harry Hinchliffe
61007	Klipspringer	61027	Madoqua	61241	Viscount Ridley
61008	Kudu	61028	Umseke	61242	Alexander Reith Gray
61009	Hartebeeste	61029	Chamois	61243	Sir Harold Mitchell
61010	Wildebeeste	61030	Nyala	61244	Strang Steel
61011	Waterbuck	61031	Reedbuck	61245	Murray of Elibank
61012	Puku	61032	Stembok	61246	Lord Balfour of Burleigh
61013	Topi	61033	Dibatag	61247	Lord Burghley
61014	Oribi	61034	Chiru	61248	Geoffrey Gibbs
61015	Duiker	61035	Pronghorn	61249	FitzHerbert Wright
61016	Inyala	61036	Ralph Assheton	61250	A. Harold Bibby
61017	Bushbuck	61037	Jairou	61251	Oliver Bury
61018	Gnu	61038	Blacktail	61379	Mayflower
61019	Nilghai	61039	Steinbok		

DAVID H. BALDWIN

"THOM(P)SON'S GAZELLES"

The antelope, gazelles and deer included in Class B1 are mostly from Africa, exceptions being **Blackbuck** (India and Pakistan), **Chamois** (Europe and South West Asia), **Chiru** (Tibet), **Pronghorn** (North America), **Jairou** (India), **Blacktail** (North America), and **Roedeer** (Europe and Asia).

They range in size from the **Eland** and **Nilghai** (largest of the antelopes) to the diminutive **Klipspringer** and the tiny antelopes which comprise *genus* **Madoqua**.

Different names are used to refer to the same animal or species viz. **Oryx/Gemsbok; Wildebeeste/Gnu; Inyala/Nyala; Reitbok/Reedbuck/Umseke; Impala/Pallah; Ourebi/Oribi; Stembok/Steinbok; Jairou/Chiru.**

Although many of the species represented in the Class remain plentiful, others are becoming increasingly endangered. **Blackbuck**, fastest of the Indian antelopes, have been over-hunted and are in danger of becoming extinct. Excessive hunting, severe droughts and tourist incursion have caused such a dramatic decline in the **Addax** population that it is now an endangered species. **Springbok** once migrated in vast herds but are now found only in relatively small numbers, where protected. Over-exploitation of the grasslands by domestic livestock, heavy poaching and poorly conceived "developmental" projects have caused the **Hirola** (also known as Hunter's Hartebeeste and the last surviving member of an ancient – circa 3 million years old – and once widespread genus of antelopes) to become Africa's most endangered antelope, with perhaps fewer than 1000 animals confined to an area bordering Kenya and Somalia.

More than one million **Chiru** may have roamed the Tibetan plateau at the beginning of the last century, but poaching has reduced the population to less than 75,000. The Chiru is threatened by hunting for its meat, magnificent horns and soft, fine wool which is used to make the extremely (and unfortunately) chic shahtoosh scarves. Similarly, excessive hunting, combined with the loss of prairies to agriculture has brought the **Pronghorn** – considered to be the fastest animal in North America – close to extinction.

On a more positive note, the Arabian variety of the **Oryx**, at one time extinct in the wild, has been successfully reintroduced into its natural habitat using stocks bred in captivity. The white-tailed **Gnu** of southern Africa was only just saved from extinction through breeding on farms.

Although obviously there are many similarities between them, "Thom(p)son's gazelles" have a wide range of unique features and behavioural characteristics. The **Wildebeeste** ("I'm a GNU, A-G-nother Gnu") is said to have been made up of the various pieces left over at the end of creation with "the forequarters of an ox,. the hindquarters of an antelope and the tail of a horse". It also has the long, mournful face of a **Hartebeeste**, a thick black mane and the horns of a buffalo.

The black markings on the tail and rump of the ubiquitous **Impala** form a distinctive letter 'M', hence the nickname "the MacDonald's antelope".

Waterbuck, which usually inhabit African swamplands and reed beds, are good swimmers and have a thick, shaggy, water-repellant coat covered in a musky secretion that not only acts as water-proofing but also has a noisome smell and taints the flesh, effectively deterring most predators.

The beautiful **Gemsbok** has very long, thin, rapier-like straight horns and striking facial markings which have made them prized hunting trophies. The horns are lowered parallel to the ground – in the manner of a fork lift truck – and the animals lunge with great accuracy when fending off lions and other predators.

The **Chamois** is a sure-footed goat antelope from mountain regions of Europe and south west Asia whose name is the origin of the word – "Shammy" – meaning a soft suede leather cloth (now obtained from the skins of sheep and goats).

Many of the antelopes featured in the B1's can display great speed and agility. When startled, or at play, the **Springbok** moves in bounds or leaps of 10 feet or more in height. Similarly, when frightened or disturbed, **Impala** scatter, making enormous bounds or leaps which can be 30 feet long and 10 feet high and cause considerable confusion to the lions and wild dogs which are their main predators.

Impala can also reach speeds in excess of 60 mph, as can the **Pronghorn** of North America and the African **Sassaby**, thought to be the swiftest hoofed animal. Although they are clumsy-looking runners, **Hartebeeste**, too, are capable of considerable speed at 40 mph or more.

Klipspringer browse and graze on rocky hillsides, bouncing on tiptoe from boulder to boulder on hooves the consistency of hard rubber. In contrast, the **Dibatag** of Somalia and Ethiopia has long, skinny legs and a pronounced ambling gait in the form of a cross-trot (opposite legs moving together).

This section would be incomplete without reference to the **Bongo**, a spiral-horned antelope belonging to the same family as the **Eland, Kudu, Nyala** and **Bushbuck** (which it closely resembles). The **Bongo** is a large, stocky, chestnut-coloured animal which inhabits dense forests and emerges only at night to graze. It was once prolific in parts of Kenya, but numbers have been reduced substantially following the introduction of lions into the game parks and reserves.

Ex-presto-Bongo?

.... "NOW DEPARTING" ....THE DIRECTORS

61036 RALPH ASSHETON

Sir Ralph Cockayne Assheton (1860-1955), 1st Baronet (cr.1946) was educated at Eton and Jesus College, Cambridge. He was a member of the Lancashire County Council from 1892 to 1949 and served as High Sheriff of the County in 1919.

Sir Ralph was appointed as a Director of the LNER in 1945. In December, 1947, his name was affixed to locomotive No. 1036 which was to have been named Korrigum (another name for **Topi**). Plates had been cast but were never fitted.

61189 Sir William Gray

William Gray (1895 – 1978), 2nd Baronet (Cr. 1919) was educated at Loretto School, Edinburgh, and saw service during the First World War as a Captain in the Yorkshire Regiment (being wounded, taken prisoner and mentioned in despatches).

He served as High Sheriff of County Durham in 1938/39 and was appointed to the Board of the LNER in 1933.

61215 William Henton Carver

Colonel William Henton Carver (1868 – 1961) served in the *King's Own Yorkshire Light Infantry* from 1889 to 1908 following education at Uppingham School.

With the onset of war in 1914, he was instrumental in raising the 10th Battalion of the *East Yorkshire Regiment* with which he saw service in Egypt and France. He retired from the army in March, 1919, with the rank of Major and subsequently became Hon. Colonel of the Regiment from 1939.

William Henton Carver served as a Member of Parliament (Howdenshire Division) from 1926 to 1945. He was a member of the East Riding County Council from 1915 to retirement (becoming an Alderman in 1940) and was President of the Hull Chamber of Commerce in 1925 and 1926.

He became a Director of the LNER in 1927 and served in that capacity for the next twenty years.

He was chairman of the Company's Property Committee.

61221 SIR ALEXANDER ERSKINE-HILL

Alexander Galloway Erskine-Hill (1894 – 1947) served in the Great War with both the *Cameronians* and the *Cameron Highlanders*. A lawyer by profession, he was appointed King's Counsel in 1935 and served as the Member of Parliament for North Edinburgh from 1935-45. He became a Director of the LNER in 1940 and was created Baronet in 1945.

Erskine-Hill was one of three Board Members whose death had occurred during his term of office as Director (in this case, six months prior to the locomotive naming ceremony in December, 1947).

61237 GEOFFREY H. KITSON

Geoffrey Herbert Kitson (1896 – 1974) was appointed to the Board of the LNER in 1937, at which time he was also a member of Leeds City Council (1930-38) and had recently been made Director of Leeds Permanent Building Society, a post he was to hold until his death in 1974.

A Company Director by profession, Geoffrey Kitson was President of the Leeds Chamber of Commerce in 1935/36. .

61238 LESLIE RUNCIMAN

Walter Leslie Runciman (1900-1989) was created 2nd Viscount Runciman of Doxford in 1937.

Educated at Eton and Trinity College, Cambridge, Runciman became a Director of Lloyd's Bank in 1932 and, subsequently, its Deputy Chairman. He was Chairman of the North of England Shipowners' Association on two occasions; President of the Chamber of Shipping of the United Kingdom; Hon. Elder Brother of Trinity House; and an Hon. Member of the Company of Master Mariners.

In addition, Viscount Runciman was Director General of BOAC

1940-43 and Air Commodore/Attache Tehran 1943-46.

He was twice appointed to the Board of Directors of the LNER, first in 1937 (resigning in the following year) and subsequently in 1946. His tenure was thus somewhat brief and his re-appointment in 1946 would probably not have taken place but for the earlier deaths of two Directors.

61240 HARRY HINCHLIFFE

Sir (Albert) Henry (Stanley) Hinchliffe (1893- 1980) Kt (1953) was educated at Cheltenham and Keble College, Oxford.

He enlisted in the *North Staffordshire Regiment* in 1914, was commissioned in the following year and was invalided out of the Army as a result of wounds received at the Battle of Loos in 1915

Sir Henry was Chairman of Glazebrook Steel and Co., Manchester, a member of Staffordshire County Council 1942-55, and held various Directorships, including Manchester Chamber of Commerce 1938-72 and Barclays Bank 1952-69. In addition, he was widely associated with matters relating to the governance of health and education, including service as a Governor of Manchester Grammar School 1940-76.

He became a Director of the LNER in 1944.

61241 VISCOUNT RIDLEY

Matthew White Ridley (1902 – 1964), 3rd Viscount (Cr 1900) and 4th Baron Wensleydale, was Chairman of the Northumberland County Council 1940-46 and 1949-52. He was Regional Controller for the North, Ministry of Production, from 1942-49.

Educated at Eton, he was married to the second daughter of Sir Edwin Lutyens RA.

He became a member of the Board of Directors of the LNER in 1938.

61242 ALEXANDER REITH GRAY

Northern Scottish Area Director of the LNER and a former Director of the *North British* Railway, with business interests in Aberdeen. He was one of only three Directors who had served continuously since Grouping in 1923.

Alexander Reith Gray died in April, 1946; his service to the Company was commemorated by the plating of locomotive No. 1242 in December of the following year.

61243 SIR HAROLD MITCHELL

Colonel Sir Harold Paton Mitchell (1900-1983), lst Bt., was educated at Eton, Sandhurst and University College, Oxford. He subsequently obtained a Doctorate in Political Sciences from the University of Geneva.

Sir Harold was M.P. for Brentford and Chiswick 1931-45 and served as Vice-Chairman of the Conservative Party during the later years of this period. He was Liaison Officer to the Polish Forces in Western Europe and Hon. Colonel of two Territorial Army Regiments.

A one-time Member of the Queen's Body Guard for Scotland, Sir Harold had also represented Great Britain at ski-ing on three occasions between the wars.

He became a Director of the LNER in 1939.

61244 STRANG STEEL

Major Sir Samuel Strang Steel (1882-1961) was educated at Eton and at Trinity College, Cambridge, and saw war service in France,

Salonika and Mesopotamia. Following the Armistice, he sat as the M.P. for the Ashford Division of Kent from 1918-1929.

Strang Steel was a Director of the Bank of Scotland and a Member of the Royal Company of Scottish Archers.

He was a Member of the LNER Board from 1938 to 1947.

61245 MURRAY OF ELIBANK

Lieutenant Colonel Arthur Cecil Murray (1879-1962), 3rd Viscount, soldier, M.P. and Diplomat served in the 2nd King Edward's Horse (despatches, DSO) from 1914-16 and was Assistant Military Attaché in Washington for the remainder of the War. Like **Strang Steel** and **Lord Balfour of Burleigh** a member of the Royal Company of Archers, Murray of Elibank was a Director of the LNER throughout the entirety of its existence from 1923 to 1947.

61246 LORD BALFOUR OF BURLEIGH

George John Gordon Bruce (1883-1967), 11th Baron, was the third of the Scottish Directors of the LNER who served as a Member of the Royal Company of Archers, the Sovereign's Body Guard for Scotland.

Lord Balfour served with distinction in the First World War, being mentioned in despatches on four occasions and awarded the Star of the Legion of Honour.

The holder of numerous Directorships, including that of Chairman of Lloyds Bank, he was appointed to the Board of the LNER in 1937.

61247 LORD BURGHLEY

David George Brownlow Cecil (1905-1981) 6th Marquess of Exeter, was an athlete of considerable distinction and renown. As a student at Magdalen College, Cambridge, (as Lord Burghley), he won the Oxford v Cambridge 120 yards hurdles and 220 yards hurdles in 1925, 1926 and 1927. In the following year, he won no fewer than eight British Championships plus Olympic Gold in the 400 metres hurdles (Amsterdam). He was President of the Amateur Athletics Association from 1936-76.

On the outbreak of the Second World War in 1939 he made a major contribution to the work of Ministries concerned with tank supply and with aircraft production/repair. He was MP for Peterborough 1939-43 and Governor and C-in-C of Bermuda 1943-45.

Lord Burghley was also the holder of numerous Directorships and served on the Board of the LNER for 17 years, having been appointed in 1930.

61248 GEOFFREY GIBBS

Hon. Sir Geoffrey Cokayne Gibbs (1901-1975), KCMG (1955), was educated at Eton College and Christ Church, Oxford.

A banker by profession, he was at one time Chairman of Antony Gibbs and Sons Ltd., Merchant Bankers, and a Director of the Australia and New Zealand Bank Ltd from 1936-74. During the Second World War, he served in the Ministry of Economic Warfare.

He became a Director of the LNER in 1938.

61249 FITZHERBERT WRIGHT

In August, 1944, in Doncaster Works Yard, the A4 'Pacific' *Merlin* was temporarily renumbered and re-named on three successive occasions for the purposes of photographs depicting the locomotive as No. 1928 Brigid; No. 1931 Davina; and No. 1934 Bryan. These were the birth dates and names of three of the children of Mr. FitzHerbert

Wright, a Midlands Company Director, who had relatively recently (in 1943) been appointed to the Board of the LNER and whose own name was subsequently to be affixed on a more permanent basis to Class B1 4-6-0 No. 61249.

It is not clear why Susan, the 7 year old younger sister of Brigid and Davina should have been excluded from these arrangements. She was to become rather better known than they following her wedding to a certain Major Ronald Ferguson and the birth of their daughter Sarah. It follows that FitzHerbert Wright was, inter alia, the maternal grandfather of the future Duchess of York.

61250 A. HAROLD BIBBY

Major Sir Arthur Harold Bibby (1889-1986) lst Bt. (Cr 1959) Kt (1956) was educated at Rugby School (of which he was a Governor from 1932-37) and served in the Royal Field Artillery during the First World War (winning the DSO at the Battle of Cambrai).

He was Senior Partner at Bibby Bros. and Co., Shipowners and Bankers 1935-73; Chairman, *Bibby Line* Ltd. 1935-69; Member of the Mersey Docks and Harbour Board 1931-65; Vice-Chairman of the National Association of Port Employers 1941-47; and a Director of the Suez Canal Company 1939-57.

He was a Director of the LNER from 1924 to 1947.

61251 OLIVER BURY

Unlike many of his fellow LNER Directors, Oliver Bury had extensive and direct experience of railway management in Great Britain and overseas.

In 1894, he was appointed Chief Engineer to the Entre Rios Railway (Argentina) and in 1900 became General Manager of the Buenos Aries and Rosario Railway.

He held the post of General Manager, *Great Northern* Railway, from 1902 to 1912, during which time he was appointed as a Commissioner to enquire into the working management of the Egyptian State Railways.

Although his appointment as a Director of the LNER dates from 1923, he had, in fact, been made a Director of one of the constituent companies (GNR) as early as 1913, giving a total of over 32 years continuous Board service.

He died in March 1946.

61379 MAYFLOWER

At a ceremony at King's Cross Station on 13th July, 1951, locomotive No. 61379 was named 'Mayflower' at the request of the Pilgrim Fathers' Association.

A small plate affixed to the cab side explained that this naming – performed by Commander Harold L. Goodwin, U.S. Navy – had been carried out "as a symbol of the ties binding the two towns of Boston and of the lasting friendship between the USA and the British Commonwealth".

61379 was cut up at Doncaster in August, 1962. The owner of the preserved and privately restored B1 No. 61306 subsequently chose to adopt the name 'Mayflower' for his locomotive.

CLASSES B17 AND B2

INTRODUCTION AND GENERAL CHARACTERISTICS

The LNER three-cylinder B17 "Sandringham" 4-6-0s were first introduced in 1928 to provide the Great Eastern section with locomotives of increased power on routes with restricted axle-loading. 73 of the class were constructed up to 1937. From 1943, most were rebuilt with Thompson's standard 100A boiler (classed B17/6) and ten were rebuilt as two-cylinder engines and reclassified B2. They were impressive-looking machines which became a familiar sight on the Eastern Counties railway scene and, for a while, on the Great Central route.

Despite some initial disappointment on the part of Great Central locomotive crews, the B17's acquired a reputation for fast running, albeit with a marked propensity to rough riding, particularly at speed. That said, some of the Class lasted over 30 years in service, a tribute to their usefulness and durability.

Post-war, with the arrival of V2's and A3 'Pacifics' on the Great Central section and 'Britannias' on the Eastern Region, the B17's were relegated to lesser duties but, prior to withdrawal, did retain some high profile work, particularly the Harwich – Manchester boat train, which they worked as far as Sheffield Victoria and back.

The first B17 was withdrawn as early as 1952, but most went between 1958 and 1960. None have been preserved.

THE NAMES

The initial batch of 10 locomotives (Class B17/1) was built in 1928 by the North British Locomotive Company to Gresley's specifications. With the consent of *King George V*, the first was named **'Sandringham'**. Eight of the remaining nine also received the names of country houses (including one castle) in the Eastern Counties; the other erroneously acquired the name of the village in North Norfolk – **Burnham Thorpe** – which was the birthplace of *Lord Nelson* and was eventually renamed.

All but two of the thirty eight locomotives then built from October, 1930, to September 1935, (Classes B17/2 and B17/3) also received the names of country houses and castles in LNER territory, (some as far north as the Scottish borders), the exceptions being No. 2845 (B.R. No. 61645) which was given a regimental name, and No. 2846 (BR No. 61646) which commemorated the Headquarters of the Boy Scout Movement. Only four of the forty eight locomotives named after country houses and castles did not retain the names originally allocated until their withdrawal from service.

The country houses commemorated in the class have no universally common characteristics other than their location in LNER territory, although the inclusion of some relatively "minor" seats may well have been influenced by their shared enjoyment of royal patronage. Some of the houses are palatial and rich in historical associations; others are far less imposing or have long since ceased to be inhabited. A handful have been demolished, some while the locomotive which carried their name was still in service. Many were created or rebuilt to satisfy the tastes and indulgences of rich men; follies and curiosities abound.

The twenty-five locomotives built between March, 1936, and July, 1937, (Class B17/4) were given the names of Association Football Clubs whose home grounds were in LNER territory. The curved nameplates on these locomotives surmounted panels painted in the Club colours either side of a cast brass half-football. Again, the majority of these engines retained the names originally allocated although some changes were made, the principal "casualties" being 'Manchester City' and 'Newcastle United'.

Notable absentees from the names of the Football Clubs commemorated in the Class were Ipswich Town, which did not acquire League (Div. 3) status until 1938, and York City which, in comparison, had been elected to the League in 1929.

THE CLASS

Seventy three locomotives numbered 61600 to 61672.

61600	Sandringham	61637	Thorpe Hall
61601	Holkham	61638	Melton Hall
61602	Walsingham	61639*	Norwich City (Rendelsham Hall)
61603*	Framlingham	61640	Somerleyton Hall
61604	Elveden	61641	Gayton Hall
61605	Lincolnshire Regiment (Burnham Thorpe)	61642	Kilverstone Hall
61606	Audley End	61643	Champion Lodge
61607*	Blickling	61644*	Earlham Hall
61608	Gunton	61645	The Suffolk Regiment
61609	Quidenham	61646	Gilwell Park
61610	Honingham Hall	61647	Helmingham Hall
61611	Raynham Hall	61648	Arsenal
61612	Houghton Hall	61649	Sheffield United
61613	Woodbastwick Hall	61650	Grimsby Town
61614*	Castle Hedingham	61651	Derby County
61615*	Culford Hall	61652	Darlington
61616*	Fallodon	61653	Huddersfield Town
61617*	Ford Castle	61654	Sunderland
61618	Wynyard Park	61655	Middlesbrough
61619	Welbeck Abbey	61656	Leeds United
61620	Clumber	61657	Doncaster Rovers
61621	Hatfield House	61658	The Essex Regiment (Newcastle United)
61622	Alnwick Castle	61659	East Anglian (Norwich City)
61623	Lambton Castle	61660	Hull City
61624	Lumley Castle	61661	Sheffield Wednesday
61625	Raby Castle	61662	Manchester United
61626	Brancepeth Castle	61663	Everton
61627	Aske Hall	61664	Liverpool
61628	Harewood House	61665	Leicester City
61629	Naworth Castle	61666	Nottingham Forest
61630	Tottenham Hotspur (Thoresby Park)	61667	Bradford
61631	Serlby Hall	61668	Bradford City
61632*	Royal Sovereign (Belvoir Castle)	61669	Barnsley
61633	Kimbolton Castle	61670	City of London (Tottenham Hotspur/ Manchester City)
61634	Hinchingbrooke	61671*	Royal Sovereign (Manchester City)
61635	Milton	61672	West Ham United
61636	Harlaxton Manor		

153

*Rebuilt and Classified 'B2'

FOOTNOTE

As previously indicated, all B17's had been withdrawn from service by 1960. The Football Club histories and achievements explored later in this section do not generally proceed beyond that date i.e. are ones with which the 'spotters' of the 1950's will have been broadly familiar.

FROM EAST ANGLIA TO EAST END

61600 SANDRINGHAM

"Dear old Sandringham, the place that I love better than anywhere else in the world", wrote the King Emperor George V, who had known it for as long as he could remember and for whom it was above all home. All of the children of George V and Queen Mary, with the exception of the future Edward VIII were born at Sandringham; he disliked the place so much that he spent only one night in the house prior to his abdication in 1936. He then sold the estate to his brother, Albert (George VI) whose affection for Sandringham was no less keen than that of his father. Both George V and George VI died here.

Situated some eight miles from King's Lynn, Sandringham is the private residence of the monarch and traditional setting for the Royal Family's Christmas and New Year holiday. The 20,000 acre estate, which takes in no fewer than seven villages, was purchased in 1862 by Edward VII (then Prince of Wales) and the present house dates from 1869. During the next 49 years, Edward made Sandringham a glittering 'Society' venue and transformed the shooting into some of the finest in the country. Clocks were set half an hour early to make the most of daylight for shooting; known as 'Sandringham time', this custom continued until 1936.

Each year during the reign of King George V rather more than 20,000 head of game were shot at Sandringham with another 10,000 or so on leased estates. Most were reared pheasants, described by one courtier as "on the whole not of the lofty nature, in fact some of them are fluffy ones", and there was much comment not only on the number of birds but also on the apparent ease with which they could be shot.

The Kaiser, the Tsar and numerous members of other royal families journeyed by train from London to the nearby (and now disused) station at Wolferton. Edward VII's eldest son celebrated his 21st birthday at the house with a command performance by an entire circus. In 1932, King George V made the first Christmas radio broadcast from here.

A small stone war memorial close to the gates of Sandringham House commemorates the 1/5th (Territorial) Battalion of the Norfolk Regiment – formed entirely of volunteers from among the workers on the Royal estate – which, on 12th August, 1915, "vanished" into the smoke and dust of a Gallipoli battle. Legend has it that the Battalion advanced into oddly-shaped clouds (in some accounts a mist); when, shortly afterwards, the clouds lifted, the Norfolks had simply disappeared. Despite extensive enquiries on behalf of *King George V* and Queen Alexandra, no trace of the men was ever discovered.

POSTSCRIPT:

In 1999, the "mystery" of the Battalion's disappearance was the subject of a BBC drama/Documentary entitled "All the King's Men" and starring David Jason as Capt. Frank Beck, formerly the Estate Manager at Sandringham.

61601 HOLKHAM

This classic eighteenth century Palladian-style mansion, home to seven generations of the Earls of Leicester, is situated in a deer park of 3,000 acres on the north Norfolk coast, close to Wells-next-the-Sea. It was founded in 1734 by the 1st Earl to house a vast collection of books, manuscripts and works of art acquired on the 'Grand Tour'.

Thomas William Coke (1754 – 1842), 1st Earl of the second creation and better known by the nickname 'Coke of Norfolk', was a leading figure in the Agrarian Revolution, being the inventor of four course crop rotation. This led to the enclosure of the hitherto open fields in order to keep livestock away from the increased yields. Between 1750 and 1850 the countryside was extensively remodelled through the planting of hedges and trees, creating the rural landscape so familiar today.

Coke, (pronounced 'Cook'), is also credited with being the 'inventor' of the bowler hat, having commissioned Lock's of St. James's to design for him a hard-domed, close-fitting, felt hat to protect his gamekeepers from injury by poachers. The first of these "billycock" hats (a corruption of Billy Coke) were made from felt supplied by Thomas and William Bowler, hence the name by which they became popularly known.

There was much rivalry between *Sandringham* and Holkham, not all of it friendly, in regard to the shooting. Although the Holkham estate was twice the size of his own, George V boasted that three times as many partridges were killed at Sandringham. It was not for the want of trying on Lord Leicester's part: when told that the churchyard at Holkham was disgracefully overgrown he apparently replied "Nonsense, best breeding ground for partridges in England."

61602 WALSINGHAM

An Augustinian Priory was established at Walsingham in 1153; although destroyed during the Reformation (1538), the remains of the building can still be seen.

John Warner, Bishop of Rochester, acquired the site of the Priory in 1666. A descendant is presumed to have built the house known to have existed here in 1791. The present house – Walsingham Abbey – was built around 1806 and purchased by the family who now own it in 1921.

Walsingham is an important centre of pilgrimage, second in

popularity only to Canterbury. It owes its celebrity to the actions of Richeldis de Faverches, a one time lady of the Manor who, in 1337, following a series of visions, built a replica of the house in Nazareth in which Jesus had been raised. This "Holy House" became a focus for those who were unable to visit the Holy Places in Palestine and caused Walsingham to become known as "England's Nazareth".

Following the dissolution of the monasteries during the reign of *King Henry VIII*, Walsingham ceased to be a pilgrim centre for some 350 years, but witnessed a modern revival from the 1890's onwards.

61603 FRAMLINGHAM

Framlingham Castle, near Saxmundham, was built by Roger Bigod, 2nd Earl of Suffolk, at the end of the twelfth Century. Its thirteen impressive towers and continuous curtain walls are still in almost perfect condition.

Under siege only once in its history, (by *King John* in 1215), Framlingham has been put to many uses – a military fortress, an Elizabethan prison, a poorhouse and a school. Inside the castle walls, the attractive seventeenth century former poorhouse is almost intact, with its carved mediaeval stone heads.

It was from Framlingham in 1553 that Mary Tudor ("Bloody Mary"), set out to depose Lady Jane Grey, who had been declared Queen following the death of *King Edward VI*.

61604 ELVEDEN

Elveden Hall, situated on the Suffolk/Norfolk border, not far from Mildenhall, was once owned by the Maharajah Duleep Singh, the last independent ruler of the Punjab, who purchased it in 1863.

In 1869, the Maharajah embarked on the demolition and reconstruction of the old Hall, formerly the seat of the 1st Earl of Albemarle. Outwardly, the result was a red brick building with stone dressings described as "very solid, respectable and dull". The elaborate and sumptuous interior, on the other hand, was in pure Indian style, with the exception of the Maharani's boudoir, which was French Renaissance.

Duleep Singh incurred heavy debts in refurbishing Elveden. Somewhat impoverished, he pleaded in vain with the British government for the return of the personal treasures bequeathed to him by his father and eventually settled as a poor refugee in Paris. He died there in 1893 but his body was returned to England and buried in the grounds of Elveden.

The first Earl of Iveagh, Edward Cecil Guinness (of the brewing family), purchased the Elveden Estate from the Executors of the Maharajah in 1894. A rich man, he indulged his own oriental fantasies and the 'Durbar' Hall erected at Elveden between 1899 and 1903 is the only interior of any consequence in this country to have been inspired by Anglo-Indian architecture.

Elveden was reputed to be one of the best sporting estates in England and throughout the Edwardian period and beyond the fame of the Elveden shoot became widespread. *King George V* was a frequent visitor, as was his son Albert, Duke of York.

During the Second World War, the Hall was occupied by the USAF as the Headquarters for Bomber Command and as a barracks. It remains the property of the Guinness Family but has been uninhabited for many years, a curiosity and relic of Empire.

61605 Lincolnshire Regiment

This locomotive entered service in 1928 as **Burnham Thorpe,** not a country house but the name of a small village near the north Norfolk coast where Horatio Nelson was born in September, 1758. In April, 1938, the locomotive emerged from Doncaster Works as LNER No. 2805 **Lincolnshire Regiment**, a name it retained until withdrawal some twenty years later.

The Lincolnshire Regiment was raised in 1685 as the Earl of Bath's Regiment and comprised eleven companies of infantry recruited in Derbyshire and Nottinghamshire together with the independent company which formed the Plymouth Garrison. It was known until 1751 by the names of eight other colonels and served with distinction in Flanders and subsequently with Marlborough in the battles of Blenheim, Ramillies, Oudenarde and Malplaquet.

In 1751 the Regiment became the 10th Regiment of Foot. In 1768, it was sent to Canada for garrison duties and shortly before the outbreak of the American War of Independence in 1775 was deployed to Boston. The 10th played a prominent part in a number of major actions in that conflict, including Bunker's Hill, and eventually returned to England in 1778, setting foot on native soil for the first time in 50 years.

In 1782, the Regiment became the 10th (the North Lincolnshire) Regiment of Foot, thereby inaugurating its territorial associations with that county. It was actively involved in the war with Revolutionary France and in the Peninsula War. The Regiment was awarded the Sphinx emblem, superscribed 'Egypt', for its part in the campaign against Napoleon in 1801. The battle honour for which it is most famous was gained at Sobraon in 1846 during the Sikh wars in India.

In July, 1881, the 10th was reorganised as the county regiment of Lincolnshire and thus became The **Lincolnshire Regiment**. It was involved in the Boer War and took part in all the major campaigns of the First and Second World Wars. In 1946, *King George VI* authorised the regiment to be known by the style and title of 'The Royal Lincolnshire Regiment'.

POSTCRIPT:

In 1948, the 1st and 2nd Battalions of the Regiment were merged. In 1960, the Regiment was amalgamated with *The Northamptonshire Regiment* to form the new 1st Battalion The 2nd East Anglian Regiment (Duchess of Gloucester's Own Royal Lincolnshire and

Northamptonshire). In September, 1964, the title was changed yet again to the 2nd Battalion, The Royal Anglian Regiment.

61606 AUDLEY END

Formerly the site of a Benedictine Monastery, Audley End, near Saffron Walden in Essex, was built on the scale of a Royal palace by Thomas Howard, first Earl of Suffolk, between 1603 and 1616, primarily for entertaining *King James I*. The King may have had his suspicions about this venture, (and may unwittingly have contributed to the cost of it) for he never stayed there; in 1619, Howard and his wife were fined and imprisoned for embezzlement and released only on payment of a substantial fine.

Charles II bought the house for £50,000 in 1668 for use as a palace and as a base when he attended the races at Newmarket.

Generations of aristocrats imprinted their taste on this former Royal residence which is now only one third of its original size. Following its return to the Suffolks, early in the eighteenth century, large parts were progressively demolished, the remaining building was repaired and the grounds were reshaped and set out by Capability Brown. The house's present interior is largely the product of ownership by the third Baron Braybrooke, who inherited Audley End in 1825 and reinstated something of the original Jacobean feel to the State Rooms.

After Audley End had been requisitioned in the Second World War, the house was sold by the Braybrooke family to the Ministry of Works, predecessor of English Heritage, the present owners.

61607 BLICKLING

Referred to in 'Country Life' (1930) as "a backwater in time ..... faint memories of famous Knights, the pomp of bishops' courts".... Blickling, near Aylsham in Norfolk, derives its name from the old English word for a water meadow around a stream.

The putative birthplace of Anne Boleyn, Blickling was formerly a large mediaeval moated house and was rebuilt between 1616 and 1627 by Sir Henry Hobart, Chief Justice to *King James I*.

From 1765 to 1782, John Hobart, 2nd Earl of Buckinghamshire, rebuilt part of the Hall, carefully imitating his ancestor's Jacobean work and preserving the unity of the original design. The result has been described as the epitome of the Jacobean House, carefully calculated to make an unforgettable impression of wealth and importance on passing travellers.

Blickling was the principal seat of the Hobart family until the death of the 2nd Earl in 1793, then passing through the female line to the Marquesses of Lothian.

In 1940, the house and estate were left to the National Trust by the unmarried Philip Kerr, 11th Marquess, who had inherited Blickling in 1930, making it his country seat in 1932. Kerr, private secretary to Lloyd George, was noted for his eccentricities, typified by his arrival at Westminster Abbey for the Coronation of *King George VI* in an Austin 7 motor car.

As might be expected, Blickling is said to be haunted by the headless ghost of Anne Boleyn and also by that of her father, Thomas, who, in the best ghostly tradition, appears each year on the anniversary of his daughter's execution, driving a coach pulled by headless horses while carrying his own head "tucked underneath his arm".

61608 GUNTON

This locomotive was the last of the B17's to be withdrawn from service in March 1960.

Gunton Hall, situated to the south of Cromer is described in the Norfolk volume of "The King's England" (1940 ed. Arthur Mee) as being "set in the heart of one of the loveliest parks in Norfolk with a thousand acres of beauty around it, trees in stately glades and massed in dark woodlands, deer flitting like shadows across pastures and herons nesting by the lake".

Gunton was settled by the Harbords in the reign of Charles I. The house was built for Sir William Harbord around 1742; the south front was extended in 1781 but was gutted by fire in 1882 and never re-built.

This was a noted sporting estate, particularly in the time of the 5th Lord Suffield, a friend of *King Edward VII*, who rented Gunton when Sandringham was being re-built in 1869-70.

Gunton serves to illustrate the close associations which existed between some of the houses – and families – included in Class B17. In 1792, William Assheton Harbord, who became 2nd Lord Suffield of Gunton in 1810, married Caroline, daughter of his near neighbour the 2nd Earl of Buckinghamshire, who lived at **Blickling** Hall (see No. 61607) to the south west of Gunton.

Caroline inherited Blickling in 1793 and, as Lady Suffield, continued to live there up to and following her husband's death in 1821. She was an enterprising gardener who had employed Humphrey Repton's son John at Gunton, and at **Blickling** after 1823. Childless, she remained at the Hall untl her own death in 1850; she was buried at Gunton and commemorated by a stained glass window at Blickling church.

POSTSCRIPT

Gunton remained the home of the Harbord family until 1980 when, following the death of the Hon. Doris Harbord, the contents were sold and the house stood empty.

Of incidental note, descendants of the Suffield family (in this case the 3rd Lord), include Mike D'Abo, former lead singer with Manfred Mann.

61609 QUIDENHAM

The village of Quidenham, in Norfolk, traces its history as far back as the Roman conquest of Britain. It is notable for its associations with *Boadicea* (Boudicca) queen of the local tribe of the Iceni, whose burial mound is reputed to stand nearby.

Quidenham Hall appears to have originated from a local manor house, first mentioned around 1000 A.D. when it belonged to a certain Guy or Guido, hence the name 'Guidenham'. In 1400 it became the property of the Bedingfield family, remaining in their possession for about 170 years.

The Bedingfields, supporters of Mary Tudor, upheld the Catholic faith during the period of the Reformation and were fined heavily for their allegiance. In 1572, the last Bedingfield was obliged to sell the manor to a Protestant gentleman named John Holland whose son, Thomas, began the construction of the present house.

During the reign of George III the house was purchased by the 3rd Earl of Albemarle and was transformed beyond recognition by his son, who greatly enlarged it with the addition of extra wings encasing the original Tudor-style mansion. It acquired its present day appearance when Georgian facings were added during the time of the 7th Earl, whose third son was married to Alice Keppel, the Edwardian beauty who became the last mistress of *King Edward VII*. Edward visited Quidenham Hall in 1907.

The Earls of Albemarle retained possession of the Hall until 1948, when it became a Carmelite nunnery.

61610 HONINGHAM HALL

This fine Elizabethan-style mansion, set in wooded parkland near Norwich, was built in 1605 by Thomas Richardson, Chief Justice in the reign of *King James I*.

Honingham was acquired in 1702 by the Townshends and subsequently inherited by the Fellowes, another prominent Norfolk family.

Ailwyn Fellowes, 1ˢᵗ Baron Ailwyn (1855-1924) served as a Conservative Member of Parliament from 1887 to 1906. Following his political career, Fellowes was Deputy Chairman of the *Great Eastern* Railway and some time Director of the LNER. He died at Honingham Hall and was buried in the grounds of the local church.

In 1936, Honingham was sold to Sir Eric Teichman, a retired diplomat, and was the setting for his murder. Hearing shots on his land he told his wife he was going to "stop this damned poaching" and set out to confront the intruders. After midnight, he was found dead with a bullet from a US Army carbine in his left cheek. The nearby presence of 10 empty cartridges and two wads of chewing gum caused the investigation to move to the nearby airbase. Two American Servicemen were subsequently arrested for Sir Eric's murder.

The Hall was demolished in 1967.

61611 RAYNHAM HALL

Raynham Hall, near Fakenham in Norfolk, was built by Sir Roger Townshend in 1630, near the site of an ancient moated hall. It was enlarged by the 2nd Viscount Townshend through the addition of a wing and alterations to the principal apartments.

Charles, 2nd Viscount Townshend (1674 – 1738) was the brother-in-law of Sir Robert Walpole (the resident of **Houghton Hall)** and a key member of his government. Professionally, the two men were at loggerheads; on a personal level they hated each other. In 1730, Townshend resigned over a foreign policy issue, retired to Raynham, and immersed himself in his true passion: agricultural improvements. A close associate of Coke of Norfolk (see 61601 **Holkham**), he was known colloquially as "Turnip" Townshend, from his introduction of turnips into the crop rotation system in collaboration with fellow agriculturalist Jethro Tull, inventor of the seed drill.

Raynham Hall is reputedly haunted by the ghost of "The Brown

Lady" identified as Lady Dorothy Walpole, sister of Sir Robert and wife of "Turnip" Townshend. The discovery by him of an earlier affair involving Lady Dorothy and a local philanderer caused Townshend to order that his wife be locked in her apartments and denied further contact with their children. She died in March, 1726, from smallpox; legend has it, however, that her death was the result of a fall – whether accidental or otherwise – down the grand oak staircase, where sightings of her ghost have generally taken place.

The most famous – and last – sighting occurred on 19th September, 1936, when two professional photographers, who were taking photographs of the interior of the house, took a picture of a misty apparition on the staircase. When the photograph was developed (and subsequently published in 'Country Life' magazine) it clearly showed a hooded female figure descending the stairs. Its authenticity was never disproved.

61612 HOUGHTON HALL

Houghton Hall is the largest country house in Norfolk and was built by Sir William Walpole, First Lord of the Treasury – a title subsequently bestowed on all British Prime Ministers – from 1721 to 1742, the longest-ever holder of that Office.

In 1700, at the age of 24, Walpole (1676 – 1746) inherited a house built or remodelled by his grandfather in the reign of Charles II. From 1722 onwards, he gradually extended and subsequently rebuilt the house on a much grander scale. While he conceived of Houghton as a monument to himself and to the Walpole family, he also saw it as a house for family living and a centre for sporting life and boisterous political entertaining.

Far from being a bluff, down-to-earth Norfolk Squire, Walpole was a cultured man with a passion for art and architecture. At Houghton, he created a magnificent showcase for the finest architects, craftsmen and painters of an elegant age. He assembled, over a period of 20 years, the great collection of old masterpieces which now form the core of the Hermitage Museum in St. Petersburg, having been sold by his impecunious grandson to Catherine the Great of Russia. Many, however, still remain at Houghton, displayed among its sumptuous interiors.

Since 1797, Houghton has been the home of the Cholmondeley family, following the marriage of Walpole's daughter, Mary, to the future 3rd Earl. Among its many attractions is the unique collection of over 20,000 model soldiers and other militaria commissioned by the 6th Marquess and featuring a reconstruction of the Battle of Waterloo.

61613 Woodbastwick Hall

Woodbastwick Hall was a large, red brick, neo-Elizabethan house with a tower, built in 1889 for Albemarle Cator to replace a burnt-out house dating from 1819.

The Hall was demolished in 1971 by the great grandson of its founder. The front door of the building was installed at Merton Hall.

61614 Castle Hedingham

Hedingham Castle, Castle Hedingham near Halstead, Essex, was built in 1140 by Aubrey de Vere, the son of a Norman Knight who had come to England with William the Conqueror. The castle remained the stronghold of this immensely rich and powerful family for over 500 years, although the splendid keep (said to be the finest example of its kind in England), and the magnificent banqueting hall with minstrels' gallery are all that remain of this great mediaeval fortress and its later Tudor additions.

The son of the Castle's founder, also named Aubrey, was created 1st Earl of Oxford by Queen Matilda. The 2nd Earl accompanied Richard *Coeur de Lion* on the Crusades and the 3rd Earl was among the barons who compelled *King John* to sign the Magna Carta at Runnymede in 1215, causing the monarch to lay siege to the Castle in the following year.

De Veres were present at the Battles of Crecy, Poitiers, Agincourt and Bosworth (where John, 13th Earl, was one of the most senior commanders in Henry Tudor's army); the 15th Earl accompanied *King Henry VIII* at the Field of the Cloth of Gold.

The 16th Earl escorted Queen Elizabeth from **Hatfield House** (see 61621) to London for her Coronation in 1559. The young Queen became the third of the Tudor Monarchs to visit Hedingham when she spent a week at the castle in the summer of 1561. Edward, the 17th Earl, a favourite at the court of Queen Elizabeth and reputedly the best of the courtier poets, has been included among the names of those suggested as the true author of Shakespeare's works!

When the 20th Earl died in 1703, there was no son to inherit the title, which became extinct. The estate was purchased in 1713 by Sir William Ashhurst MP, Lord Mayor of London, who landscaped the grounds and built a country mansion within the inner bailey.

The title subsequently passed to the Majendie family who owned Hedingham for the next 250 years before it reverted to a latter-day descendant of the de Veres.

61615 CULFORD HALL

Now a school, Culford was formerly the seat of the Earls of Cadogan.

The Hall remains basically as built for Sir Nathaniel Bacon but was remodelled by Samuel Wyatt for the 1st Marquess Cornwallis, whose surrender at Yorktown in 1781 signalled victory for the Americans in the War of Independence.

Distinguished visitors to Culford during its heyday included *King Edward VII* and Queen Alexandra in 1904 and Princess Mary, (the *Princess Royal*) in 1926.

61616 FALLODON

Although the Estate dates from the time of Henry I (1068-1135) Fallodon Hall, near Embleton in Northumberland, originates from the eighteenth century with later additions and alterations (and twentieth century reconstruction following a major fire).

Built of red brick, "a material rarely used in the buildings of the neighbourhood" (Northumberland County History), Fallodon was the home of General Sir Charles Grey (1729-1807), afterwards 1st Earl Grey, a younger son of the house of Grey of Howick, one of the most important families in Northumberland. Charles Grey (1764-1845), 2nd Earl and prominent English statesman, was born at Fallodon, by then his father's residence, but spent much of his life at Howick Hall.

Charles Grey was elected as Whig MP for Northumberland at the age of only 22. As Foreign Secretary in 1806 he played a prominent part in the abolition of the African Slave trade and as Prime Minister (1830 to 1834) was responsible for the passing of the Reform Act which brought the principle of "one man, one vote" into the British Parliamentary system.

In gratitude for the services of an envoy sent to China by Grey as part of a diplomatic mission, a grateful Mandarin sent the Earl a specially scented tea, flavoured with oil of Bergamot. Earl Grey is now the world's most popular blend of scented tea.

Ownership of Fallodon passed through successive generations of the family including Sir George Grey, grandson of the 1st Earl, who was for twenty years Home Secretary, and Sir Edward Grey (1862-1933), MP for Berwick-upon-Tweed who served twice as Foreign Secretary, firstly from 1892-95 in Gladstone's final administration and then from 1905-16 in the Liberal governments of Campbell-Bannerman and Asquith.

Grey is perhaps best remembered for a remark made to a friend one evening just before the outbreak of the First World War as he watched lights being extinguished on the street below his office: "The lamps are going out all over Europe; we shall not see them lit again in our lifetime."

Raised to the Lords as Viscount Grey of Fallodon in 1916, he continued to play an active part in politics, serving briefly as Liberal leader in that House, 1923-24.

Viscount Grey was also a director of the *North Eastern* Railway and, subsequently, a member of the Board of Directors of the LNER. (Chairman: Traffic Committee)

61617 FORD CASTLE

The history of Ford Castle, near Berwick-upon-Tweed, dates back to the early fourteenth century when Sir William Heron fortified his residence by the addition of a tower to each corner. Three of the towers still survive, although one now stands detached from the main building.

The northern part of the castle dates mainly from the sixteenth century but was rebuilt, together with the forecourt and gateway, in 1861. The main building was converted into a Country House in 1694 and restored in 1862.

King James IV of Scotland stayed at Ford Castle before his fatal incursion into Northumberland and death at the Battle of Flodden Field in 1513.

61618 WYNYARD PARK

Wynyard Hall and its adjacent parkland stand in an Estate of 5400 acres, located seven miles north east of Middlesbrough and Stockton.

The earliest recorded inhabitants of the Estate were the de Chapell family, circa 1230. It eventually came into the possession of the Vane Tempest family towards the end of the eighteenth century. Frances Vane Tempest inherited the Estate in 1813 and subsequently married the future 3rd Marquess of Londonderry.

Wynyard flourished under the 3rd Marquess and his wife, who demolished the existing Hall (dating from the fifteenth century), and replaced it with a new one funded mainly from the earnings of the family coal mines, regarded as the best in the north. To cut the cost of exporting his coal, Londonderry built a harbour at Seaham, connected to the pits by railway, and over the years 1835-37 exported over 250,000 tons.

Following its completion in 1827, Wynyard Hall was visited by many famous people, including the Duke of Wellington, who had given away Frances Vane Tempest on her wedding day. Unfortunately, disaster struck the Hall in 1841, when two-thirds of the House was gutted by fire. Reconstruction commenced almost immediately and was completed in 1848 at a cost of £40,000 including £100 for a new fire engine!

On completion, glittering society balls were still the order of the day, catering for as many as 800 guests and celebrating famous visitors such as Sir Robert Peel, *Sir Walter Scott*, and Benjamin Disraeli.

By the beginning of the twentieth century, the Estate had no fewer than eighteen farms within its boundaries, which also included a dairy, hunt kennels for the *South Durham*, gas house, (using coal transported from the Londonderrys' collieries), and a wide range of facilities for recreation and leisure pursuits. The Estate also had its own stud farm which produced Polemarch, winner of the 1921 St. Leger as a 50-1 outsider.

In the best traditions of country houses, Wynyard also possessed a resident Ghost – the seemingly ubiquitous 'Grey Lady' – who is reported to have wandered many times through the grounds of the Estate, before emerging from large mirrors in the Duke's Gallery in the Hall.

This once bustling and largely self-sufficient community neither had, nor needed much contact with the outside world: it was rare for anyone to venture out of the Estate except for major shopping trips to Stockton or to transport people to and from the local railway stations.

The 4th and 5th Marquesses had shown little interest in the Estate or its workforce but, during the reign of the 6th Marquess (1884 to 1915), political prominence returned to Wynyard and major shooting parties were the order of the day, with no fewer than eighteen gamekeepers in employment. In 1903, *King Edward VII* visited the Hall to hold a Privy Council Meeting, the first of six visits by that Monarch during his reign.

The 7th Marquess had a particular prominence in political circles and was Air Minister in the 1930's. He was visited at Wynyard on several occasions by Joachim von Ribbentrop, his German opposite number, who became Hitler's Foreign Minister and was hanged after the Nuremberg trials. Other prominent visitors to the Hall during the 1920's and 1930's included Winston Churchill, Harold MacMillan and Anthony Eden. The Prince of Wales (later Edward VIII) visited in 1930, as did his brother Albert, Duke of York, in 1934.

The Hall was taken over in 1942 by the War Ministry and transformed into an army camp for the duration of the War. *Princess Elizabeth* stayed at Wynyard in 1947, at a time when it was in use as a Teacher Training College. Its role as a "temporary" college was intended to last for only two years in order to assist in training the large number of teachers required after 1945. In the event, the College lasted until 1961.

Despite its popularity with the Royal family, Wynyard gradually became second in preference to the Londonderrys' other seat in Ireland where the 8th Marquess, who succeeded in 1949, spent much of his time. (Lady Jane Vane Tempest Stewart, his elder daughter, was one of the attendants to Queen Elizabeth II during her Coronation).

The 9th Marquess, who succeeded to the title in 1955, made extensive alterations to the Hall and landscaped the grounds. It has to be said, however, that by this time the Estate was in a very run down condition. The decline in Wynyard's fortunes had begun in 1915 with the death of the 6th Marquess and the heavy financial burdens imposed by death duties had virtually crippled the Estate.

Contemporary Note ("Modern Image")

Considerable sums were spent on the farms and cottages during the 1960's but it proved no easy task keeping the Estate in pristine condition and in 1987 it was sold to Mr. John Hall, knighted in 1991 for his contribution to northern industrial life. Sir John, a multi-millionaire, masterminded the creation of the highly successful MetroCentre at Gateshead and, as Chairman, brought about the resurgence of Newcastle United F.C.

61619 Welbeck Abbey

Welbeck Abbey, ancestral home of the Dukes of Portland, is built on the site of an abbey founded in 1153. After the Dissolution, the estate eventually came into the possession of Sir Charles Cavendish, son of Bess of Hardwick, who began construction of the present house.

In 1734, marriage brought Welbeck into the possession of the Dukes of Portland, the most enigmatic of whom was the kindly but eccentric (and unmarried) 5th Duke (1800 – 1879), who shunned the company of his peers and spent a small fortune building a network of underground rooms and passages connecting the Abbey with different parts of the Estate. The tunnel connecting the house with the stables was over one and a quarter miles long; it meant that the Duke could be driven in his coach almost to the edge of Workshop unseen by his employees or local inhabitants.

The subterranean burrowings – most of which still exist – were heated by hot air and illuminated by thousands of gas lights, the library alone containing eleven hundred. The underground ballroom is said to be the largest room in Europe without supporting pillars. The riding school was second only in size to the Spanish Riding School in Vienna.

Despite his lavish building programmes and immense wealth, the 5th Duke occupied only 3 or 4 rooms at Welbeck where he dined almost exclusively on roast chicken and rice pudding. His day time apartment was fitted with a trap door via which he could descend into the underground tunnels and "pop up" without warning at some other part of the estate. Servants and the army of workmen excavating and building at Welbeck had orders not to greet or salute him and to treat him "as if he were a tree". In later life, he contrived to travel unseen from the Abbey to his London home behind the closed blinds of his horse-drawn carriage, which was rolled onto a specially-built flat railway trailer at Worksop Station.

When his cousin, the 6th Duke, succeeded, far from being the home of a strange recluse, Welbeck became one of the great social centres of England. *King Edward VII* and Queen Alexandra visited the Abbey as did the ill-fated Archduke Franz Ferdinand, two years before his assassination at Sarajevo.

The 6th Duke was a prominent racing man who won the Derby twice, (including once with *Donovan*), and whose thoroughbred *St. Simon* sired numerous champions. He spent much of his gains on charitable objects, including almshouses at Welbeck named, appropriately, "The Winnings".

The 6th Duke died in 1943 and was succeeded by his elder son, who had already built and continued to live in a large modern country house one mile north east of Welbeck Abbey. The dowager Duchess remained in the Abbey until her death in 1954.

Welbeck continued to provide accommodation and state rooms for the use of the family but, since 1953, was largely leased to the Ministry of Defence as a Sixth Form College and boarding school for students intending to make a career in the Army.

61620 CLUMBER

Duke's Drive at Clumber, Notts, is a tree-lined avenue, over a mile in length, leading towards what was once a substantial mansion – the former seat of the Dukes of Newcastle.

Sadly, the end of the drive is something of an anti-climax. The great house, with its classical arcades, its cupolas and its balustraded terraces along the lakeside, has all but vanished. Only a tiny fragment is left standing, together with the stables and clocktower; the rest is history.

In 1707, John Holles, 1st Duke of Newcastle, was authorised to enclose 3,000 acres at Clumber to create a park for Queen Anne. Although there was a hunting lodge in the park from this early date, Clumber House was not built until the 2nd Duke succeeded in 1768. The new house was built to the designs of Stephen Wright and was enlarged by Sir Charles Barry, architect of the Houses of Parliament.

Even after the house was built, however, much of the surrounding grounds – retrieved from primeval forest – remained wet and soggy. Horace Walpole, son of Sir Robert (see 61612 **Houghton Hall**), who visited in 1772, was not impressed, describing it as "a bleak heath, full of rabbits".

The 4th Duke, who succeeded in 1795, was a knowledgeable art collector but was also a die-hard opponent of political reform. With the failure of the Reform Bill in 1831, his principal seat at Nottingham Castle was burnt to the ground by an angry mob – hence the less than imposing Victorian replacement which now adorns the Castle rock. Fearing that Clumber would also be attacked, he fortified the house with cannon, but the rioters dispersed without further incident.

On 26th March, 1879, a disastrous fire swept through Clumber House. Fortunately, the Fire Brigade arrived quickly, controlling the fire in about six hours, and the greater part of the Newcastle art collection was saved. The fire destroyed the oldest part of the building including the west front, the Grand Staircase and the Great Hall. The 7th Duke restored and greatly improved the house, making it even more palatial than previously.

The first two decades of the twentieth Century were the heyday of both house and estate but, after the economic slump of the 1920's, matters went into sharp decline. In 1937, the contents of the house were sold piecemeal, including the marble staircase, the magnificent fountain, and the half-mile of balustrading which had adorned the terraces. A year later – within ten years of the plating of the locomotive which bore its name – Clumber itself was demolished. Sic transit gloria mundi.

Following its wartime use as an ammunition dump, in 1945 the estate was offered for sale and eventually became the property of The National Trust.

61621 HATFIELD HOUSE

Built originally in the late fifteenth century as a palace for the Bishop of Ely, *King Henry VIII* retained the property as a childhood home for his daughters Mary and Elizabeth.

Hatfield remained a Royal palace until 1603 when, in a somewhat bizarre transaction, *King James I* exchanged it for a property near Waltham Cross owned by his Chief Minister, Robert Cecil, 1st Earl of Salisbury. It has been the home of the Cecils ever since.

In 1607, Robert Cecil set about demolishing the Tudor palace and replaced it with a fine Jacobean manor house, constructed on an 'E'-shaped plan to commemorate the significance of Queen Elizabeth I at Hatfield. Within the grounds stands the surviving wing of the former Royal palace, incorporating the great Tudor banqueting hall where Elizabeth held her first Council of State in 1558 following the death of her sister Mary. Some of her possessions are on display in the House.

The principal designer of Hatfield House was Robert Lyminge assisted, possibly, by the young Inigo Jones. The interior design was the work of English, Flemish and French craftsmen.

The State Rooms at Hatfield are rich in world famous paintings, including the Rainbow Portrait of Queen Elizabeth I and the Ermine Portrait by Nicholas Hilliard. Also displayed in the House are many historic momentoes associated with the Cecils, one of England's foremost political families. Robert's father, William Cecil, Lord

Burghley, was a loyal servant and Chief Adviser to Elizabeth I for over 40 years. The 3rd Marquess of Salisbury was three times Prime Minister during the closing years of Queen Victoria's reign.

Under the influence of successive generations of Cecils, Hatfield was progressively transformed, renovated, partly re-built after a fire and, finally, largely restored to its original splendid appearance.

61622 ALNWICK CASTLE

Alnwick Castle, sometimes referred to as "the Windsor of the North", is the second largest inhabited castle in England (the largest being Windsor itself), and has been the home of the Percy's, Earls and Dukes of Northumberland, since 1309.

The earliest recorded mention of Alnwick occurs around 1096 when Yves de Vesay erected the original castle buildings, described as being "very strongly fortified" in about 1134. De Vesay's descendant Eustace was one of the leaders of the barons' revolt against *King John* in 1212 and was forced to flee to Scotland. John gave orders for the destruction of Alnwick Castle, but subsequently appears to have rescinded them for they were never carried out.

Having been ruined during a particularly violent phase of Border warfare, the Castle was restored to military effectiveness by the 1st Lord Percy of Alnwick in the early 1300's and the major features of its design date from that time.

Alnwick Castle was repeatedly battered by Border strife spanning the next 250 years, following which the 7th Earl undertook considerable restoration work in the mid-sixteenth century.

When the 1st Duke of Northumberland took his seat in 1750, he restored the Castle as a family residence. The interior was subsequently refurbished in the classical Renaissance style.

Alnwick ranks as one of the most magnificent buildings of its type in the Country. The gateway is guarded by an impressive barbican and the outline of its massive keep, walls and towers completely dominates the town's horizon. The Castle houses the Regimental Museum of the Northumberland Fusiliers.

Contemporary Note ("Modern Image"):

Alnwick Castle doubles for Hogwarts School of Witchcraft and Wizardry in the screen adaptations of the first two 'Harry Potter' novels and Harry's first flying lesson was shot in the Castle grounds. The Guest Hall provided the setting for Hogwart's school library in "The Chamber of Secrets".

61623 Lambton Castle

Lambton Castle commemorates one of County Durham's great families, who rose to prominence through wealth founded on coal, but dates only from 1797 when construction began on the site of an earlier fortification at which the 68th Regiment of Foot (*Durham Light Infantry*) had been raised in 1758. Lambton, completed in 1833, is thus a nineteenth century creation, although the design was in part influenced by that of **Brancepeth Castle.**

The Castle was built for "Radical Jack" Lambton, 1st Earl of Durham and the driving force behind the Reform Act of 1832. He also became the first Governor General of Canada.

Underlying coal seams threatened the castle with collapse; in 1865, part of it was dismantled and replaced by a Great Hall and various other additions (which largely disappeared again in 1932).

The Lambton story was not always one of success or good fortune. Local legend tells of the Lambton worm (or dragon) which was slain by a bygone Lambton heir after he had taken advice from a local witch. Because he reneged on his promise to the witch to kill the first living thing he subsequently met – his father, as it happens – she condemned his family to a curse of violent or untimely deaths said to have continued for nine generations.

The Castle has remained in private ownership.

61624 LUMLEY CASTLE

Lumley Castle dominates the countryside near Chester-le-Street, County Durham. It was built in 1392 as a manor house and later fortified by Sir Ralph Lumley, who was heavily involved in the many Border skirmishes between England and Scotland during that period. He was lauded for his defence of Berwick-on-Tweed, but this and other successes "went to his head" and he was executed for treason in 1400.

The castle was for centuries the seat of the Lumley family, including 'Lily of Lumley', whose ghost reputedly haunts this magnificent building.

Richard, Viscount Lumley, was created 1st Earl of Scarborough in 1690 for his part in putting down the Monmouth rebellion. The Lumleys prospered as mine owners until the end of the eighteenth century but subsequently fell on hard times such that, in 1807, they were obliged to sell most of the family possessions, including rare tapestries, pictures and furniture to raise money.

The castle became largely unoccupied until the beginning of the twentieth century when Frederica, Countess of Scarborough, took up residence. It subsequently became, and remains, a luxury hotel with golf course fashioned from the grounds originally landscaped by Sir John Vanbrugh and others.

61625 RABY CASTLE

This impressive pile stands in a 170 acre deer park with two lakes and matches exactly the popular conception of how a castle should look, right down to its moat and nine great towers. Its history can be traced back to King Canute, who owned the estate in the early eleventh century, and may well have built a manor house here, but its distinctive appearance is due largely to fourteenth century construction by the Neville family.

Over the centuries, Raby has played a major role in British politics. The huge Barons hall was the scene of plotting – the so-called 'Rising of the North' – aimed at putting Mary Queen of Scots on the throne in place of Elizabeth I, but when the rebellion failed the castle was forfeited by the Nevilles and held by the Crown until 1626, when it was purchased by Sir Henry Vane the Elder, MP and important member of the household of *King Charles I.*

Raby Castle was besieged in the Civil War but suffered little damage, and it was not until the eighteenth century that the first major alterations were made to the mediaeval structure. The dramatic Entrance Hall was created in its present form for the 2nd Earl of Darlington, to celebrate the coming of age of his heir in 1787. The roof was raised to enable carriages to pass through the Hall, resulting in a quite stunning interior in the Gothic Revival style. The castle was further restored in the nineteenth century but has remained largely unaltered since then.

61626 BRANCEPETH CASTLE

"Bobby Shafto's gone to sea

Silver buckles on his knee,

When he comes back he'll marry me,

Bonny Bobby Shafto."

The origins of Brancepeth Castle, County Durham, can be traced back to Anglo-Saxon times. The castle passed by marriage into the hands of one Gilbert de Neuville, a Norman baron who had come to England with William the Conqueror. De Neuville's descendants – as the Nevilles, Earls of Westmoreland – owned and greatly enlarged Brancepeth until 1569 when along with **Raby Castle**, it was confiscated following the unsuccessful 'Rising of the North'.

The Castle remained in the hands of the Crown for a number of years until *King James I* gave it to Robert Carr, Earl of Somerset. Subsequent owners included Sir Henry Bellasyse, whose daughter Mary fell in love with Bobby Shafto of Whitworth Hall, just across the River Wear from Brancepeth. Her love for Bobby became the subject of a famous north country song; sadly, he had eyes for another and Mary is said to have died of a broken heart.

In 1796, William Russell, a Sunderland banker, bought Brancepeth for £75,000. His son Matthew, who re-built the Castle at a cost of £12,000, was reputed to be the richest commoner in England, his wealth being derived from coal mining. Later, through marriage, the Castle became the property of Lord Boyne whose family remained in Brancepeth until the First World War when it became a military hospital.

After the 1914-18 war, the Castle stood empty for the first time and its contents were sold: the Great Hall contained a suit of armour, inlaid with gold, taken from King David of Scotland at the Battle of Neville's Cross – together with a picture by Hogarth.

During the Second World War, Brancepeth Castle was put to new use as the home of the *Durham Light Infantry*, whose Regimental Headquarters it was until 1960.

61627 ASKE HALL

Aske Hall, located near Richmond, North Yorkshire, is the country seat of the Marquess of Zetland.

The estate, which is mentioned in the Domesday Book, was owned for more than 500 years by the Aske family, long-established in Yorkshire. In the sixteenth century, the last male member of the family died and the estate subsequently passed via the Bowes (1530) and Wharton (1640) families to the D'Arcy's (1727). Sir Conyers D'Arcy built the present Hall, which incorporates the original thirteenth century Peel Tower.

Nestling in Capability Brown landscaped parkland, this Georgian treasure house and its estates were acquired in 1763 by the founder of the Dundas family in Yorkshire, whose wealth was derived from Army contracts, particularly during the Seven Years War (1756-

63). Laurence Dundas, son of Thomas, 1st Baron Dundas, who served as Vice-Admiral of Orkney and Shetland, became 1st Earl of Zetland in 1838; his grandson, also named Laurence, became the 1st Marquess of Zetland in 1892.

Aske, a spacious and elegant stone mansion which was extended and remodelled by the Dundas family has been described as an "architectural kaleidoscope"; the stable block, built in 1765, was later converted into a chapel with Italianate interior.

King Edward VII and Queen Alexandra, as Prince and Princess of Wales, stayed at Aske Hall in January, 1889, during an official visit to Yorkshire.

61628 HAREWOOD HOUSE

Built between 1759 and 1772, Harewood House, near Leeds, is one of England's most imposing stately homes.

The estate was purchased by the Lascelles family in 1738. Edwin Lascelles, the 1st Lord Harewood, commissioned both John Carr and Robert Adam as architects, with the result that the central part of the house was designed by Carr while the two wings (and the interiors) were created by Adam. Harewood stands in 1,000 acres of parkland, landscaped by Capability Brown.

During the nineteenth century, many changes were made to the house, most notably the extensions and alterations made by Charles Barry. These included the addition of a third storey and the construction of the Terrace Garden between 1844 and 1848.

Between 1919 and 1939, the house was further remodelled by the 6th Earl, largely with an eye to restoration and improvement. His wife, Princess Mary, the *Princess Royal*, daughter of *King George V*, lived at Harewood for 35 years until her death in 1965.

61629 NAWORTH CASTLE

Naworth Castle, Cumberland, home of the Dacre and Howard families for over 700 years, was begun in 1335, originally as a Peel Tower. It was subsequently enlarged and extended into a border fortress by Thomas, Lord Dacre, who played a prominent part in the defeat of the Scots at the Battle of Flodden.

The Dacre estates eventually came into the possession of the Howard family following the marriage of Thomas Howard, 4th Duke of Norfolk and cousin of Queen Elizabeth I, to the widowed Lady Dacre. The 4th Duke foolishly became embroiled in a plot to further the cause of Mary, Queen of Scots, and went to the scaffold in 1572. His third son, Lord William Howard, eventually managed to raise sufficient funds to re-claim ownership and possession of the Naworth estate, which had been forfeited to an angry Queen Elizabeth. He then set about restoring the castle.

Lord William served both James I and Charles I and was responsible for the maintenance locally of law and order. In the castle grounds stands the stump of the renowned oak tree where he used to hang Scottish Reivers and wrongdoers; it is said that he hanged 62 Armstrongs in two years.

Lord William's great grandson, Charles Howard, was a great friend and ally of General Monck. Together with George Downing, they were instrumental in restoring Charles II to the throne in 1660. As a result, Charles Howard was made Earl of Carlisle (and George Downing gave his name to the most famous street in London). Howard became governor of *Jamaica* and even owned St. Lucia personally, amassing an enormous fortune which enabled his grandson to commission Vanbrugh to build Castle Howard.

Increasingly, the Earls of Carlisle used Castle Howard as their main residence and Naworth became very much a secondary home, left as an old mediaeval fortification. In 1844, the east wing of the castle was engulfed by fire; fire engines were brought from Carlisle (by train!) but arrived too late to save the Tower, although the residential areas did escape destruction.

The reconstruction of the castle commenced in the 1850's. Much of the interior was restored by the 9th Earl of Carlisle, George Howard. George was primarily a painter; his circle of friends included Philip Webb, Edward Burne-Jones, William Morris and many other eminent pre-Raphaelites, all of whom were regular house guests.

George died in 1911; Naworth, still playing "second fiddle" to Castle Howard, eventually became the property of the 12th Earl, who moved back into the castle after it had been leased out and neglected in the years following the Second World War.

Naworth has long been a much-used location for film and T.V. productions. In 1935, Walt Disney was a house guest of the 10th Earl.

61630 TOTTENHAM HOTSPUR

Originally (and incorrectly) named Thoresby Park (the location of Thoresby **Hall**), in January, 1938, LNER No. 2830 was re-named **Tottenham Hotspur**, a name formerly carried on No. 2870 from May, 1937, to September, 1937, when it was fitted with a streamlined boiler casing, re-named **City of London** and set to work on the new "East Anglian" express service linking Norwich, Ipswich and London.

The "glory days" of Tottenham Hotspur F.C. – the days of Blanchflower, Greaves and other legends – had yet to come when the last of the B17's was withdrawn in 1960. Prior to that, the Club's achievements during its eighty year history were not particularly noteworthy, apart from a brief spell from 1949 to 1952 when, in three consecutive seasons, 'Spurs' were Champions of Divison 2; Champions of Division 1; and Division 1 Runners-up.

The Hotspur Football Club was formed from an existing cricket club in 1882 by the old boys of two local schools. Tottenham Hotspur F.C., as it was by then known, turned professional in 1895. Seven years earlier, in 1888, the Club had moved from its first ground at Tottenham Marshes to Northumberland Park; in 1899 it moved to its present location at White Hart Lane. Its first Football League game (Division 2) on 1st September, 1908, brought a 3-0 victory over Wolverhampton Wanderers.

Tottenham Hotspur won the F.A. Cup in 1901 and, again, in 1921, having achieved promotion as Division 2 Champions in the previous Season. This brief "purple patch" continued into the 1921-22 season, when Spurs came second in Division 1. That apart, the inter-war years brought little noteworthy success to the Club, other than its participation (as the losing side) in the 1933 Cup Final.

61631 SERLBY HALL

Serlby Hall in North Notts., situated not far from **Welbeck Abbey** and **Clumber**, was the family residence of the Moncktons, Earls of Galway.

The Hall dates from the beginning of the eighteenth Century, although there had been a mansion on that site from earlier times. In 1727, John Monckton was created a Peer of Ireland - Viscount Galway and Baron Killard – and in that year purchased the Serlby estate shortly after his marriage to the daughter of the Duke of Rutland. Almost immediately following the acquisition of the estate, the village of Farworth was evacuated, and the buildings demolished, to create space for Lord Galway's planned gardens and promenades.

Successive generations of the Earls of Galway were Members of Parliament and held various Offices in the Service of the Crown. John Monckton, 1st Viscount, was the Member for York and Pontefract and also served as a Privy Councillor. His son, the 2nd Viscount, represented Pontefract and Thirsk. The 6th and 7th Viscounts were Members of Parliament for Bassetlaw and North Nottinghamshire, respectively.

POSTSCRIPT:

Serlby Hall is no longer the country seat of the Earls of Galway, but does remain in private ownership.

61632 BELVOIR CASTLE/ROYAL SOVEREIGN

Belvoir Castle, located south west of Grantham, is the ancestral home of the Duke and Duchess of Rutland and commands an outstanding view of the Vale of Belvoir. The name, meaning "beautiful view", dates back to Norman times when Robert de Todeni, William the Conqueror's standard bearer, built the first fortress on this superb site.

In the early sixteenth century, the Castle passed by marriage to the Manners family, who later became Earls and then Dukes of Rutland.

Belvoir was seriously damaged in the Civil War. Between 1655 and 1658 a new, classically-proportioned house was built on the old foundations. In 1801, the 5th Duke commissioned James Wyatt to remodel the Castle in castellated style. Wyatt also designed the new Gallery where the Duke entertained on a grand scale. However, in 1813 the north and west ranges were destroyed by fire and most of the pictures and furniture were lost.

The Duke's chaplain, the Rev. Sir John Thoroton, who had worked closely with Wyatt on the earlier remodelling, was entrusted with the re-building work. His designs were bolder, with a great tower projecting from the centre of the north-east range. The entrance hall, staircase and passages were also created by Thoroton and the new series of state rooms he designed for this Victorian "castle" were decorated after his death in 1820 by the sons of James Wyatt.

Belvoir Castle houses the Regimental Museum of the 17th/21st Lancers, the "Death or Glory Boys" of Light Brigade fame (now the Queen's Royal Lancers).

For a brief period prior to its withdrawal from service, this locomotive assumed a change of identity. In October, 1958, No. 61632 was re-named **Royal Sovereign** following the withdrawal of No. 61671 and took over the Royal train duty at Cambridge shed. It was, however, called upon to convey the Royal family to King's Lynn (for **Sandringham)** only once before it, too, was taken out of service in February, 1959.

61633 KIMBOLTON CASTLE

Kimbolton Castle, *Huntingdonshire*, was built before 1201 as a fortified manor house and was subsequently modified and improved in Tudor times. In 1615, the castle came into the possession of the Montagu family, who became the Earls (and eventually Dukes) of Manchester, and remained their country seat until 1950.

In 1707, the old south wing collapsed and the castle was rebuilt by Vanbrugh, Hawskmoor and Adam. The Pellegrini mural paintings at Kimbolton which date from this period are said to be the best examples in England of the work of this gifted Venetian painter.

Kimbolton Castle is best known as the final home (or prison) of Henry VIII's first queen, Katharine of Aragon ("**Divorced**, beheaded, died ......") who was sent here in April, 1534, for refusing to give up her status or deny the validity of her marriage. She died in January, 1536, in what is now known as the Queen's Room – the setting for a scene in Shakespeare's "Henry VIII".

The building has undergone several phases of restoration since the eighteenth century but remains essentially as rebuilt by Vanbrugh and others. In 1950, it became part of Kimbolton School.

61634 HINCHINGBROOKE

The mediaeval priory at Hinchingbrooke was closed in 1538 as part of the Dissolution. Shortly afterwards, Sir Richard Cromwell acquired the property and began conversion of the nunnery into a dwelling. His son, Henry, pulled down part of the nunnery and constructed a fine Elizabethan house surrounded by an open courtyard and designed to reflect his increasing self-importance (as county sheriff and Member of Parliament). He entertained Queen Elizabeth I here in 1564, when she knighted him.

Henry's son, Oliver, (uncle of his rather more famous namesake, who played here as a child), feted James I at Hinchingbrooke on his journey south from Scotland to take possession of the English throne. Made a Knight of the Bath, Sir Oliver carried on the family tradition of entertaining royalty and James I was a frequent visitor. Unfortunately, Oliver's lavish lifestyle was not matched by his means and Hinchingbrooke was eventually sold to Sir Sidney Montagu in 1627.

The Montagus were destined to become the Earls of Sandwich and to play an important part in British history. Charles I was held prisoner at Hinchingbrooke for one night in June, 1647, and the lst Earl (created 1660) was second cousin to – and patron of –Samuel Pepys. Both Hinchingbrooke and its owner feature prominently in the celebrated Diary.

The widely-travelled 4th Earl became First Lord of the Admiralty and was patron to Captain James Cook. He is probably best remembered now for the convenience food which took his name (the "sandwich"). It is more likely that he ate this as part of his working day at the Admiralty than, as has been suggested, because he spent so much time at the gaming tables. The original sandwich was a piece of salt beef between two slices of toasted bread.

The north-east corner of Hinchingbrooke was severely damaged by fire in January, 1830. Reconstruction commenced in 1832 and was completed in 1836.

The 8th Earl was a personal friend of *King Edward VII* who visited twice. The Earl also entertained the opera singer Dame Nellie Melba as his houseguest. According to a local newspaper, in February, 1900, "imbued with patriotic fervour" he expressed his readiness to convert Hinchingbrooke into a convalescent home for officers invalided home from the Boer War. He was not seemingly called upon to do so.

The 9th, and last, Earl succeeded to the title in 1916. His son and intended successor, as Lord Hinchingbrooke, relinquished his title and his seat in the House of Lords in order to continue an active life in the Commons. Sadly, he lost his Parliamentary seat at the next election.

The 9th Earl died in 1962. In the following year, after 500 years as a home, the house was put up for sale and in 1970, became

Hinchingbrooke School. The following extract (1921) from a local newspaper, although not intended as such, serves as a fitting epitaph:-

"Hinchingbrooke can rightly be called a memory haunted place, filled as it is with recollections of battles and victories by sea and land; of men and women who have attained the highest pinnacles of earthly glory, and who long hundreds of years ago were filled with passionate human purpose, and who had a prominent part in shaping the destinies of our Empire."

61635 MILTON

Milton Hall and the Fitzwilliam estate in which it stands are located some two miles from Peterborough, Cambs.

Sir William Fitzwilliam, a London Merchant, purchased the Manor of Milton in 1502. His grandson, the third Sir William, Lord Deputy of Ireland from 1588 to 1594, is thought likely to have begun the construction of Milton Hall, which was progressively enlarged and modernised during the eighteenth and nineteenth centuries.

Designs for a new mansion were commissioned in 1726 and 1750 but came to nothing: new wings were added in 1725 and 1750-51. The park in which the Hall stands was landscaped in the mid-eighteenth century.

The 5th Sir William (d. 1644) was made Lord Fitzwilliam in 1620. The 3rd Lord was created Earl Fitzwilliam in 1716 and was awarded an English earldom in 1746, the original grant being an Irish title. William, the 4th Earl (d.1833) was an important Whig politician who was briefly Viceroy of Ireland. The 5th Earl (d.1857) left Milton to his second son; the Hall and estate passed eventually to his great grandson, who succeeded as 10th Earl in 1952. (On his death in 1979 the Earldom became extinct).

During the First World War, Milton was used as a military hospital. During the Second, it became the focus for Jedburgh Team training and the permanent 'home' for the Jedburghs from February, 1944.

A Jedburgh Team was a special forces unit typically consisting of three men (two officers and a wireless operator), whose role was to parachute into enemy territory ahead of the advancing Allied armies and contact the local resistance groups. The JED's were part of the Special Operations Executive (S.O.E.); the arrival of US forces led to the formation of their own equivalent of S.O.E., the Office of Strategic Services (O.S.S.).

The Jedburgh Teams were predominantly British, American and French; most were designed for deployment in France and their scope for future missions was substantially reduced following the liberation of that country.

61636 HARLAXTON MANOR

Harlaxton Manor, near Grantham, Lincs, is a Grade I listed country house built between 1832 and 1844 for Mr. Gregory Gregory, a bachelor, on the site of an earlier ruined manor house which was demolished to make way for his own pretentious grand creation.

The imposing exterior in the Elizabethan style (mixed with Jacobean and Baroque) was designed by Anthony Salvin and William Burn; the interior has been described as an "architectural tour de force" in various styles and with an unparalleled Cedar staircase. The building even incorporates a copy of the Elizabethan Great Hall at **Audley End**.

No one knows why Gregory Gregory commissioned Salvin and Burn to create this somewhat over-blown, if beautiful, fusion of architectural styles and tastes. Since he had no children to succeed him, it has even been suggested that he built Harlaxton to "cock a snook" at his neighbours, including those at nearby **Belvoir Castle**, Harlaxton somewhat pointedly being one room bigger.

Following Gregory's death, Harlaxton Manor became increasingly neglected by his heirs and successors and virtually derelict. In the desperate hope of saving it from demolition, in 1937 it was advertised for sale in 'The Times' and in 'Country Life', seeking someone to save "the labour of an age in piled stones", and was purchased for £78,000 by a Mrs. Violet Van der Elst.

Mrs. Van der Elst, born Violet Dodge in 1882, was the daughter of a coal porter and a washer woman. After starting work as a scullery maid, she became a successful business woman by developing 'Shavex' the first brushless shaving cream, which she manufactured initially in her own kitchen. By the end of the 1930's, and now married to the Belgian, Jean Van der Elst, she had amassed a huge personal fortune (and earned some notoriety for her vocal campaigning against capital punishment).

The new owner's first acts were to re-name the place 'Grantham Castle' and to forbid shooting on the estate, promising to preserve the grounds as a sanctuary "for the dear birds and the wild creatures". She then set about the not-inexpensive task of restoring the interior of her new home, including the permanent installation of electricity. The massive chandelier in the Great Hall was originally destined for a palace in Madrid, but was diverted to Harlaxton on the outbreak of the Spanish Civil War; the fountain on the rear terraces was flanked by a pair of marble lions obtained from **Clumber** Park. Mrs. Van der Elst spent £250,000 modernising and furnishing the Manor only to find herself confined to a few rooms during the War years when members of the First Airborne Division were billeted in the house.

Having dissipated her fortune on various causes, Mrs. Van der Elst – a compulsive litigant – was, in 1948, obliged to sell Harlaxton Manor for £60,000 to the Society of Jesus, who proceeded to use it as a seminary.

POSTSCRIPT:

The Jesuits' occupation was brief and in 1966 – the year in which Mrs. Van der Elst died penniless in a Kent nursing home – the Society leased the property to Stanford University of California.

Stanford remained at Harlaxton for four years and the lease was then assumed by the University of Evansville, Indiana.

61637 THORPE HALL

Although there are at least three Thorpe Halls in the territory served by the LNER, it appears to be generally accepted that Locomotive No. 2837 (BR No. 61637) was named for the large, plain, white-brick house at Thorpe-le-Soken, Essex, dating from 1823, which was the one time seat of Field Marshal Lord Byng, 1st and last Viscount Byng of Vimy.

The Manor of Thorpe dates back to medieval times. After several changes of ownership following the Dissolution, it was bought in 1723 by Stephen Martin, who assumed the name and arms of Leake upon inheriting an estate from Admiral Sir John Leake. He was succeeded by his son Stephen Martin Leake. Successive generations of Leakes then lived at Thorpe Hall until 1830, when it was leased to various tenants before being put up for sale in 1913.

The remarkable Leake family included Lieutenant-Colonel Arthur Martin-Leake, Army Medical Department, one of only three men ever to be awarded the Victoria Cross twice, in his case during the Boer War (1902) and, subsequently, at the First Battle of Ypres (1914)

Martin-Leake's five brothers included a naval officer who captained the first ship in World War I to be torpedoed by the Germans. The other four were all army officers; one was killed in a ballooning accident in the English Channel.

When the Hall was put on the market in 1913, it was purchased by Julian Byng, whose wife laid out new gardens around the Georgian-style villa which had been built to replace the old manor house in 1823.

Following an education at Eton College, Julian Hedworth George Byng (1862-1935) embarked upon a military career which saw early service in *India* and in *South Africa* during the Boer War, 1899-1900.

Following the outbreak of war in 1914, *Byng* first campaigned in France with the B.E.F. as Commander of the Cavalry Corps. Later, he commanded the 9th Army Corps in the ill-fated Dardanelles Campaign and supervised the withdrawal from the Straits. In 1916, he was given command of the Canadian Army Corps on the Western Front, gaining his greatest glory with the Canadian victory at Vimy Ridge in April, 1917. He then assumed command of the British 3rd Army and conducted the first surprise attack using tanks at Cambrai, considered to be a turning point in the war. For these services, he was promoted to the rank of General, and after the war was elevated to the peerage as 1st Baron Byng of Vimy of Thorpe-le-Soken, Essex.

Lord Byng served as Governor General of *Canada* from 1921 to 1926. Following his return to England, he was raised in the peerage and became Viscount Byng. He served as Commissioner of the London Metropolitan Police and was promoted to the rank of Field Marshal, finally retiring to Thorpe Hall, where he died in June, 1935. His widow remained in Essex until the Second World War, when she returned to Canada to live with friends.

During the war, the Hall was occupied by the Ministry of Defence. When hostilities ceased, Lady Byng returned and remained in occupation until her own death in 1949. The estate was then sold to Sir George Nelson for use as a Lady Nelson Convalescent Home for employees of English Electric.

It remained as such until 1988, when it was sold to developers. The Hall has been unoccupied since that date, although the gardens laid out by Lady Byng continue to be maintained by the corporate owners of the estate.

A second Thorpe Hall, situated near Peterborough, might almost equally have been considered for inclusion in Class B17.

The house was built for Oliver St. John, Lord Chief Justice to Oliver Cromwell, during the 1650's. Ornamental stones from the old Minster at Peterborough, which had taken a severe battering from the Parliamentary army, were used in the construction of Thorpe

Hall, alongside local stone. The Hall is a splendid example of a Cromwellian mansion – the only one in the country still standing in its own grounds.

St. John died in exile following the Restoration. Ownership eventually passed to the Bernard family through the marriage of Oliver's daughter to Sir John Bernard, M.P. for Huntingdon. In the mid-nineteenth century the Hall was purchased by Rev. William Strong whose family occupied it until 1926, when it was again sold. During the Second World War, the house was requisitioned for use as a hospital and later became a maternity home. It is now a hospice and palliative care unit run by the Sue Ryder Foundation.

61638 MELTON HALL

The history of Melton Constable, Norfolk, seat of the Astley family for centuries, dates back to the time of the Norman Conquest. Although there was a manor house here in the thirteenth century, the present Melton Hall was erected or rebuilt by Sir Joseph Astley between 1664 and 1670. There were many subsequent additions or alterations. The grounds and gardens were landscaped in the eighteenth century by Capability Brown, and Melton was only the second estate in England to witness the introduction of red deer into the parkland.

To the north of the house, about a mile away, is a lookout tower, named Belle-vue, built at the time of the Spanish Armada. This commands extensive views of the surrounding countryside and of the distant coastline, even though it stands more than ten miles inland.

In the late nineteenth century the parish of Melton Constable, some six miles from Fakenham, was served by the (then) Eastern and Midlands Railway and, with a population of only 118 inhabitants in 1881, was the surprising location for a railway locomotive works, or 'plant' covering an area of 14 acres.

The house and most of the estate were sold in the 1950's to the Grosvenor Estate.

DAVID H. BALDWIN

POSTSCRIPT:

Melton Hall features in the 1971 Joseph Losey film "The Go-Between", starring Alan Bates, Edward Fox and Julie Christie.

61639 NORWICH CITY

This locomotive entered service as No. 2839 **Rendelsham Hall** but, in January, 1938, acquired the name **Norwich City**, in turn displaced from LNER No. 2859 which, like No. 2870, had been streamlined for duty on the "East Anglian" service between Norwich and Liverpool Street and re-named **East Anglian** (see 61630).

The re-naming of No. 2839 presented the LNER with an opportunity to dispense with a name which had been spelt incorrectly and should have read **Rendlesham.**

(It transpires that the mis-spelling may not have been the only reason for the change of name. Apparently the Hall had recently been sold by its owner and had been converted into a treatment centre for alcoholism and drug addiction; the 'grandees' of the LNER did not consider this to be a suitable venture with which to publicly associate one of their locomotives).

Formed in 1902, largely through the initiative of two local schoolmasters, Norwich City acquired professional status in March, 1905, but did not play its first Football League game (Division 3(S)) until August, 1920, drawing 1-1 with Plymouth Argyle. The Club moved to its present location at Carrow Road in 1935.

During the period under review, the 'Canaries' alternated between League Divisions 2 and 3. (Elevation to the former Division 1 did not come until 1972). Honours were few; Norwich were Champions of Division 3(S) in 1933-34 and Division 3 Runners-up in 1959-60.

The Club's performance in the F.A. Cup is not impressive, although it did reach the semi-final in 1959 and, in January, 1935, beat First Division Leeds United 2-1 in a fourth round replay at Elland Road, having been two goals down in the first game before drawing 3-3.

61640 SOMERLEYTON HALL

Situated between Lowestoft and Great Yarmouth, Suffolk, Somerleyton Hall is a splendid early Victorian mansion created in Anglo-Italian style by Sir Morton Peto, (Bart. 1855), to make a grand show of the immense wealth accumulated by him as a building and railway contractor.

Built between 1844 and 1851 on the site of an earlier Jacobean house, it boasts lavish architectural features and magnificent carved stonework together with fine state rooms, paintings and carvings by Grinling Gibbons. A highlight of the 12-acre grounds and gardens is the famous 1846 yew hedge maze, among the finest in Britain.

Charles Dickens was a house guest at Somerleyton Hall in the late 1840's. 'David Copperfield' is set partly at Blunderston, an outlying village, and the people living in upturned boats in that novel are based upon Dickens' observation of "boat dwellers" on the beach at Lowestoft.

In 1863, the Hall was sold to Sir Francis Crossley, (later Baron Somerleyton), the Halifax carpet manufacturer. Ownership and occupation has remained with his descendants since that time.

61641 GAYTON HALL

Gayton Hall, near King's Lynn, Norfolk, dates from the nineteenth century and was first erected as a shooting box by a gentleman named St. Andrew St. John. The property was sold in 1877 and subsequently rented by the 4th Earl of Romney, who became the owner in 1891.

Constructed in grey stone and set in spacious grounds with a lake, Gayton Hall was one of the country houses in the vicinity of **Sandringham** which enjoyed Royal patronage during the reign of King George V, when it was often visited by the King and Queen Mary for shooting parties.

The Hall remains in private ownership.

61642 KILVERSTONE HALL

Kilverstone Hall, near Thetford, Norfolk, was built around 1620 by Thomas Wright, who had acquired the manor in 1587.

Kilverstone was inherited by the Davy family in 1849 and sold around the turn of the century to Josiah Vavasseur, the armaments magnate, who greatly enlarged the original medieval manor and added what was described by Nikolaus Pevsner as "a crazy-looking water tower".

Vavasour devised the Hall in 1908 to the future 2nd Lord Fisher, at that time simply Cecil Fisher, son of Admiral of the Fleet Lord "Jacky" *Fisher* (1841-1920) one of the greatest reformers in the history of the Royal Navy.

Fisher's modernisation and re-building programme for the Royal Navy had brought him into contact with Vavasseur, who was technical director of William Armstrong Ltd., one of Europe's leading arms and munitions manufacturers, and also an inventor, patenting several mounting devices for artillery and machine guns.

Their acquaintance blossomed into friendship, and Vavasseur, who was married, but childless, became particularly fond of Cecil, adopting the boy as his heir in return for his taking his name (becoming Cecil Fisher Vavasseur) and adopting his coat of arms. When Vavasseur died, in 1908, his mansion at Kilverstone Hall, and its 3000 acre estate, came into the possession of Cecil, recently retired from a career with the Indian Civil Service.

His father, Lord Fisher, who was created baronet in 1910 when he left the Admiralty, enthusiastically adopted Kilverstone as his own country home, with a little financial help from Cecil's rich American wife. The mailed fist and trident which surmounted his baronial crest appeared over the gateway, the bedrooms of the house were named after ships formerly in his command, the figurehead of his first seagoing ship was displayed in the garden and the avenue of yew trees which led to it became known as the Admiral's Walk.

The house now stands empty and forlorn, although it still belongs to the Fisher family. The outbuildings are derelict and have been partly damaged by fire. Following the Second World War, the estate had been used as a wildlife park, specialising in the breeding of miniature horses, but that enterprise has long since come to an end.

The mortal remains of Admiral Lord Fisher and his wife Kitty lie in the shade of a tree in the graveyard of the nearby country church.

61643 Champion Lodge

Champion Lodge, Heybridge, near Maldon in Essex, became best known as the home of Sir Claude Champion de Crespigny, Bart., (1847-1935), a 'larger than life' Victorian adventurer, regarded with admiration by some and with considerable distaste by others.

The family was of Norman/Huguenot descent, but the baronetcy was of relatively recent origin, having been conferred upon Sir Claude's great-grandfather following a visit to Champion Lodge by the Prince Regent in 1805.

Sir Claude Champion de Crespigny espoused Spartan values and enjoyed in particular shooting, riding, boxing, swimming, ballooning, sailing and 'a cold tub before breakfast'. He swam the Nile rapids and rode a winner in the Indian Grand National. He achieved a certain notoriety for horse-whipping members of the Salvation Army and for boxing his servants; he appeared more than once before fellow magistrates on charges of assault.

For Sir Claude, aristocratic sporting pleasures and military duty went hand in hand. 'Featherbed aristocrats', particularly those who declined duty, were likened to the effeminate French aristocracy and had no rightful place in the British social hierarchy.

De Crespigny served in both the Royal Navy and the Army. At the age of 14 years he was a naval rating aboard the first ironclad warship, HMS Warrior, now preserved at Portsmouth. From 1865 to 1870 he was commissioned into the 60th Rifles, later the Hussars

197

(Yeomanry Cavalry) and, still later, held a militia command.

Sir Claude remained in later life "one of the hardest and pluckiest men in England ….. ready to box, ride, walk, run, shoot, fence, sail or swim with anyone of over 50 years on equal terms."

The greatest controversy involving de Crespigny related to his presence at and, in one case, participation in the execution of convicted criminals.

In May, 1885, a man was hanged for the murder of a Police Inspector. The hangman described the execution in some detail, referring to a titled Essex Magistrate as being present at the 'drop'. Six months later, the same executioner carried out a triple hanging, (again for the murder of a policeman), at Carlisle prison. He was assisted by a "Charles Maldon" who was subsequently revealed to be Sir Claude Champion de Crespigny. He defended his involvement by saying that, as a possible future High Sheriff, "he would not care to ask a man to do what he himself was afraid of doing" and claimed that it was necessary for him to have the knowledge and ability to supervise the way in which the sentence of the law (i.e. the execution) was carried out. He also admitted to having been present at the earlier hanging in his capacity as a magistrate, an involvement which was fiercely attacked by the then equivalent of the Magistrates' Association.

Outwardly, the scandal appeared to quickly subside although there does seem to have been some residual damage to Sir Claude's social standing and reputation.

POSTSCRIPT:
Champion Lodge – re-named Totham Lodge – subsequently became, and remains, a care home for the elderly.

61644 EARLHAM HALL
Earlham Hall stands in the grounds of Earlham Park, Norwich,

and dates from the early seventeenth Century. In 1785, the Hall was leased by its owners to the Gurney family and remained their home until 1912.

The Gurneys were Quakers whose wealth came from banking. They were also active social reformers, whose many visitors included Amelia Opie and William Wilberforce.

Earlham Hall was the childhood home of Elizabeth Gurney Fry, whose work with prisoners, the "insane" and the homeless, brought her international recognition and renown.

The Hall was sold to Norwich Corporation in 1925 and is now part of the University of East Anglia.

61645 THE SUFFOLK REGIMENT

This locomotive was the only one of the first forty-eight in the Class not to be named originally after a country seat or castle.

The Suffolk Regiment was raised by the Duke of Norfolk in 1685, as the 12th Regiment of Foot, to suppress the threatened Monmouth Rebellion. In 1782, it became the East Suffolk Regiment and the Suffolk Regiment in 1881.

On 27th June, 1743 the 12th Foot fought against the French at Dettingen, the last battle in which an English King (George II) led troops into the fray. Ensign James Wolfe served with the Regiment at Dettingen, aged 16 years; he was later to achieve fame as Wolfe of Quebec in 1759.

One of the most celebrated engagements involving the Regiment was the Battle of Minden, fought on 1st August, 1759, during the Seven Years War. Six British Regiments, including the 12th Foot, marched through withering cannon fire and, largely unsupported, repulsed six elite French cavalry charges. The event is commemorated by a parade and by the wearing of red and yellow roses on 1st August each year.

The Regiment was involved in the Siege of Gibraltar by Spanish and French forces from 1779 to 1783 and for its part in the action was awarded the emblem of the Castle and Key, later incorporated within the cap badge and colours of the Suffolks.

In 1852, a draft of one sergeant and 79 private soldiers of the First Battalion was sent to *South Africa* on board HMS Birkenhead. They were shipwrecked off the Cape and stood steady on parade on deck as the ship went down, to allow the women and children into the lifeboats. This event gave rise to the famous expression "women and children first" although, sadly, 55 soldiers were drowned in this act of self-sacrifice.

The second half of the nineteenth century saw service in *New Zealand, India* and Afghanistan. The 2nd Battalion was part of the British Expeditionary Force in France following the outbreak of the First World War and the Regiment fought in all subsequent major engagements, being awarded two Victoria Crosses.

In the Second World War, the First Battalion was sent to France with the B.E.F. and was evacuated from Dunkirk. It returned to France in June, 1944, as part of the D-Day landings and eventually recovered the Battalion's drum which had been hidden at Roubaix in 1940 during the retreat.

When Singapore fell, men of the 4th and 5th Battalions became prisoners of war and were coerced into building the *Burma* Railway.

The 7th Battalion was converted to armour and fought in the battles of Tunis and Monte Cassino.

In the post-war period, the Regiment was involved in peace keeping duties in Palestine and in anti-terrorist operations in Malaya and *Cyprus*.

In August, 1959, the First Battalion, Suffolk Regiment amalgamated with the First Battalion, Royal Norfolk Regiment to form the First Batalion, the First East Anglian Regiment (subsequently the Royal Anglian Regiment).

61646 GILWELL PARK

The home of Scouting and of Scout Training, Gilwell Park was purchased in 1919 for the U.K. Scout Association. It was at Gilwell that Baden-Powell experimented with and devised training programmes for the adults who would lead and support the newly formed Scout Troops and Patrols.

The first recorded history of the land which now comprises the Gilwell estate dates back to 1407. Through time, the estate was progressively extended and developed under various private owners, but fell into disrepair around the beginning of the twentieth century.

Gilwell was purchased for the Scout Association in 1919 by William F. de Bois Maclaren, the owner of an Edinburgh publishing company and himself a Scout Commissioner, who was searching for a suitable camping ground for Scouts from the East End of London. The purchase price of £7000 acquired an estate of 53 acres, which was gradually cleared, restored and renovated. Baden-Powell persuaded Maclaren that his own vision of a training centre for Scoutmasters could be accommodated alongside the provision of a training camp.

Gilwell was officially opened on 26th July, 1919. New buildings and facilities were constructed, (and some older ones demolished), during the 1920's.

During the Second World War, the estate was requisitioned by the War Ministry and was used as a base and training centre for Anti-Aircraft gunnery. During the Blitz, in September, 1940, a number of incendiary devices fell on Gilwell but did no significant damage. The surrounding area was heavily bombed by the Luftwaffe, with the Lee Enfield armaments factory and the Royal Ordnance depot being key local targets.

In the post-war years, the estate was further expanded to the present site of 108 acres.

The Greenwich Meridian (the line of zero degrees longitude) passes through the campsite.

61647 HELMINGHAM HALL

This large, moated house, near Stowmarket in Suffolk, has been the seat of the Tollemache family since the late fifteenth century.

Construction commenced in 1510, in traditional half-timbered style. Subsequent additions and alterations, mainly carried out in phases between 1750 and 1840, have preserved the basic form of a courtyard manor house.

Queen Elizabeth I is said to have visited twice, first in 1561 and later to attend the christening of her godchild. She left as a gift on the second of these visits the Helmingham lute or orpharion, (after Orpheus and Arion, musicians in Greek mythology), built by John Rose in 1580. This is unique and has been exhibited all over the world.

John Constable lived for some time at Helmingham Rectory and painted a number of versions of a dell in Helmingham Park. The oak tree featured in that scene is one of many still in the Park, some thought to be up to 900 years old.

61648 ARSENAL

Beginning life as Dial Square (one of the workshops), and playing in a set of red jerseys begged from **Nottingham Forest**, the Club was formed in 1886 by workers at the Woolwich Royal Arsenal. Known initially as the 'Woolwich Reds', their official title soon after formation was Woolwich Arsenal and, in 1914, simply 'Arsenal'. The Club made use of five different grounds before moving to Highbury in 1913.

The first Football League game (Division 2) took place on 2nd September, 1893, when the then Woolwich Arsenal drew 2-2 at home to Newcastle United. Seven years later, also in a Division 2 fixture, the club achieved a Record League Victory by beating Loughborough Town 12-0, sweet revenge for a 0-8 drubbing by the same opponents four years previously.

A Division 1 side from 1919 onwards, the "Gunners" dominated English football in the 1930's, winning the League Championship on no fewer than five occasions and the F.A. Cup twice. Finishing second in the 1931 –32 Season denied them what would otherwise have been an unbroken sequence of five consecutive Championships between 1930 and 1935.

The accomplishments of that supremely talented side became the stuff of football legend; records set then remain unbroken to this day and include a club record attendance of 73,295 for a match against **Sunderland** on 9th March, 1935.

In the 1930-31 Season, Arsenal won the Division 1 Championship with a Club Record of 66 points (based on 2 for a win), scoring 127 league goals in the process (also a Club Record). "Heroes" of the time included Cliff Bastin, who holds the record for the most league goals (150) scored for the Club in total aggregate; Alex James, a Scottish International who joined Arsenal from Preston in 1929 for £9000; and Ted Drake, a £6000 signing from Southampton who, with 42 goals, set the record for the Highest League score in Season (1934-35) and, with 7 goals against Aston Villa in December, 1935, (a hat-trick in each half), became the record holder for the most League goals scored in one match. In the following season, Drake scored Arsenal's Cup-winning goal against **Sheffield United** at Wembley.

Arsenal's "glory days" continued into the immediate post-war era. They were again Division 1 Champions in 1947-48 and 1952-53 and won the F.A. Cup in 1950 by playing seven matches, including the Cup Final, in London.

61649 SHEFFIELD UNITED

An F.A. Cup semi-final, played at Bramall Lane in 1889, caused local soccer enthusiasts to pursue the formation of a football section of the Sheffield United Cricket Club.

Initially, it seemed that the new club would not find it easy to become established. **Sheffield Wednesday** was already in existence (having turned professional in 1887), and other Sheffield clubs viewed the newcomers with suspicion. Advertisements in the local newspapers resulted in the acquisition of only 3 players; United tactfully recruited outside Sheffield, relying particularly on Scotland.

The first Football League (Division 2) game in September, 1892, resulted in a 4-0 win over Lincoln City. United went on to become Division 1 Champions in 1897-98 and were twice Runners-up in the closing years of the nineteenth century. They won the F.A. Cup on four occasions between 1899 and 1925 and lost by the solitary goal to **Arsenal,** in 1936.

Overall, the 'Blades' acquired something of a 'yo-yo' reputation, alternating between Divisions 1 and 2 and failing consistently to achieve distinction. A total of 102 League goals in 1925 – 26, despite being a Club record, was insufficient to bring Division 1 Honours. Although the aggregate total of 105 League goals scored by Harry Johnson over the period 1919-30 greatly exceeded the number scored by Arsenal's Cliff Bastin over a 17 year career with that Club, United won only one Honour during that time in the form of the 1925 FA Cup.

61650 GRIMSBY TOWN

Formed in 1878 as Grimsby Pelham F.C., the name was changed to Grimsby Town in the following year. The Club acquired professional status in 1890 and moved to Blundell Park in 1899.

The 'Mariners' had three spells as a Division 1 side in the first half of the twentieth century. But for two consecutive Seasons spent in Division 2 (of which they were Champions in 1933-34), they would have enjoyed unbroken Division 1 status from 1919 to 1948, a period during which they twice (1936 and 1939) reached the semi-finals of the F.A. Cup. In January, 1931, during their second brief spell in Division 1, they suffered their heaviest ever defeat, losing 1-9 to **Arsenal**, that Season's Champions.

When not in Division 1, Grimsby alternated between Division 2 and Division 3 (N), of which they were Champions in 1925-26 and 1955-56 (with a Club Record of 68 League points, based on 2 for a win).

The Club's most prolific goal scorer (and capped player) was the Welshman, Pat Glover, who scored 42 goals in Grimsby's Division 2 Championship Season of 1933-34 and 180 goals over the period 1930-39.

61651 DERBY COUNTY

Derby County F.C. was formed by members of the Derbyshire County Cricket Club in 1884 to help boost finances for the Summer game. The Club turned professional in the same year and was a founder member of the Football League in 1888. The move to the venue associated with the Club during most of its subsequent history – the Baseball Ground – took place in 1895.

In the pre-Clough era, Derby County alternated between Division 1 and Division 2, except for a brief spell in the mid-fifties when the Club spent two Seasons in Division 3 (N).

The 'Rams' were Division 1 Runners-up on three occasions but never succeeded in winning the Championship. They gained promotion as Champions of Division 2 in 1911-12 and 1914-15 and were Runners-up in that Division in 1925-26. As a Division 1 side, they won the FA Cup once, in 1946.

In 1955-56, Derby County narrowly missed promotion from Division 3 (N), to which they had been relegated at the end of the previous season, but were successful in their attempt in the following year, emerging as Champions of that Division with 111 League goals.

As LNER No. 2851, this locomotive briefly became No. 2854 **Sunderland** for three weeks in April/May, 1937, because the real 2854 was under repair and not available to haul the Sunderland supporters Cup Final Special!

61652 DARLINGTON

The first fourteen "Footballer" locomotives were built at Darlington Works and the intended names were published in advance. The Darlington workforce insisted that the name of their local Club should be included so 'Manchester City' was omitted – not for the only time – in order to make way for lowly **Darlington,** languishing in Division 3 (N). The locomotive nameplate was displayed on No. 2849 **Sheffield United** for the purposes of the official photograph, and then removed.

Formed in 1883, Darlington won the Durham Senior Cup in the Second Season of their existence and was for many years one of the leading amateur clubs in the North East before turning professional in 1908.

Apart from a brief spell in Division 2 (1925 to 1927), the 'Quakers' spent most of their time in Division 3 (N), of which the Club was an original member in 1921. Darlington were Champions of Division 3(N) in 1924-25, when David Brown achieved a Club record as the Highest League scorer in Season with 39 goals, and Runners-up in 1921-22.

Darlington reached the fifth round of the FA Cup in 1958.

61653 HUDDERSFIELD TOWN

Huddersfield Town was formed as a professional Club in 1908 and after two years in the North Eastern League was elected to Division 2 in 1910.

Arsenal's supremacy in the 1930's and beyond was almost matched by Huddersfield's achievements in the previous decade. Ironically, in November, 1919, the newly-formed **Leeds United** F.C. was in discussion with the Directors of a near-bankrupt Huddersfield Town about a possible merger. The Club survived the crisis to become one of the "household names" of the inter-war years.

Having achieved promotion to Division 1 in 1919-20 (when Sam Taylor became the Club's joint highest League scorer in Season with 35 goals), Huddersfield went on to win the Division 1

Championship three times in the next decade and were runners-up on two occasions. In their Championship Season 1925-26, George Brown, also with 35 League goals in Season, equalled Taylor's earlier record. Brown is also the joint holder of the Club record for scoring the most League goals in aggregate, (142 over the period 1921-29), a feat equalled by Jimmy Glazzard between 1946 and 1956.

In the FA Cup, the "Terriers" beat Preston North End 1 – 0 in the 1922 Final (when Preston's goalkeeper, J.F. Mitchell, achieved the distinction of being the only footballer ever to play a Cup Final wearing spectacles), and were losing finalists at Wembley in 1920 and 1928.

Huddersfield continued to be a side to be reckoned with throughout the 1930's, although largely as "also-rans" compared with their earlier successes. They were Division 1 runners-up in 1933-34 and were losing FA Cup Finalists in 1930, (the Season in which they achieved their record League victory by beating Blackpool 10-1) and again in 1938. Perhaps not surprisingly, the Club's record home attendance of 67,037 was achieved in an FA Cup 6th round match against Arsenal (the losing Finalists) on 27th February, 1932.

The post-war years witnessed a steady decline in the Club's fortunes, their only notable achievement being to "bounce back" as Division 2 runners-up in 1952-53, following relegation in the previous Season. From 1956 onwards they remained a Second Division side.

Other points of interest: in a fixture against Notts County played on Christmas Eve, 1956, Dennis Law, then some two months short of his seventeenth birthday, became the Club's youngest League player. Twelve months later, in December, 1957, Huddersfield achieved the doubtful distinction of losing 7-6 away to Charlton Athletic, having led 5-1 and with Charlton down to ten men!

61654 SUNDERLAND

Formed in 1879 as Sunderland and District Teachers AFC, the name of the Club was shortened to 'Sunderland' in 1880 following the admission of members from outside the teaching profession.

The "glory days" of Sunderland F.C. were mainly in the period between their acquisition of professional status in 1886 and the First World War.

The Club enjoyed Division 1 status from 1890 to 1958 followed by a brief spell in Division 2 (1958-64). Sunderland were six times Division 1 Champions and runners-up on five occasions. All but three of these successes occurred before 1914, (five before the turn of the Century), although, in a brief "purple patch", they were runners-up in 1934-35 and Champions in 1935-36. During this latter season, the team set a Club record of 109 League goals, including 5 scored by Bobby Gurney in a match against Bolton Wanderers to equal the 5 scored by Charlie Buchan against Liverpool in December, 1919. Buchan remains the holder of the Club record for the most League goals in Aggregate, with no fewer than 209 over the period 1911-25.

Despite this impressive League record, particularly in the early years, Sunderland won the F.A. Cup only once (in 1937), having been runners-up in 1913. The Club moved to Roker Park in 1898 and played there for the next 99 years.

61655 MIDDLESBROUGH

From the time it first acquired League status in 1899, up to 1960, Middlesbrough FC spent a total of 50 years in Division 1, with only brief spells in Division 2, including four seasons between 1924 and 1929 and the period from 1954 onwards.

Put another way, Middlesbrough enjoyed an unbroken spell of First Division football from 1927 to 1954, save for one season (1928-29) in Division 2. Despite this achievement, the Club never won the Division 1 Championship (or the FA Cup), but were Division 2 Champions in the Seasons in which they booked their return ticket to Division 1 following brief spells in the lower Division (1924-27 and 1928-29).

The Division 2 Championship Season of 1926-27 saw the Club score its highest ever number of League goals (122), 59 of which were netted by George Camsell to set a Division 2 record. Over the period 1925-39, Camsell scored the most League goals in total Aggregate for Middlesbrough (325 goals). This feat included 5 against Manchester City in December 1926 (Division 2) and the same number against Aston Villa in September, 1935 (Division 1).

In November, 1954, Middlesbrough suffered its greatest ever defeat in losing 9-0 to Blackburn Rovers. Five years later, the Club achieved its record League victory in beating Brighton and Hove Albion by a similar margin , Brian Clough scoring 5. But for injury, Clough, a prolific goal scorer, might well have gone on to equal the 26 international appearances by Wilf Mannion, Middesbrough's most capped player.

61656 LEEDS UNITED

Leeds United was founded in 1919 following the disbandment by the F.A. of Leeds City Club (formed in 1904) because of allegations of illegal payments to players. United joined the Midland League in the year of their formation and turned professional in 1920, when they were elected to Division 2.

Up to 1932, Leeds alternated between Divisions 1 & 2, spending an average of three or four seasons at a time in one or the other. During this period, they were Division 2 Champions only once in 1923-24, and twice achieved promotion to Division 1 as runners-up, including 1927-28, when they set a Club record of 98 League goals.

From 1932 to 1947, Leeds United played in Division 1, achieving a record League victory for the Club (8-0 v. Leicester City) on 7th April, 1934. Paradoxically, that same Season witnessed the Club's record defeat, 1-8 to Stoke City, on 27th August, 1934.

Leeds were relegated to Division 2 in 1947 and remained there until they next achieved promotion, again as runners-up, in 1956.

In 1953-54, John Charles became the Club's highest League scorer in Season with 42 goals; 1953 also saw the first of Jack Charlton's 629 League appearances for Leeds, another Club record.

It is interesting to note that, for three consecutive years in the F.A. Cup (1955-56; 1956-57; 1957-58), Leeds were drawn at home to Cardiff City. They lost all three games 1-2!

The "glory days" (1964-75) were, of course, yet to come.

61657 DONCASTER ROVERS

Doncaster Rovers F.C. – representing another prominent railway town – was founded in 1879 and turned professional in 1885. In 1901, the Club was elected to the Football League (Division 2) and re-elected in 1904-05.

Between 1923 and 1959,Rovers alternated between Division 3 (N) and Division 2, although until 1950 (when they achieved promotion to the higher Division and managed to stay there until 1958), they had spent all but three seasons in the Third Division.

In 1946-47, their "Champagne" Season, Doncaster achieved promotion to Division 2 as Champions of Division 3 (N) with their highest ever number of League points (72) and a Club record for the most League goals scored (123, of which 42 were netted by Clarrie Jordan – another record). Despite these successes, Rovers found themselves back in Division 3 (N) at the end of the following Season and remained there until 1950.

In March, 1946, Doncaster Rovers met Stockport County in a Division 3 (N) cup-tie. The tie had two legs. The first, at Doncaster, ended in a 2-2 draw, as did the return match at Stockport. The competition rules stipulated extra-time of 10 minutes each way, which was duly played without either side scoring. The teams then played on until the first goal i.e. a "sudden death" eliminator.

After 203 goal-less minutes had been played, the referee abandoned the game because of bad light. The two teams tossed a coin for choice of ground in the reply. Doncaster won and, not surprisingly, chose their own ground. The following Wednesday they beat Stockport 4-0.

61658 THE ESSEX REGIMENT

Turned out from Darlington Works in May, 1936, as LNER No. 2858, this locomotive briefly carried the name **'Newcastle United'** while on running-in turns, but was officially renamed **The Essex Regiment** at a railway exhibition at Romford, Essex, on 6th June, 1936.

In view of the initial intention, it remains a mystery why the name **'Newcastle United'** should not have been permanently affixed to one or other of the B17's, given that Football Club's prominence and the City's importance to the LNER as a railway interchange.

The Essex Regiment was raised in 1741 as Long's Regiment. In 1751, it became the 44th Foot and in 1748 was designated the 44th, or East Essex, Regiment. In 1881, it was amalgamated with the West Essex (56th Foot) and was designated the 1st Battalion The Essex Regiment.

Members of the Regiment were referred to as 'The Pompadours' because of their rose-purple facings, a colour popular with Mme de Pompadour, Mistress of Louis XV.

The Regiment has a distinguished history. It took part in the seige of *Gibraltar* from 1779 to 1783 and, like **The Suffolk Regiment**, was awarded the Castle and Key emblem for its part in the action.

At Salamanca in 1812, during the Peninsular War against Napoleon, the Regiment captured and carried away a highly treasured 'Eagle' emblem from a French Regiment. That emblem, or a replica of it, is still carried on parade.

In January, 1842, during the British Army's disastrous retreat from

Kabul in the First Afghan War, the 44th lost 22 Officers and 632 other ranks killed (out of a total of 684).

The 44th fought at Waterloo in 1815 and throughout the Crimean War (1854-1856). At Waterloo, a French lancer attempted to seize one of the Regimental Colours from Ensign Christie (recently promoted from Sergeant-Major). Despite being severely wounded by a lance thrust that entered his left eye and penetrated to the lower jaw, Christie managed to save the Colour and the Frenchman was shot dead.

In August, 1857, the Regiment deployed to *Madras* following the Indian Mutiny and later took part in the China War of 1860 (Taku Forts). In total, the 44th was overseas for fifty of the sixty years from 1822 to 1881.

The Regiment served in the Boer War (1899-1902) and was involved in all the major campaigns of the First World War, including Gallipoli (1915-16). In the Second World War, the Regiment played a prominent part in the North African Campaign and was present at both the siege of Tobruk and the Battle of El Alamein.

A total of three Victoria Crosses were awarded to members of The Essex Regiment: at Paardeberg, South Africa (1900); Loos, France (1917); and St. Nazaire, France (1942).

In June, 1958, The Essex Regiment was amalgamated with The Bedfordshire and *Hertfordshire Regiment* to form the 3rd Battalion, East Anglian Regiment (16th/44th Foot).

61659 EAST ANGLIAN (NORWICH CITY)

In September, 1937, this locomotive (as LNER No. 2859), in company with No. 2870 (later No. 61670) was streamlined for working "East Anglian" service between Norwich and Liverpool Street, became Class B17/5 and was named **East Anglian** via the fitting of A4-style straight nameplates to the streamlined casing. The curved nameplate formerly carried by this locomotive was transferred to the incorrectly named **Rendelsham Hall** (See 61639 **Norwich City**).

It seems that consideration may have been given to naming the two streamlined locomotives **City of London**, (the name actually given to No. 2870 in September 1937), and **City of Norwich** (which would, presumably, have resulted in the withdrawal and discontinuance of the existing football club nameplate). Since the new service linked Norwich, Ipswich and London, it was probably considered 'politically' inappropriate and a potential public relations disaster to name the locomotives after only two of those cities, hence the adoption of **East Anglian** for No. 2859.

This service was discontinued with the outbreak of war; by the time of its reinstatement in October, 1946, the new B1's were available.

In April, 1951, the streamlining was removed and the locomotive was re-classified as B17/6. The name **East Anglian** was retained, but was now displayed on a curved nameplate over the centre wheel splasher.

61660 HULL CITY

The "Tigers", so called because of their amber and black vertically-striped jerseys, were formed in 1904 and for the first year of their existence rented the Boulevard Ground of Hull R.F.C. They entered the F.A. Cup in that first Season and were elected to the Football League (Division 2) after only one year.

Between 1905 and 1960, Hull City alternated between Division 2 and Division 3(N). They were Champions of Division 3 (N) in 1932-33 (when Bill McNaughton became the Club's highest League scorer in Season with 39 goals), and again in 1948-49. They were runners-up in the newly-formed Division 3 in 1958-59.

Hull's best Season in Division 2 was 1909-10, when they finished third in the table. In the following Season, the Club suffered a record defeat, losing 0-8 to Wolves in November, 1911.

The "Tigers" record League victory came in January, 1939, when they thrashed Carlisle United 11-1 in a Division 3(N) fixture, (having lost their previous two away games 6-1 and 6-2).

The Club Record for the most League goals in one match, (5), is shared by Ken McDonald (v. Bristol City, Division 2, November 1928), and Simon "Slim" Raleigh (v. Halifax Town, Division 3(N), December 1930).

Success in the F.A. Cup is limited to a solitary (and losing) semi-final appearance in 1930.

61661 SHEFFIELD WEDNESDAY

The "Owls", known until 1929 as "The Wednesday", were formed in 1867 by Sheffield Wednesday Cricket Club, whose own formation dated from 1825.

The Football Club, which turned professional in 1887, played at a variety of grounds, (including Bramall Lane, home of **Sheffield United),** until 1899, when it took up permanent residence at Owlerton (since 1912 known as Hillsborough).

Like their neighbours at Bramall Lane, Wednesday regularly alternated between Divisions 1 and 2, particularly during the 1950's when they shuttled back and forth on no fewer than seven occasions.

They were Division 1 Champions in the consecutive Seasons 1902-03 and 1903-04 and repeated that feat in 1928-29 and 1929-30 (when they achieved a Club Record League victory, hammering Birmingham City 9-1).

Wednesday were Division 2 Champions on five occasions, including 1925-26 when they were captained by Frank Froggatt whose son, Redfearn, led the "Owls" in their 1958-59 Championship season. In 1951-52, when they again achieved promotion to Division 1, the prolific goal scoring Derek Dooley set a Club Record for the Highest

Scorer in Season, (46 goals), before a broken leg and gangrene at Deepdale tragically ended his playing career.

In 1958-59, Wednesday emerged as Division 2 Champions with a Club Record for the number of League points (62), based on 2 for a win. In that same Season they also achieved a Club Record for the number of League goals scored (106). After the "yo-yoing" of the 1950's, their return to Division 1 heralded a decade of relative stability; indeed, they were runners-up in that Division in 1960-61, only their second Season since returning to the top flight.

The 'Owls' were F.A. Cup winners in 1896, 1907 and 1935, but enjoyed little success in that competition in the following two decades.

61662 MANCHESTER UNITED

Manchester United F.C. was formed comparatively late in the day (1902) after their predecessors, Newton Health L & YR (Lancashire and Yorkshire Railway) Cricket and Football Club (formed 1878) were declared bankrupt. They won the Manchester Cup in 1886 and, as Newton Health F.C., were admitted to the Second Division in 1892.

Between 1902 and 1938, Manchester United had alternating spells in Divisions 1 and 2. They were Division 1 Champions in 1907-08 and in 1910-11, and won the F.A. Cup in 1909. Beyond that, they achieved little of any distinction until the years following the Second World War.

Both the Triumph and the Tragedy of English soccer in the post-war era and during the 1950's can be summed up in two words – Manchester United. The record speaks for itself. United were Division 1 Champions in 1951-52; 1955-56; and 1956-57. They were runners-up in 1946-47; 1947-48; 1950-51; and 1958-59. They won the F.A. Cup in 1948 and were the losing Finalists in 1957 and 1958. They reached the semi-finals of the European Cup in 1956-57, (losing 3-5 on Aggregate to Real Madrid), having achieved a Record Cup Victory for the Club of 10-0 v. RSC Anderlecht in a fixture played on 26th September, 1956. Sixteen months later, seven members of that winning side were dead.

In 1952, United won the League Championship for the first time in 40 years. Their early slump to the bottom of the table in the following season led to the rapid promotion of United's youth team members who helped the Club rise to a respectable eighth position by the Season's end. United were 4th and 5th respectively in the following two Seasons, and in 1956 again won the Championship with a team which included only two members (Berry and Byrne) of the 1952 side and whose average age was only 22 years (hence the "Busby Babes"). Apart from Tommy Taylor, who was acquired from Burnley, this was largely a 'home-grown' side.

The Championship Season of 1956-57 saw the Club debut of Bobby Charlton who, over a career spanning 17 years, became United's most capped player (106 for England), the holder of the Record for the most League appearances (606) and the highest goal scorer (199 League goals in total aggregate).

On 6th February, 1958, the BEA Elizabethan charter airliner carrying the players and backroom staff of United and a number of journalists and supporters, crashed in a blizzard on its third attempt to take off from Munich airport. Twenty three of the forty three passengers on board lost their lives, including the following players:-

Roger Byrne	28	Left Back and Captain	33 Caps
Mark Jones	24	Centre Half	
Duncan Edwards	21	Wing Half	18 Caps
Eddie Colman	21	Right Half	
Tommy Taylor	26	Centre Forward	19 Caps
Liam Whelan	22	Inside Right	4 Caps (Eire)
David Pegg	22	Outside Left	1 Cap
Geoff Bent	25	Left Back	

Survivors included Matt Busby (Manager), John Berry, Jackie Blanchflower, Bobby Charlton, Bill Foulkes, Harry Gregg, Ken Morgans, Albert Scanlon, Dennis Viollet and Ray Wood. Happily, two years later, Dennis Viollet achieved the Club Record for the

Highest League Scorer in season with 32 goals.

61663 EVERTON

Formed in 1878 by St. Domingo Church Sunday School as St. Domingo F.C. Everton adopted their present name in the following-year, playing in black shirts with a scarlet sash and nicknamed "the Black Watch". The Club changed to royal blue shirts in 1901, having turned professional in 1885, and played briefly at Anfield Road, (1884-1892), before moving to Goodison Park. As the principal landmark of Everton village was 'Ye Ancient Toffee House', it was not long before the sobriquet "Toffees" became attached to the Club, which was a founder member of the Football League.

From 1888 to 1930, Everton was a First Division Club, winning the Championship three times and finishing as runners-up on six other occasions. During this period the club also played in four F.A. Cup Finals, winning only once (1906).

In Everton's Championship Season of 1927-28, William Ralph "Dixie" Dean scored 60 goals, an all-time League record. Dean also holds the Club Record for the most League goals in total Aggregate (349 goals over the period 1925-1937).

Strange to tell, after these successes Everton were relegated to Division 2 in 1930, but spent only one Season in the lower Division before bouncing back as Champions in 1930 –31. On their way up they thrashed Plymouth Argyle 9-1 ("Dixie" Dean scoring 4), to equal a Club Record set in 1906. They also set a Club Record for the most League goals (121).

Equally strange to tell, having returned to the upper reaches, they promptly won the Division 1 Championship in 1931-32 – their first Season back – and went on to win the FA Cup in 1933.

Everton remained in Division 1 until 1951, followed by three seasons in Division 2. They achieved promotion in 1953-54 and again became an established Division 1 side. Not that all went smoothly, however; in October, 1958, the Club sustained its record defeat, losing 4-10 to **Tottenham Hotspur.**

61664 LIVERPOOL

Because of a dispute with their landlord at Anfield Road in 1892, **Everton** F.C. moved on to Goodison Park and the landlord, John Houlding, formed a new Club to take their place. Having failed in his attempt to retain the name 'Everton', he founded Liverpool A.F.C. on 15th March, 1892.

Liverpool were elected to the League (Division 2) in 1893-94 and promptly achieved promotion to Division 1, where they remained for just one Season (1894-95) before returning to the lower Division.

True to form, in 1896 they bounced back into Division 1 at the end of only one Season in Division 2, having set a Club Record for the most League goals scored (106). With the exception of one further Season in Division 2 (1904-05), they finally "got into gear" and remained in Division 1 until 1954, winning the Championship five times – mostly in the early years – and finishing as runners-up on two other occasions.

For a Club with such a distinguished League history, it is interesting to note that they did not win the F.A. Cup before 1965, although they were losing Finalists on two previous occasions (1914 and 1950).

In 1954, Liverpool were relegated to Division 2 and remained there until 1962. During their first Season in the lower Division, they sustained a Club Record Defeat, losing 1-9 to Birmingham City in December, 1954.

For Liverpool, the halcyon days of the 1970's and 1980's were yet to come. Their most prolific scorer, Roger Hunt, made his debut in 1959 – the year in which Bill Shankly became Manager – at the start of a career that would bring a total of 245 League goals while playing for the Club.

61665 LEICESTER CITY

The "Filberts", (sometimes "Nuts"), were founded in 1884 as Leicester Fosse by a number of young footballers who were mostly old boys of Wyggeston School. Professional status was acquired in 1888, three years before the Club moved from its original ground at Victoria Park to Filbert Street. In 1919, Leicester Fosse became Leicester City.

From 1894 to 1925, Leicester was a Division 2 side, with the solitary exception of one Season (1908-09) spent in Division 1. Having gained promotion to the higher Division in 1925, they remained there for the next ten years, achieving runner-up status in 1928-29.

The Club's post-war years were spent mostly in Division 2 (1946-57) except for yet another solitary Season (1954-55) in Division 1.

Leicester's best Season was demonstrably that in which they next achieved promotion to Division 1 (1956-57) as Division 2 Champions, with Club Records for the highest number of League points (61) and for the most League goals scored (109). Arthur Rowley set a further record for the most League goals scored for the Club in Season by an individual player (44).

Leicester do not have a distinguished record in the F.A. Cup; they were losing Finalists in 1949.

61666 NOTTINGHAM FOREST

One of the oldest football clubs in the world, Nottingham Forest was formed as Forest F.C. at a meeting in the Clinton Arms in 1865. The Club played at six grounds (including Trent Bridge Cricket Ground) before moving to the City Ground in 1898.

The "Foresters" were elected to Division 1 in 1892 and achieved the first of their two F.A. Cup wins in 1898. During most of the first half of the twentieth century, the Club played in Division 2, including an unbroken spell from 1925 – 1949. Worthy of note is the fact that in 1935 on 9th November (v. Barnsley), 23rd November (v.

Port Vale) and 26th December (v. Doncaster Rovers), Tom Peacock scored 4 goals for Forest (i.e. a feat achieved on three occasions in less than seven weeks!).

A remarkable downturn in the Club's fortunes brought relegation to Division 3(S) in 1949. Forest bounced back as Champions in 1950-51, achieving Club Records for the most League points (70, based on 2 for a win), and for the most League goals scored in Season (110, of which Wally Ardron scored 36).

Forest spent the next six years in Division 2 and achieved promotion to Division 1 in 1956-57. They won the FA Cup for the second time in the Club's history in 1959.

61667 BRADFORD

Now receding rapidly into distant memory, Bradford Park Avenue A.F.C. was formed in 1907 and elected to Division 2 of the Football League in the following year. In 1913, the club narrowly won promotion to Division 1, as runners-up to Notts County, by defeating Blackpool on the last day of the Season and thereby finishing with a goal average superior to that of third-placed **Arsenal.**

In 1922, Bradford were relegated to Division 2, and in the following Season, were demoted further to Division 3(N), where they remained for six years. In 1928, a revival in the Club's fortunes brought promotion to Division 2 and Bradford went on to reach the 5th round of the F.A. Cup four years in succession between 1928 and 1932.

Sadly, the Club's history in the post-war years was one of steady decline. Relegation to Division 3(N) in 1950 was followed, from 1958, by twelve years in Division 4. In 1969-70, Bradford Park Avenue lost its Football League status and was voted out of Division 4, largely because of the insistent demands of Cambridge United for recognition. In that Season, Bradford came bottom of the table with 23 points, having won only 6 of their 46 League games, and having conceded more goals (96) than any other League side.

61668 BRADFORD CITY

Bradford City A.F.C. was formed in 1903, in succession to Manningham R.F.C., the then occupants of Valley Parade. The Football League immediately accepted the new Club's application for membership of Division 2.

With the exception of the years between 1908 and 1922, when they were a First Division side (and Winners of the F.A. Cup in 1911), Bradford had alternating spells in Divisions 2 and 3, although they were anchored permanently in the latter from 1937 to 1961.

Bradford's most successful Season by far was 1928-29, when they achieved promotion as Champions of Division 3(N). That Season brought Club Records for the most League points (63, based on 2 for a win), the highest number of League goals (128) and the most League goals (7) netted by an individual player (Albert Whitehouse) in a single fixture (v. Tranmere Rovers on 6th March, 1929). In that same Season, Bradford also achieved a Record League victory in thrashing Rotherham United 11-1 on 25th August, 1928.

This locomotive was the last of the "Footballers" to remain in service with British Railways.

61669 BARNSLEY

Barnsley Football Club was formed in 1887 by the Reverend T.T. Preedy, curate of Barnsley St. Peter's, and went under that name until it was dropped in 1887, a year before the Club was admitted to Division 2 of the Football League.

The "Tykes" are yet another Club which, in the period between their acquisition of League status and the beginning of the 1960's, alternated between Division 2 and Division 3(N). That said, they did enjoy continuous Division 2 status from 1898 to 1932, during which period they were F.A. Cup winners in 1912, (beating West Bromwich Albion in a replay), and runners-up in 1910 (losing to Newcastle United, also in a replay).

Barnsley were promoted as Champions of Division 3(N) in 1933-34 (setting a Club Record for the most League goals scored – 118); in 1938-39 (with a Club Record of 67 League points); and in 1953-54.

61670 CITY OF LONDON (TOTTENHAM HOTSPUR/MANCHESTER CITY)

In September, 1937, LNER No. 2870 (formerly **Tottenham Hotspur)** was fitted with a streamlined boiler casing, re-named **City of London** and, in company with No. 2859, was set to work on the new "East Anglian" express service linking Norwich, Ipswich and London.

(See   61659 **East Anglian**

       61630 **Tottenham Hotspur**

       61639 **Norwich City**)

In April, 1951, the streamlining was removed and the locomotive was re-classified as B17/6. The name **City of London** was retained but, like 61659 **East Anglian,** was now displayed on a curved nameplate over the centre wheel splasher.

This locomotive is a further illustration of the mixed fortunes which dogged the name **Manchester City**. Reference has already been made (see 61652) to the late substitution of **Darlington** for the name originally intended for LNER No. 2852. Subsequently, No. 2870 entered service on 13th May, 1937, as **Manchester City**. The next B17 in the series, No. 2871, was still in production and was not delivered in sufficient time for an official naming ceremony organised for 29th May (and at which it was to be named **Tottenham Hotspur**). In consequence, No. 2870 – carrying substitute **Tottenham Hotspur** nameplates – took its place at the ceremony, and the **Manchester City** plates thus displaced were switched to the unfinished No. 2871, which entered service in June, 1937.

The name "City of London" had formerly been carried by Robinson 'Sir Sam Fay' Class B2 No. 5427. It was also carried contemporaneously with No. 61670 by LMS " Princess Coronation" Class Pacific No. 46245.

61671 ROYAL SOVEREIGN (MANCHESTER CITY)

Third time lucky! LNER No. 2871 (BR No. 61671) entered service in June, 1937, as **Manchester City** and, having been re-built in August, 1945, to Class B2, managed to retain that name until April, 1946, when it was renamed **Royal Sovereign** and became the Royal train engine. It was finally withdrawn from service in October, 1958, the name **Royal Sovereign** passing to No. 61632 (formerly **Belvoir Castle).**

Manchester City F.C. was formed in 1894 as a limited company after its predecessor, Ardwick F.C. (formed 1887), had been declared bankrupt. The Club took up residence at Maine Road in 1923.

Between 1900 and 1938, City spent all but five Seasons in Division 1; from 1938 to 1947, (the date from which the name **Manchester City** ceased to be affixed to a locomotive), they were members of Division 2.

The "Blues" (or "Citizens") enjoyed their most successful Seasons between the years 1926-29 and 1933-37. They won the FA Cup in 1926 (for the second time in their history) as a Division 2 side, and in the following year were Division 2 Champions after just two Seasons in the lower reaches. In 1926-27, their first Season in Division 2, City set a club record for the most League goals scored (108); in 1928-29, their first year back in Division 1, Tommy Johnson became the Club's highest League Scorer in Season with 38 goals.

City were FA Cup Winners in 1934, having been the losing Finalists in 1933. On 3rd March, 1934, they achieved a record attendance of 84,569 in an FA Cup 6th Round fixture v. Stoke City at Maine Road (a British record for any game played outside London or Glasgow). They were Division 1 Champions in 1936-37.

In September, 1906, on the first day of the new Season and long before substitutes were allowed, Manchester City met Woolwich Arsenal in a fixture at Maine Road. The game was played in temperatures exceeding 90°F in the shade; City fielded a makeshift side, 17 players (and ex-players) having recently been suspended by the FA, which was investigating alleged financial irregularities.

At half-time, the home side were down to eight men, two players having left the pitch suffering from sunstroke and a third – Conlin – having sought refuge in the dressing room. **Arsenal**, seemingly unaffected by the conditions, were winning 0-2.

After half-time, the depleted City side adopted a 1-3-3 formation in the hope of repeatedly catching Arsenal in the "offside trap". In the 50th minute, with the return of the gritty Conlin, they even managed to reduce the deficit to 1-2. Unfortunately, however, three more Manchester players succumbed to the heat and the five "fit" members of the side – plus Conlin – eventually lost 1-4, the referee and linesmen apparently seeing no good reason to abandon the game.

It took City some time to recover from this setback; two days later they lost 1-9 at **Everton**, but the 'new look' side pulled together sufficiently to keep the Club in Division 1.

61672 WEST HAM UNITED

Thames Iron Works F.C. was formed by employees of this famous shipbuilding company in 1895, entered the F.A. Cup in its first Season (at Chatham) and joined the London League in its second. In July, 1900, the Club was re-launched, with professional status, as **West Ham United**.

Comparative newcomers to the Football League, the "Hammers" were elected to Division 2 in 1919. Within four years, they had not only achieved promotion to Division 1, but had also taken part, as the losing side, in an F.A. Cup Final at Wembley. They remained a Division 2 side until 1932 when they were relegated to Division 2, their abode for the next 25 years.

In 1957-58, West Ham achieved promotion as Champions of Division 2, with a Club Record for the most League goals scored (101). Their promotion Season also included an 8-0 victory over Rotherham United, setting a further Club record unequalled for ten years.

From the loser's point of view, some Records are best forgotten. In November, 1931, mid-way through the Season in which they were relegated to Division 2 after nine years in the top flight, West Ham lost 1-5 at home to West Bromwich Albion. W.G. Richardson, Albion's centre forward, had two good chances in the first five minutes of the game and missed them. He then scored four times in the next five minutes to equal a record for the greatest number of goals scored in the shortest time set by Blackburn Rovers a decade earlier.

CLASS K2

INTRODUCTION AND GENERAL CHARACTERISTICS

The LNER Class K2 mixed traffic 2-6-0s were designed by H.N. (later Sir Nigel) Gresley for the *Great Northern* Railway and first introduced in 1914. A total of 75 locomotives were constructed up to 1921.

The majority (66 engines) were built to the basic design and classified K2/2. Some were later fitted with a side-window cab to provide added protection from the elements over the more exposed Scottish routes.

The remaining 9 engines were a rebuild (from 1931) of Class K1 locomotives originating from 1912 and were re-classified K2/1.

Scrapping commenced in 1955 and by 1963 all had gone.

THE NAMES

Over the period December, 1924, to August, 1925, 14 engines of this Class were transferred from the Great Northern section of the newly-formed LNER to work on the West Highland line from Glasgow to Fort William and Mallaig in order to provide increased motive power and, hopefully, reduce the need for double-heading of the increasingly heavy passenger trains. (In 1908, the West Highland Railway had become part of the *North British* Railway which, in turn, was absorbed into the LNER in 1923).

By January, 1932, following some "toing and froing" and reallocation of locomotives between depots, the number of K2's at Eastfield shed had been reduced to 13. Between February, 1933, and June 1934, all 13 were fitted with curved nameplates over the centre driving wheel carrying the names of lochs bordering upon or in the vicinity of the West Highland line.

61764	Loch Arkaig	61787	Loch Quoich
61772	Loch Lochy	61788	Loch Rannoch
61774	Loch Garry	61789	Loch Laidon
61775	Loch Treig	61790	Loch Lomond
61781	Loch Morar	61791	Loch Laggan
61782	Loch Eil	61794	Loch Oich
61783	Loch Sheil		

(For some, a surprising omission was *Loch Long*, later rectified in the naming of the first locomotive of Class K4.)

THE ROAD TO THE ISLES

A far croonin' is pullin' me away
As take I wi' my cromack to the road.
The far Coolins are puttin' love on me
As step I wi' the sunlight for my load.
It's by Shiel water the track is to the west
By Aillort and by Morar to the sea
The cool cresses I am thinkin' of for pluck
And bracken for a wink on Mother knee.

Chorus

Sure by Tummel and Loch Rannoch and Lochaber I will go
By heather tracks wi' heaven in their wiles.
If it's thinkin' in your inner heart the braggart's in my step
You've never smelled the tangle o' the Isles.
Sure by Tummel and Loch Rannoch and Lochaber I will go
By heather tracks wi' heaven in their wiles.
Oh the far Coolins are puttin' love on me
As step I wi' my cromack to the Isles.

In Scotland, the word "loch" is used to describe any large, enclosed expanse of water, including areas coming in from the sea (the equivalent of Norwegian 'fjords').

Covering an area of 27½ square miles, Loch **Lomond** is by far the largest and most magnificent of the lochs, its "bonnie banks and braes" celebrated in song. Formed during the Ice Age by the action of glaciers and shaped by the Highland boundary line – a massive geological fault that separates the Scottish highlands from the lowlands – Loch **Lomond** is the largest single inland waterway in Britain. There are 30 islands in the loch, most of them privately owned.

Other lochs were also created along geographical fault lines. The Great Glen, a slip fault which completely divides Scotland along a line running from north-east to south-west, was created over 400 million years ago, and is home to the waters of a series of canal-connected lochs, including Lochs **Oich** and **Lochy**, which form the Caledonian Canal.

Loch **Garry** lies in *Glenn Garry* to the west of the Great Glen. It receives water via the river Garry from Loch **Quoich**, two miles further west, and drains eastwards into Loch **Oich** at Invergarry. Close by are the ruins of Invergarry Castle – once a stronghold of the MacDonnells – destroyed by the Duke of Cumberland because of its use as a refuge for Bonnie Prince Charlie, both before and after his defeat at Culloden.

Also close by is the Well of Seven Heads, a monument erected in 1812 by Alastair MacDonnell to commemorate the revenge taken on seven murderers of his clansmen in 1665. The monument depicts a hand holding a dagger and seven severed heads. The well is said to have been the one in which the heads of seven murderers were washed in revenge for the killing of two of the Keppoch family. The two men were murdered by their own uncle, Alasdair MacDonnell, because they stood in the way of his aspirations to chieftainship. All those responsible were captured and beheaded, their severed heads being washed in the well before being presented to MacDonnell Glengarry at Glengarry Castle. (Seven headless bodies were later

disinterred from a mound that was said to hold the murderers'
remains).

The area is also rich in Jacobite history. Loch **Arkaig**, to the west of
Loch **Lochy** lies in Cameron country. Achnacarry House, the seat of
Locheil (see LNER Class K1 No. 61995 *Cameron of Locheil*) is situated
on the river Arkaig, close by the loch. The old castle was another
building demolished by the Duke of Cumberland after the '45, but
a few ruins remain. After Culloden, Prince Charles Edward found
temporary shelter in a cave on the Black (or Dark) Mile, the road
between Lochs **Arkaig** and **Lochy**. Strathan at the west end of the
former was the location of a redcoat barracks after the Rising had
been put down by Cumberland's soldiers.

During the Rebellion, an unspecified but large amount of gold was
sent from France to help the Jacobite cause but arrived too late. The
treasure was buried somewhere in Arkaig and never (apparently)
found.

The gateway to Loch **Arkaig**, symbolically at least, is the Commando
Memorial, a mile or so north of Spean Bridge, which commemorates
the use made of the area, and Loch **Arkaig** in particular, for
commando training between 1942 and 1945.

To the south of Loch **Arkaig**, and running parallel with it, is Loch
Eil, one of the many east-west lochs scoured out by glaciers across
the Western Highlands. Loch **Eil** is a sea loch, seven miles long,
opening into Loch Linnhe at the head of the Caledonian Canal,
opposite Fort William. It gives its name, Locheil, to the style of the
chiefs of the *Clan Cameron*.

Further to the west, Loch **Sheil** (sometimes 'Shiel), extends for
17 miles in dog-leg fashion from *Glenfinnan* (and the Glenfinnan
Monument) at its northern tip. The 'Road to the Isles' passes the
head of Loch **Sheil** on its way to Morar and Mallaig.

Apart from their attraction to ramblers, climbers and fisherman,
the lochs serve a variety of purposes including reservoir storage
and hydro-electric power. To the east of the Great Glen, a tunnel

from the western end of Loch **Treig** passes under Ben Nevis to supply water to the aluminium smelting works 14 miles away in Fort William. Loch **Laggan**, to the north east of Loch **Treig**, was dammed in 1926 to form a reservoir providing hydro-electric power to the same plant.

The West Highland Railway line skirts the eastern shore of Loch **Treig** before describing a wide semi-circle to reach Fort William to the west. Loch **Laggan** boasts the largest fresh water beach in the country and, on its southern shore, the splendid Victorian pile of Ardverikie where Queen Victoria spent her first long Highland holiday in 1847, allegedly driven to distraction by the unwelcome attention of the midges.

Also to the east of the Great Glen, in what was Highland *Perthshire* lies Loch **Rannoch**, famous for both its fishing and rough water. The main road along the north shore of the loch continues westwards to end abruptly at Rannoch station, between Loch **Rannoch** and Loch **Laidon**, where the west Highland railway line makes a great curve around the east side of the vast empty wilderness of Rannoch Moor.

Finally, and perhaps inevitably, it appears that Loch Ness is not the only expanse of water in the area to house a resident monster. "Nessie" may be the best-known, but his/her relatives include Morag in Loch **Morar**, Shielagh in Loch **Sheil** and Lizzie in Loch **Lochy**. Sitings have also been claimed in Lochs **Arkaig, Oich** and **Quoich.**

Loch **Morar**, almost at journey's end for the West Highland extension to Mallaig, is as likely a candidate as any for the home of a sea monster, being deeper than Loch Ness (over 1000 ft in places) if not as large a body of water.

In August, 1969, Duncan McDonnell and Bill Simpson were fishing on the loch in a motor cruiser. They became aware of a loud splashing in the water behind them and turned to see a large object in the water, which rammed the boat side-on "in a deliberate manner". Simpson grabbed his shotgun from the boat and fired at the creature which was described as 25 to 30 feet long, with dirty brown rough skin, 3 large black humps and a snake-like head. The creature slowly slipped back under the water after it had been shot at, much to the relief of the two men.

Since the loch is remote, (there is no road around it), it has been suggested that there have been fewer sightings than would have been the case if it was more accessible. This situation is probably just as well because Morag's sinister reputation is apparently based on the belief that whenever she is sighted it heralds the death of a member of the local branch of the clan MacDonald. One tourist brochure advises that "over the years many reliable sightings have been reported, a high proportion from local residents" (none of them, presumably, MacDonalds!).

CLASS K4

INTRODUCTION AND GENERAL CHARACTERISTICS

Although the Gresley K2 2-6-0's had been introduced onto the West Highland line in an attempt to reduce costly and uneconomical double-heading, by the mid-1930's passenger train loadings over that line were proving too much for the K2's and double-heading had become commonplace.

Locomotive design limitations imposed by the sharp curvature of the West Highland route ruled out the introduction of any eight-coupled machines; consequently, Gresley opted for a 'hybrid' solution which amalgamated proven components – including wheelbase, boiler and firebox – from earlier successful designs. The result was a 3-cylinder, 2-6-0 locomotive with 5 ft. 2 in. coupled wheels, capable of hauling 300 ton trains over the gradients on the West Highland route with only a marginal increase in coal consumption compared with the K2's on much lighter loads.

The prototype, No. 3441, entered traffic in January, 1937. Successful trials led to an order for five more engines although only one – No. 3442 – was completed in time for the summer traffic of 1938. The remaining four locomotives were turned out from Darlington Works in December of that year.

The K4's were popular with their footplate crews and quickly established a pre-eminence on the West Highland line which was to last until 1947 and the arrival of the Thompson B1's. The further introduction of other new types post-nationalisation resulted in the K4's being used increasingly on freight traffic.

In the following decade, they were given a much wider route availability than previously and appeared at Scottish locations far removed from the West Highland line. In 1959, they were brought together at Thornton Junction depot in Fife and from there were collectively withdrawn from service in October, 1961.

No. 3442 (BR No. 61994) **The Great Marquess** was purchased from British Railways and preserved.

THE NAMES

The prototype was named **Loch Long**, possibly to rectify an omission in the names previously given to the K2's. The remainder were named after Highland chieftains and grandees, with the exception of No. 3442 which continued the earlier practice (see LNER Class A2/2) of using "heroic" names associated with Scottish history.

61993	(3441)	Loch Long
61994	(3442)	The Great Marquess (MacCailein Mor)
61995	(3443)	Cameron of Lochiel
61996	(3444)	Lord of the Isles
61997*	(3445)	MacCailin Mor
61998	(3446)	MacLeod of MacLeod (Lord of Dunvegan)

*Rebuilt by *Edward Thompson* to Class K1 in December, 1945. The prototype for Thompson's K1's of which 70 were built post-nationalisation but the only one to carry a name.

"GREAT SCOT(S)!!"

61993 Loch Long

A salt water inlet of the *Firth of Clyde* extending for 17 miles from north east to south west and varying in width from 2 miles at its mouth to three-quarters of a mile in its upper reach. A traditional dumping place for the dredgers preserving the tideway of the Clyde – much to the annoyance of anglers.

61994 THE GREAT MARQUESS

James Graham, 1st Marquess of Montrose (1612-50) succeeded his father as 5th Earl of Montrose in 1626.

In 1637, he took an active part in drawing up the National Covenant in response to the attempt by *King Charles I* to introduce an Episcopal 'Book of Common Prayer', seen as an attempt to anglicise the Scottish Church. Montrose did not, however, agree with the extremist views of the Presbyterian leaders and soon found himself in opposition to the Covenanters and the foremost champion of the Crown in Scotland. In 1643, he was arrested and briefly imprisoned in Edinburgh Castle.

In 1644, the Scots army entered England and joined forces with the English Parliament and Puritans against Charles I. Still loyal to the King, Montrose obtained from him a commission as Lieutenant General in Scotland and raised a small force of disaffected clansmen – plus some trained Irish soldiers – on his behalf. Now elevated to the title of Marquess by the King, Montrose met and defeated his often numerically superior opponents in a series of battles. It is claimed that his strategy, tactics and daring marked him out as the greatest soldier of the war, with the sole exception of Cromwell.

After the Battle of Kilsyth (1645), Montrose was appointed Lord-lieutenant and Captain-general of Scotland by Charles I and set off south to assist the King after his defeat at Naseby. Unfortunately for Montrose, he was deserted by the majority of his clansmen as he advanced into the Borders and his depleted force was cut to pieces by a numerically superior army led by David Leslie, the best of the Scottish generals, who had been despatched by Cromwell to head off the invasion. With the royalist cause in Scotland now hopelessly lost, Montrose was ordered by the King to abandon his efforts and escaped abroad to Norway.

Having served Charles I so well, Montrose was sacrificed by Charles II, who had been accepted as King of Scotland in 1649 on condition that he agreed to the Covenant; while he negotiated with the Covenanters, Charles sent Montrose back to Scotland, hoping to overthrow them by force. Montrose failed to raise any significant support and was quickly defeated. He was subsequently betrayed to the Scots government, taken to Edinburgh and, without trial, was sentenced to be executed and dismembered as a traitor. He was hanged on 21st May, 1650, with Wishart's laudatory biography of him put round his neck. Eleven years later, the remains of the **"Great Marquess"** were buried in St. Giles' Cathedral, where a monument was erected to him in 1888, inscribed:

> "Scotland's glory, Britain's pride,
>
> As brave a subject as ere for monarch dy'd
>
> Kingdoms in Ruins lye
>
> But great Montrose's Acts will never dye."

This locomotive briefly entered service as 'MacCailein Mor'. The apparent mis-spelling offended Gaelic scholars and led to the re-naming of No. 3442 within less than two weeks.

61995 CAMERON OF LOCHIEL

The Camerons consisted originally of three separate family branches in Lochaber. The first chief of the combined families was Donald Dubh (born around 1400) whose marriage to a daughter of one of the branches brought about the federation. The Camerons' estates in Lochaber expanded into the hills of *Loch Lochy, Loch Arkaig* and *Loch Eil* (see LNER Class K2) as the clan's power grew. The Camerons became embroiled in a territorial dispute with the powerful *Clan MacKintosh* and the two remained in conflict – and combat – for over 200 years. Donald Dubh and his successors were known as captains of Clan Cameron until 1528 when the lands of Lochiel were united by charter into the Barony of Lochiel by Allan Cameron, the 12th chief.

Perhaps the most famous Cameron of Lochiel was Sir Ewan (1629-1719) who became chief of the clan after 1647. Ewan was loyal to the cause of the Stuart monarchs and a firm supporter of Charles II. He led his clan in an uprising against the Commonwealth in

1653 and only in 1658 did he submit to the Puritan general George Monck, who was instrumental in bringing about the Restoration of the Monarchy (see LNER Class V2 No. 60873 *Coldstreamer*). Ewan accompanied Monck to London in 1660 and was received at the Court of the restored *King Charles II*; he was knighted in 1682. A supporter of James II, Sir Ewan took part in the Jacobite victory over the forces of William III at Killiecrankie in 1689 and sent his clan to aid the Jacobite Uprising of 1715.

Ewan of Lochiel built Achnacarry Castle, the ancestral home of the Camerons. He was reputedly a warrior of great strength who is attributed with slaying the last wolf in Scotland and, in a role reversal not wholly in keeping with the 'romantic' tradition, with biting out the throat of a Roundhead officer during an attack on a government castle. From one of his feats, *Sir Walter Scott* drew his description of the fight between *Roderick Dhu* and *James Fitzjames* in *The Lady of the Lake* (see LNER Class D11).

Sir Ewan's grandson, Donald, known as "the gentle Lochiel", was persuaded, through loyalty to the Crown and the honeyed words of Prince Charles Edward Stewart, to support the 1745 Jacobite Uprising and led the clan at Culloden under the Prince's banner. It is claimed that, but for the support of Cameron of Lochiel – who survived Culloden and was exiled to France – the rising might never have taken off, such was his influence. During the Jacobite retreat, Lochiel prevented the Highlanders from sacking Glasgow and tradition has it that the church bells in that city were subsequently rung in greeting and gratitude whenever a Cameron of Lochiel entered it.

The Cameron lands were restored in the General Amnesty of 1784 and Donald's grandson, also Donald, became the 22nd Cameron of Lochiel.

In 1793, Sir Allan Cameron of Lochiel maintained the fighting tradition of the clan by raising the 79th Regiment of Foot which, in 1881, became the *Cameron Highlanders*.

DAVID H. BALDWIN

61996 Lord of the Isles

The MacDonalds, known also as Clan Donald, have been one of the most powerful and influential families in the Scottish Highlands since mediaeval times.

The clan traces its descent from Somerled, King of the Isles, who expelled the Vikings from the Western Isles in the twelfth century. His grandson, Donald, was the first to be styled 'Lord of the Isles' and it is from him that the main branch of the family descends. Divided into a number of branches, the clan held vast territories in the Western Highlands and islands of Scotland, and also in Ulster.

Donald's great-grandson, John, formally assumed the title of **Lord of the Isles** in 1354. Later holders of the title became powerful enough to challenge the Kings of Scotland and had their own Parliament at Finlaggan on Islay. John's son, also Donald, became the 2nd Lord of the Isles; his grandson Alexander became the 3rd Lord and also Earl of Ross, a title acknowledged by the Crown. Alexander died in 1448 and was succeeded by the 4th, and final, Lord of the Isles, John MacDonald, Earl of Ross, who was created a Lord of Parliament as Lord of the Isles. During the next half century John increasingly rebelled against the Crown and sought to declare his independence; in consequence, the Earldom of Ross was annexed to the Crown followed, in 1493, by forfeiture of the title 'Lord of the Isles' which has, since that time, been reserved for the eldest son of the reigning Scottish/British monarch.

61997 MacCailin Mor

The name Campbell is apparently associated with the Gaelic, 'Cam Beul' which translates as 'crooked (or wry) mouth'.

The origins of the name can be traced back to the ancient kingdom of Dalriada, which eventually evolved into the territories of Argyll and Lorne.

In 1296, the Campbells were under the jurisdiction of the MacDougals, Lords of Lorne. The MacDougals killed the Campbell

WHAT'S IN A NAME

chief and founder of the Argyll family, Sir Cailean Mor of Loch Awe. Since then, all Campbell chiefs have taken the patronymic of **MacCailin Mor** meaning 'son of Colin the great'.

Sir Cailean Mor's son, Neil, was a supporter of *Robert the Bruce* and married his daughter. He had his revenge for his father's murder when his loyalty was rewarded by the gift of extensive lands taken from the Lords of Lorne and others in Argyll who had been the Bruce's enemies. The power and influence of the *Clan Campbell* grew steadily from this point onwards. The chiefs of the clan acquired the titles of Lord Campbell (1445), Earl of Argyll (1457), Marquess of Argyll (1641) and Duke of Argyll in Scotland (1701).

The family home had been a castle which occupied the entire surface area of a small island situated in Loch Awe. In 1474, the 1st Earl of Argyll moved to Inveraray on Loch Fyne.

The 8th Earl of Argyll, created Marquess in 1641, was executed for treason in 1661 because of his leadership of the western Covenanters and support for the Parliamentary cause in the Civil War. His title and lands were forfeited but were restored to his son, albeit briefly, by Charles II. The 9th Earl was executed for his part in the Monmouth Rebellion, his head being afterwards displayed on the very same spike in the Edinburgh Tollbooth which had hosted (and hoisted) that of his father 25 years earlier.

The family's fortunes were restored when Archibald Campbell, 10th Earl, was created Duke of Argyll in 1701 for his part in bringing William of Orange to the throne.

61997 MacLeod of MacLeod

The Clan MacLeod traces its descent to one Leod, who lived in the thirteenth century. The clan had two main branches independent of each other, the MacLeods of Harris, (whose chief, Tormod, was Leod's eldest son), and the MacLeods of Lewis, founded by another son, Torquil. Tormod established the clan seat at Dunvegan and adopted the title MacLeod of Dunvegan or **MacLeod of MacLeod**.

Tormod's son supported *Robert the Bruce* in the War of Scottish Independence but, by and large, the MacLeods succeeded in not becoming embroiled in the tortuous politics of fourteenth and fifteenth century Scotland.

The MacLeods served under the Lords of the Isles and when James IV set out to break the power of the MacDonalds, began to assert their own influence and independence.

The MacLeods of Lewis, who had never fully accepted the ascendancy of their cousins at Dunvegan, were forced to do so when the head of that branch of the family was killed in 1597. Two years earlier, Rory Mor had succeeded as the fifteenth chief. He was knighted by James VI and continued the work of establishing Dunvegan as the cultural centre of the Isles. No chief of the MacLeods can avoid at least once calling Rory Mor to memory. A great drinking horn, named after him, is kept at Dunvegan and forms an integral part of the rite of passage of every MacLeod chief. The horn, which holds a bottle and a half of claret, must be drained at one draft "without setting down or falling down".

In 1650, the name MacLeod became synonymous with treachery when a member of the family betrayed **The Great Marquess** to claim the reward on his head (see No. 61994).

Clan MacLeod supported the Royalist cause in the Civil War and took part in the Battle of Worcester (1651) where Cromwell's forces inflicted a crushing defeat and over 500 MacLeods were killed. Although loyal to the Stuarts, this terrible loss prevented the clan from taking a leading role in the Rising of 1715. The MacLeods believed the arrival of Prince Charles Edward in 1745, without a substantial French army, to be ill-conceived and bluntly refused to join him. Dunvegan's official rebuff to the "Young Pretender" saved the clan from the wrath of the Hanoverian Government following the disaster at Culloden and their estates were spared.

Sir Reginald MacLeod, 24th chief, who died in 1935, was the last of the male line of the Dunvegan MacLeods, but his daughter Flora (who died in 1977 aged 98 years) was recognised as his successor, becoming Dame Flora MacLeod of MacLeod.

This locomotive was named 'Lord of Dunvegan' when it first entered service in January, 1939, but was re-named **MacLeod of MacLeod** in March of that year, in deference to the wishes of Dame Flora as clan chief.

CLASS D34

INTRODUCTION AND GENERAL CHARACTERISTICS

During World War 1, the North British Railway, like other Companies, experienced an exceptional increase in traffic. Shortages of men, many of whom had enlisted, and backlogs of maintenance created immense strain, and the War left the NBR greatly weakened, a situation made worse by shortages of coal and engines. Nevertheless, the Company did recover; services were reinstated and locomotive deficiencies remedied, including the construction of a further 17 'Glen' Class 4-4-0's in 1919-20 to add to the engines already in service (dating mostly from 1913).

The 32 locomotives of the 'Glen' Class (NBR Class K), built at Cowlairs between 1913 and 1920, were a small-wheeled version of the earlier 'Scott' Class and were allocated to all parts of the NBR system. Two of the Class were scrapped prior to Nationalisation (Nos. 9287/62486 **Glen Gyle** and 9505/62491 **Glen Cona**); three more had gone by 1951 (Nos. 62473 **Glen Spean**, 62476 **Glen Sloy**, and 62481 **Glen Ogle**). General withdrawal began in 1959 and was completed by 1962, No. 62496 **Glen Loy** being the last to be withdrawn from service.

No. 62469 **Glen Douglas** has been restored in working condition as NBR No. 256; it is currently preserved as a static museum exhibit.

THE NAMES

The Class was named after Scottish Glens bordering upon or, in some cases, traversed by the West Highland line. All the locomotives in the Class retained the names originally allocated, the only exception being No. 62494 **Glen Gour,** which began life as Glen Gau (no such place existed) and was re-named in July, 1925.

THE CLASS

32 locomotives numbered 62467 to 62498

62467	Glenfinnan	62483	Glen Garry
62468	Glen Orchy	62484	Glen Lyon
62469	Glen Douglas	62485	Glen Murran
62470	Glen Roy	(62486)	Glen Gyle
62471	Glen Falloch	62487	Glen Arklet
62472	Glen Nevis	62488	Glen Aladale
62473	Glen Spean	62489	Glen Dessary
62474	Glen Croe	62490	Glen Fintaig
62475	Glen Beasdale	(62491)	Glen Cona
62476	Glen Sloy	62492	Glen Garvin
62477	Glen Dochart	62493	Glen Gloy
62478	Glen Quoich	62494	Glen Gour (Gau)
62479	Glen Sheil	62495	Glen Luss
62480	Glen Fruin	62496	Glen Loy
62481	Glen Ogle	62497	Glen Maillie
62482	Glen Mamie	62498	Glen Moidart

MONARCHS OF THE GLEN (MORE OR LUSS)

Although all Scottish glens – from the Gaelic 'gleann' – are, in essence, narrow and deep mountain valleys, each one has unique characteristics which set it apart from the others. These range from fierce grandeur and solitary peaks, through moorland hills, crags and steep wooded gullies to gentle tranquillity, and peaceful walks by meandering rivers. Some are traditionally popular locations, attracting campers, climbers, anglers and walkers, as well as many artists. Other, more isolated areas are not easily accessible and are less amendable to the passage of rivers, roads, railways…. and ramblers.

Many of the glens were carved out by glacial movement. **Glen Roy,** near to the Great Glen (or Glen More), has various glacial features, but is best known for its striking parallel "roads", which are unique in Britain for their excellent preservation. During the last ice age, advancing glaciers dammed a series of large lakes in the glen. These left behind a set of shorelines, all indicating different lake levels that can be clearly seen on the hillsides. Others can be found in nearby **Glen Gloy**, but only at one level.

Glen Croe is a further example of glacial movement during the ice age. The roads and bridges built here by General Wade following the Jacobite rebellion of 1745 made the region more easily controllable for Government forces, but also opened up the area for tourists. At the highest point on the road through the glen is a flat resting place named "Rest and Be Thankful". Boswell and Dr. Johnson stopped here in 1773 and wrote of terrible weather. Dorothy and *William Wordsworth* visited in 1803.

Military roads and, later, railways traversed many of the glens. **Glen Ogle**, often referred to as the Khyber Pass of Scotland, contains the remains of a railway line (and viaduct) that were once part of the Stirling-Crianlarich route. The line passes the end of Balquhidder Glen, burial site of the famous Rob Roy MacGregor (**Glen Gyle**, at the head of Loch Katrine, being his birthplace). **Glen Ogle** is also the location of a former military road, built in 1749 by Major Caulfield, a successor to General Wade.

Not surprisingly, other glens in this Highland region have associations with the Jacobite Rebellion. **Glen Finnan**, for example, is one of the most beautiful and "romantic" places in the West Highlands where the 'Road to the Isles' passes the head of *Loch Shiel* on the way to Morar and Mallaig. This is the location of the prominent Glenfinnan Monument that commemorates the raising by the Marquess of Tullibardine of Prince Charles Edward's Standard on 19th August, 1745, as a rallying point for the clans. It was over the hill to the north that *Locheil* and his clansmen marched to join the Prince, and helped convince many other clans to do the same. During the Rising, **Glen Nevis** was the location of an English garrison to which the Highlanders laid siege in April, 1746. After his defeat at Culloden, Bonnie Prince Charlie hid for some days in

Glen Beasdale before his celebrated escape to Skye. **Glen Sheil** is the location of Eilean Donan Castle, which dates from the thirteenth century and which was briefly occupied by Spanish troops fighting alongside the Jacobites. Their main invasion fleet having been destroyed by a storm before it even set sail for England, only a small diversionary force made it to the north west of Scotland. They then garrisoned Eilean Donan Castle before being scattered by the prompt and energetic response of the local Hanoverian Commander at the Battle of **Glen Sheil.**

Several of the glens have associations with other periods and aspects of Scottish history. In 1645, Montrose's army (see LNER Class K4 No. 61994 – *The Great Marquess*), crept stealthily up **Glen Nevis** to surprise Argyll's forces. (More recently, this glen was the location for the filming of both "Braveheart" and "Rob Roy"). **Glen Fruin** is memorable as the scene of the bloody conflict in 1603 in which 800 Colquhouns (consisting of 300 mounted men, plus 500 on foot), were virtually exterminated by a MacGregor contingent of 300 men. As a result of this savage encounter, an order of the Privy Council proscribed the use of the names Gregor or MacGregor and prohibited those who had borne these names from carrying weapons.

Glen Lyon is the site of Meggernie Castle (sixteenth century) said to be haunted by the wife of a Menzies laird, who murdered her in a fit of jealousy and cut her body into halves for easier disposal. Perhaps for the best, it is apparently her upper half which haunts the castle.

Last, but by no means least, Glen Garry, to the west of *Loch Oich,* gave its name to the well-known cap or bonnet worn in both the Highlands and the Lowlands of Scotland. This glen has been described as the longest and most beautiful cul-de-sac in Britain and contains a single-track road which twists and turns for 22 glorious miles along the shores of *Loch Garry* and *Loch Quoich*. It is now virtually deserted but was once home to some 5000 people who were driven out in the infamous Highland Clearances of the nineteenth century. It was reputedly **Glen Garry** that gave Sir Edwin Landseer the inspiration for his famous painting "The Monarch of the Glen".

CLASS D10 AND D11

INTRODUCTION AND GENERAL CHARACTERISTICS

In 1899, the *Great Central* Railway's 'London Extension' transformed what had been a cross-country railway linking *Lancashire* with *Lincolnshire* and the East Coast into a north-south main line express service.

The London (Marylebone) – Manchester run was at first entrusted to "Atlantic" and 4-6-0 types, but their poor performances led John Robinson, the Locomotive Superintendent of the GCR, to design a new 4-4-0 locomotive with superheating, improved steam-raising capability and consequent lower fuel consumption. The new design proved to be at least the equal of the 4-6-0's and was soon in regular and preferred use on the expresses.

The first of the new Class (D10) was delivered from Gorton Works in 1913 and nine more engines were completed in the same year. Construction was suspended during the First World War, but 1919 saw the introduction of a further eleven locomotives (Class D11/1) with altered cabs and even better steam-raising ability.

Following the Grouping, Nigel Gresley ordered an additional 24 of the Robinson 4-4-0's (Class D11/2) to meet a critical shortage of motive power on former *North British* routes in Scotland.

Withdrawal of Class D10 locomotives commenced in 1953 and all had gone by 1955. By 1958, all but one of the engines which comprised Class D11/1 were based at Darnall in Sheffield. They were gradually withdrawn during 1959-60 but one, No. 62660 (GCR No. 506) **Butler-Henderson**, the sole-surviving ex-Great Central passenger locomotive, is preserved in the National Collection in original GCR condition.

Class D11/2 locomotives, which had been introduced post-Grouping with cut-down boiler mountings to meet the requirements of the Scottish loading gauge, were all taken out of service and scrapped between 1958 and 1962.

THE NAMES

The ten locomotives turned out in 1913 (Class D10) were named after Directors of the Great Central Railway.

The first two locomotives in the second (post war) batch of eleven (Class D11/1) were also named after Directors who had joined the Board of the GCR in its later years. The next three were named after members of the Royal family (the first and second sons of the reigning monarch together with his third child and only daughter). The final series of six D11/1's built for the GCR in 1922 were named after major engagements in the World War which had only just ended and evoked such painful memories. All eleven locomotives were referred to collectively as "Enlarged Directors".

The final batch of twenty four locomotives introduced from 1924 for service in Scotland continued the time-honoured North British Railway tradition of naming locomotives after characters from the works of *Sir Walter Scott*.

CLASS D10

429	62650	Prince Henry (Sir Alexander Henderson/Sir Douglas Haig)
430	62651	Purdon Viccars
431	62652	Edwin A. Beazley
432	62653	Sir Edward Fraser
433	62654	Walter Burgh Gair
434	62655	The Earl of Kerry
435	62656	Sir Clement Royds
436	62657	Sir Berkeley Sheffield
437	62658	Prince George (Charles Stuart-Wortley)
438	62659	Worsley Taylor

As previously indicated, the ten locomotives of Class D10 originally took the names of the Chairman and nine other Directors on the Board of the Great Central Railway. As there were eleven Directors, the one omission from this list of splendid Victorian names – which might almost have been taken from the pages of an even earlier Jane Austen novel – had to be accommodated elsewhere. Consequently, Sutton Nelthorpe, a Director from 1901 to the end of 1922, had his name affixed to one of four named locomotives in Class 1A and thereby found himself in the illustrious company of none other than Earl Kitchener of Khartoum and Earl Roberts of Kandahar.

The fourth named locomotive in this Class of eleven – Glenalmond – took the name of Sir Alexander Henderson's Scottish residence.

In 1917, following Sir Alexander's elevation to the peerage as *Lord Faringdon*, locomotive No. 429 was re-named Sir Douglas Haig. In 1920, after Haig's own ennoblement to the rank of earl, No. 429 became **Prince Henry** (the future *Duke of Gloucester)*, continuing a tradition established in the naming of post-war Class D11/1 locomotives, which already carried the names of King George V's three eldest children.

Locomotive No. 437 bore the name Charles Stuart-Wortley until October, 1920, when he became Lord Stuart of Wortley and his name was affixed to a new 4-6-0 of Class 9P. No. 437 then took the name of **Prince George**, the future Duke of Kent and "black sheep" of the Royal family, who was killed in an air crash in 1942.

Nos. 429 and 437 might have undergone further changes of name in 1935 when Prince Henry and Prince George were created Duke of Gloucester and Duke of Kent respectively. As it was, the names affixed in 1920 remained unchanged up to the withdrawal of these locomotives in the mid-1950's as B.R. Nos. 62650 and 62658.

CLASS D11/1

62660	Butler-Henderson	62666	Zebrugge
62661	Gerard Powys Dewhurst	62667	Somme
62662	Prince of Wales	62668	Jutland
62663	Prince Albert	62669	Ypres
62664	Princess Mary	62670	Marne
62665	Mons		

62660 BUTLER-HENDERSON

The Hon. Eric Brand Butler-Henderson (1884-1953) joined the Board of the Great Central Railway in 1918 at the comparatively youthful age of 34 years and remained a Director until the end of 1922.

Perhaps significantly, he was the sixth and youngest son of *Lord Faringdon* (Sir Alexander Henderson), Chairman of the GCR from 1899 to 1922 and, subsequently, Deputy Chairman of the LNER.

This locomotive is preserved as part of the National Collection.

62661 GERARD POWYS DEWHURST

Captain Gerard Powys Dewhurst (1872 – 1956) was a Director of the Great Central Railway from 1914 to 1922. Educated at *Repton* and at Trinity College, Cambridge, he was Chairman of a number of Manchester-based companies, including his own family business, held directorships in several banks and was a Director of the London Assurance Corporation.

62662 PRINCE OF WALES

Born at White Lodge, Richmond Park, on 23rd June, 1894, the first child of the then Duke and Duchess of York was christened Edward Albert Christian George Andrew Patrick David. The last four names are those of the patron saints of the countries which comprise the

United Kingdom, and it was by the last of these, David, that he was known to his family. Gaining four brothers and a sister before he was 11 years old, as a boy he spent much of his time on the *Sandringham* estate, where York Cottage was home. He was educated by private tutors before enrolling at naval college; after a short time at sea the prince went to Oxford University. From there he moved on to a life in the Officers' Training Corps. Then came the horrors of the First World War. Pressing for active involvement Edward became an army officer and served (albeit largely desk-bound) throughout the 'Great War' of 1914-18 and for a year beyond.

With his military service at an end, the 25-year-old, unmarried prince set out on the next phase of his life as heir to the throne. Slight and dapper, Edward possessed an easy charm and soon became popular as he travelled from country to country as a royal ambassador. Relations were less easy with his father, as the King viewed with disdain his eldest son's liking for parties and the company of married women such as Wallis Simpson, who the prince first met in 1930.

Raised in Baltimore by her widowed mother, in 1916 Wallis Warfield (as she then was) married her first husband, a naval officer. This marriage lasted until 1927 and the following summer she married her second husband, Ernest Simpson. Transferring to London, it was there that she met the Prince of Wales. On 20th January, 1936, George V died and the prince succeeded his father as Edward VIII.

Torn between the crown and the woman he loved, Edward abdicated after just 11 months as King and before he had even been crowned. His duties were taken on by his brother, who became George VI, and in 1937 Edward married Wallis Simpson three months after being given the title Duke of Windsor. He served during the Second World War as Governor of the Bahamas and spent the remainder of his life in retirement in Paris, where he died in 1972.

62663 PRINCE ALBERT

Born Albert Frederick Arthur George on 14th December, 1895, the birthplace of the future George VI was the family home of York

Cottage on the *Sandringham* estate in Norfolk. Commonly referred to as "Bertie", he was a sickly boy who was also afflicted with a stammer.

Following his elder brother, Edward, to the naval colleges at Osborne and Dartmouth, George was not a gifted student, preferring instead to play the fool and sports such as cricket.

However, by 1913 white flannels had been cast off in favour of a naval uniform as the future king enrolled as a midshipman in the Royal Navy. When World War 1 broke out in August, 1914, George played his part and saw front-line service in the battleship *Collingwood* at the Battle of **Jutland** in 1916. By then a sub-lieutenant, later the prince transferred to the Royal Naval Air Reserve before becoming a pilot in 1918 with the newly formed Royal Army Flying Corps.

With the War finally at an end, George once again followed his brother's footsteps by spending a year as a University student. Becoming Duke of York in 1920, he renewed acquaintances with Lady Elizabeth Bowes-Lyon, who would soon become his future wife. The young couple were married in 1923; their first child, Elizabeth (later Elizabeth II), was born in April, 1926, and their second, Margaret in August 1930.

Content with a place in the shadows, the duke went about his royal duties, diligently and without fuss. A devoted family man, a move to Royal Lodge at Windsor saw George develop an interest in gardening. In 1936, however, such simple pleasures were forced to take second place as the monarchy lurched from one crisis to another. The turbulent year for the Windsors began with the death of the duke's father, George V, and ended with his own accession as George VI. For a shy man, who disliked public speaking, such a sudden elevation came as a huge shock. However, once his elder brother had decided to abdicate, George was forced to adjust. He persevered to become a popular king.

62664 PRINCESS MARY

The third child and only daughter of King George V and Queen Mary, the future *Princess Royal* was born at York Cottage, *Sandringham* on 25th April, 1897. Christened Victoria Alexandra Alice Mary, the Princess was always known by her last name. She was to prove the brightest of the family; her eldest brother once said that it was a pity that she would not succeed (to the throne) for "she was much cleverer than me".

The wife of the 6th Earl of Harewood, Princess Mary lived at *Harewood House* in Yorkshire from her marriage in 1930 to her sudden and unexpected death in March 1965.

In November 1914, by which time it was already clear that the war involving the European powers would not soon be over, an advertisement was placed in the national press inviting monetary contributions to a 'Sailors and Soldiers Christmas Fund' which had been created by Princess Mary, the then 17 year old daughter of the King and Queen. The purpose was to provide everyone who would be wearing the King's uniform on Christmas Day, 1914, with "a gift from the nation".

The response was overwhelming. It was decided to spend the money on a hinged brass box, embossed to depict the profiled head of the Princess surrounded by a laurel wreath and flanked on either side by the 'M' monogram. The contents of the box varied according to the intended recipient: Officers and men on active service at sea or at the front received a box containing a combination of pipe, lighter, 1oz of tobacco and twenty cigarettes. Non-smokers and boys received a bullet pencil and a packet of sweets instead. Indian troops often got sweets and spices and nurses were treated to chocolate.

Many of these items were despatched separately from the tins themselves, because once the standard issue of tobacco and cigarettes had been placed in the tin there was little room for much else apart from a Christmas card and a picture of the Princess.

More than 355,000 tins were successfully delivered by the deadline. Those which were not distributed until after Christmas were sent out with a card wishing the recipient a "victorious new year". When the fund finally closed in 1920, almost £200,000 had been donated for the provision of more than two and a half million boxes with contents.

62665 MONS

On 12th August, 1914, as German troops fought to overcome the last Belgian resistance, the first soldiers of the all-regular and highly-trained British Expeditionary Force (BEF) crossed the English Channel. In ten days, 120,000 men were transported by the Royal Navy without the loss of a single man or ship. Units of this "contemptible little army" reached the town of Mons at the very moment when the First German Army of 580,000 men was driving southward through the area in a thrust towards the French frontier. The Allied force opposing them totalled less than 360,000 of whom almost 36,000 were British.

At 7 o'clock on the morning of 22nd August, 1914, just outside the village of Le Casteau, north-east of Mons, a squadron of British soldiers of the Royal Irish Dragoon Guards encountered a group of German soldiers. Shots were exchanged: the first fired in battle by British soldiers on the continent of Europe for almost one hundred years.

The French Fifth Army to the east of the British line was driven back by the German advance. In order to enable the French to avoid being outflanked, the British Commander-in-Chief, Sir John French, determined to hold his position on the Mons-Condé Canal for twenty four hours. Throughout 23rd August, in mist and rain, the German and British armies were in violent conflict as the BEF fought to hold the line. The numerically superior Germans were surprised by the intensity of British rifle fire and suffered heavy losses at the hands of an opposing force not much larger than that commanded by Wellington at Waterloo.

The battle gave rise to the legend than an angel had appeared, on the traditional white horse and dressed all in white with flaming sword, to curtail the German advance. Whatever the Angel of Mons might have destined, however, the hard-pressed British had already lost 1600 men killed or wounded. French was still inclined to stand his ground but, in order to avoid being isolated and cut off by the Fifth Army's retreat, ordered a tactical withdrawal. The BEF fell back towards Paris, fighting a series of spirited rearguard actions, particularly at Le Cateau. Having retreated nearly 150 miles in thirteen days, they crossed the **Marne** on 3rd September, 1914, blowing up the bridges behind them.

62666 ZEEBRUGGE

In April,1918, as the struggle on the Western Front continued and with the imminent transportation across the Atlantic of considerable numbers of American troops and their supplies, the Royal Navy devised a plan to prevent German submarines from using the shelter of the canal at Zeebrugge as a base for their attacks on Allied shipping. Despite the growing British success in hunting submarines, they continued to be built almost as swiftly as they were being destroyed.

Six miles inland from Zeebrugge, and linked to it by canal, were concrete submarine shelters so thick as to be impervious to air attack. The base at Bruges also contained the necessary facilities to maintain, repair and arm the U-boat fleet.

On April 23rd, St. George's Day, three old British cruisers (Thetis, Intrepid and Iphigenia), with a large supporting naval force commanded by Vice-Admiral Roger *Keyes*, were sent across the North Sea to be sunk as blockships at the entrance to the canal. The fortified mole guarding Zeebrugge was rammed by a British submarine packed with explosives and subsequently stormed. Many of its facilities were destroyed and the railway viaduct leading to it was broken.

Although this daring raid caught the public imagination and resulted in the award of 8 Victoria Crosses, it was by no means an unqualified or lasting success. Within three weeks, the Germans had dredged a channel around the sunken blockships at the entrance to the canal and were able to renew their forays into the North Sea and beyond. The British losses in the raid had been 200 killed and 400 wounded.

62667 SOMME

Just as the Battle of Verdun reached its climax, the Allies launched a major attack on the German lines near the River Somme. On 1st July, 1916, after a ferocious 5-day artillery bombardment intended to destroy the German trenches and cut the wire, 13 Divisions of British troops, aided by 5 French Divisions, assaulted German positions on an 18 mile front. Since nothing and no-one had been expected to survive the bombardment by over 1½million shells, the British were told to simply walk over no-man's-land and occupy the devastated German trenches. Unfortunately for them, the bombardment had failed. The German fortifications had remained largely intact and the wire had not been cut.

The result was the blackest day in the history of the British Army. Wave upon wave of infantrymen went "over the top" on that fine July morning to be slaughtered by German machine-gunners. By the end of the first day, the British had suffered nearly 60,000 casualties, of whom one third (i.e. 20,000) had been killed or were to die of wounds received, mostly in the first hour of the assault.

Where the British troops did achieve breakthroughs, they had no orders to exploit their advantage or proceed beyond their first day objective. As a result, ground taken on the first day was given up and re-occupied by the astonished German defenders. The aftermath was several months of bloody fighting and painfully slow progress over ground which had already once been taken by the British.

The worst part of the story is that it continued in the same pattern, if not with the same intensity, for the next five months. The conflict finally ground to a halt as torrential rain turned the battlefield into a vast quagmire. Some first day objectives had still not been taken by the time the battle petered out. British and French casualties together exceeded 620,000; German losses reached perhaps 450,000.

The Somme was an Allied and, in particular, a British disaster which tore the heart out of Kitchener's New Army and brought about the destruction of so many of the volunteer 'Pals' battalions. "Two years in the making; ten minutes in the destroying."

In February, 1917, the Germans withdrew to a new defensive system, over ten miles behind the front line, and thereby voluntarily gave up territory ten times greater in area than the Allies had succeeded in capturing in 1916. When the British and French troops reached this new line, they found a perfectly sited defensive system waiting for them, as strong as the one they had so painfully forced the previous year. They would have to start all over again.

Ironically, it was the Germans who next attacked on the Somme. In March, 1918, the ground between Albert and Bapaume, defended by under-strength British Divisions further depleted by the slaughter of 1917, and over which Kitchener's volunteers had struggled for more than four months in 1916, was recaptured by the Germans in just one day.

62668 JUTLAND

On 31st May and 1st June, 1916, the British Grand Fleet and the German High Seas Fleet met in battle in the only full-scale naval action of the War. The British fleet entered the battle with a numerical superiority which allowed the Germans little hope of victory. If, however, the Admiralty was hoping to inflict a decisive, Trafalgar-style defeat, it was to be profoundly disappointed.

On 31st May, the Grand Fleet sailed to confront a German sortie detected by radio intercepts. Poor communications and an imperfect grasp of the tactical situation on both sides resulted in a confused series of encounters beginning in the afternoon with a clash between the rival battle cruiser forces. In this engagement, the outnumbered Germans destroyed two British vessels (*Indefatigable* and *Queen Mary*) – prompting *Beatty's* famous remark "There seems to be something wrong with our bloody ships today" – while drawing the remainder south towards their own main body.

British forces then turned north in the face of superior numbers, bringing the Germans into contact with the full might of the Grand Fleet's 'Dreadnought' squadrons. Although the British lost a third battle cruiser – HMS *Invincible*, broken in half by an explosion in the magazine which killed all but six of the 1031 man crew – they inflicted a severe mauling on leading elements of the High Seas Fleet before clever tactics by Admiral Scheer enabled the Germans to break off the engagement and make good their escape during the night. *Jellicoe* declined to pursue them, fearing the possibility of greater losses from U-boat activity.

In the final analysis, Jutland proved a disappointment to both sides. The Germans failed to isolate and destroy a small detachment of the British fleet, and in the end only extracted their own fleet from a disastrous engagement with a superior force by the narrowest of margins. The Royal Navy not only failed (through signalling errors and poor gunnery) to destroy the enemy they had waited to catch away from base for almost two years, but suffered the more serious ship losses in the process. In addition to the loss of three of its nine battle cruisers, which were torn apart by devastating explosions, the Grand Fleet lost the armoured cruisers *Black Prince, Defence* and *Warrior* plus 7 destroyers at a cost of nearly 7000 casualties, including 5914 men killed.

Overall, however, Jutland was a strategic victory for the Royal Navy, simply because it maintained a balance of sea power already heavily in its favour. As an American journalist put it: "The German fleet has assaulted its jailer but it is still in jail." The High Seas Fleet played no further significant part in the war until, in November, 1918, its demoralised crews broke into open mutiny.

The Boy Hero of Jutland – John Travers ("Jack") Cornwell, aged 16 years – was the youngest winner of the Victoria Cross in the twentieth century. He served as a sight-setter on board the light cruiser HMS Chester and although mortally wounded in a shell burst which had killed the rest of the gun crew, remained at his post awaiting orders.

The future *King George VI* saw active service as a gunnery midshipman in the battleship *Collingwood* during the Battle of Jutland.

(The name 'Jutland' was also carried by LMS ' Jubilee' Class locomotive No. 45684).

62669 YPRES

Although there were three Battles of Ypres ("Wipers" to the Tommies), the name is most often associated with the Third Battle, sometimes referred to simply as 'Passchendaele'.

The Battle of the Marne in 1914 was followed by the so-called "race to the sea" and the construction of trenchlines all the way from the Channel ports to the Franco-Swiss Border. In the First Battle of Ypres (October 1914), the Germans attempted to bludgeon their way through the new Allied line so as to re-establish a war of movement, but found it impossible to do so.

In the Second Battle of Ypres (22nd April – 27th May, 1915) the Germans used gas against the French for the first time but succeeded in advancing only 3 miles.

The Third Battle of Ypres (31st July to 10th November, 1917) involved attempts to breakout of the Ypres salient by the British, Australians and Canadians.

Despite profound doubts and misgivings on the part of Lloyd George about the likely success of such a venture, the War Cabinet authorised Haig to proceed. The main offensive was preceded by a successful attack on the strong German position on the Messines Ridge in which both sides lost a combined total of over 40,000 men killed or wounded. Haig's plan was to strike north east from the salient and seize the rim of high ground running through Passchendaele. He would then exploit the advantage thus gained by driving north towards Ostend and Bruges.

The massive preliminary bombardment smashed up ground being made sodden by the heaviest August rainfall for years. With all the ditches and land drains destroyed, the battlefield became one vast quagmire. Haig instructed Gough's Fifth Army to continue with the attacks. When these failed in the incessant rains, the emphasis of the attack was switched to Plumer's Second Army. During September, aided by fine and dry weather and step-by-step tactics, Plumer made significant advances. Unfortunately, the rains returned and the battlefield reverted to swamp conditions. Men, horses and machines were literally swallowed up in the mud; this last stage of the Third Battle of Ypres provided the scene of the living nightmare that inspired some of the most deeply felt of all war poetry from the likes of Wilfred Owen and Siegfried Sassoon.

In the October fighting, the *Anzac* forces almost made it to the crest of the Passchendaele Ridge before being withdrawn, utterly exhausted. The obliterated village, some 5 miles from the original start line, finally fell to the Canadians on 20th November. Six days later, Haig closed down the Battle.

By any standard, the offensive must be counted a complete failure and a monumental exercise in futility, with around 250,000 men killed, wounded or missing on each side.

62670 MARNE

The First Battle of the Marne (6th-9th September, 1914) was a decisive engagement that halted the German advance near the River Marne, less than 30 miles from Paris.

The German First Army had been checked by the BEF at **Mons** and Le Cateau and the Second Army by the French at Guise. Although the German advance had continued and the Allied armies were obliged to retreat, both German Armies were forced to turn inward to keep in touch with each other, so that the "right hook" (the First Army) swung east of Paris.

General Gallieni, the military governor of Paris, persuaded Joseph Joffre, Commander-in-Chief of the French forces, to attack the flank thus exposed. Under Joffre's orders, troops were rushed to the front by all available means including Paris taxi cabs and the Allied attack on the German First Army was begun on 6th September.

The German Commander wheeled his entire force to meet the attack, opening a 30 mile gap between his own troops and those of the German Second Army. The BEF and the French Fifth Army advanced into the gap that had been created, effectively splitting the two German Armies.

On 19th September, the Germans began to retreat, stablising their line on the River Aisne. The threat to Paris was ended and the German hope of a swift and decisive victory (the Schlieffen Plan) was frustrated and abandoned. The First World War had begun.

CLASS D11/2

62671	Bailie MacWheeble	62683	Hobbie Elliott
62672	Baron of Bradwardine	62684	Wizard of the Moor
62673	Evan Dhu	62685	Malcolm Graeme
62674	Flora MacIvor	62686	The Fiery Cross
62675	Colonel Gardiner	62687	Lord James of Douglas
62676	Jonathan Oldbuck	62688	Ellen Douglas
62677	Edie Ochiltree	62689	Maid of Lorn
62678	Luckie Mucklebackit	62690	The Lady of the Lake
62679	Lord Glenallan	62691	Laird of Balmawhapple
62680	Lucy Ashton	62692	Allan-Bane
62681	Captain Craigengelt	62693	Roderick Dhu
62682	Haystoun of Bucklow	62694	James Fitzjames

When these locomotives entered service with the newly-formed LNER in 1924, they did not carry names. Within a year, however, all but two had received names which continued the North British tradition of naming passenger service locomotives after characters from the works of *Sir Walter Scott*. The remaining two engines in the Class received names of a similar nature – applied by means of shaded transfers – during the Summer of 1926.

The first of Scott's novels, "Waverley", dealt with the Jacobite

261

rebellion of 1745; published anonymously in 1814, it was hugely successful. During the 15 years that followed, Scott produced a succession of works of fiction which became known collectively as the Waverley novels, even though they had many subjects, characters and settings.

Scott's work was very popular during the nineteenth century and was extensively read. His popularity subsequently declined and his novels are now largely ignored.

There is little point or purpose in attempting to isolate Scott's characters from the novels or poems they inhabit and which give them life. Suffice it to say that they represent all facets of society – hero and villain; highbrow and lowbrow: rich and poor – in the Scotland of the mid-eighteenth century onwards. Scott, like *Charles Dickens*, was a master story-teller. Like Dickens, the names of his characters – including those selected for display on the earlier Class D30 locomotives – often clearly evoke a picture of the person to whom they refer. It is almost possible to *see* Cuddie Headrigg straining at the plough or Luckie Mucklebackitt gutting fish. Unlike Dickens, however, and with few exceptions, Scott's characters have not stood the test of time and are not instantly recognisable. There are no Fagins, Scrooges or Pickwicks here!

CLASS D49

INTRODUCTION AND GENERAL CHARACTERISTICS

The Gresley three-cylinder D49 4-4-0's were designed for use on secondary express passenger duties. A total of 76 locomotives were built at Darlington between October, 1927 and February, 1935. The D49's were used mostly on routes in the north east of England and in Scotland. They were generally regarded as successful, although they did acquire a reputation for rough-riding at speed.

There were two main variants:-

Class D49/1	Piston valve engines (except as referred to below) of which 36 were constructed between October, 1927, and June, 1929.
	(Five locomotives (Nos. 62720 to 62724) were at first built with oscillating cam valve gear and classified D49/3. This proved unsatisfactory and from 1938 all five were converted to piston valve engines and assimilated into Class D49/1).
Class D49/2	Constructed with rotary cam operated poppet valves. 10 were built between April and October, 1932, and a further 30 between August, 1933, and February, 1935.

No. 62768, The **Morpeth**, was the only member of the Class ever to be substantially altered from the original design. In 1942, this locomotive was re-built by *Edward Thompson* from three cylinders to two inside cylinders and remained in service without further modification until withdrawal in 1952 following damage sustained in a collision.

All the D49's had been withdrawn by 1961. One locomotive has been preserved.

THE NAMES

The class D49/1 locomotives (36 in total) were named after most of the English and Scottish counties served by the LNER. For some reason, the list included **Berkshire** (not in LNER territory), but excluded County Durham, where all of the D49's were built, as well as the major counties of East Anglia.

The Class D49/2 locomotives (42 in total) were named after foxhunts, all but six of which were in, or bordered upon, LNER territory.

In May/June 1932, the names of Nos. 62727 and 62726 were changed. Although named initially as "Shires", both had been built to the same specification as the D49/2's (i.e. with poppet valves) and their names were changed to "Hunts", to match those of like type. Thus, No. 62726 **Leicestershire** became The **Meynell** and No. 62727 **Buckinghamshire** became The **Quorn**, thereby reducing the number of "Shires" from 36 to 34.

In 1952, of the 20 locomotives in this Class allocated to Scotland, 11 (mostly "Shires) were shedded in Edinburgh (at St. Margaret's and Haymarket).

Of the remaining 56 locomotives, no fewer than 52 (including 37 of the 42 "Hunts") were allocated to Yorkshire (mostly at York, Hull and Starbeck sheds). They were set to work mainly on the cross-country services of that county, which territory embraced 15 of the hunts whose names were carried on these locomotives. 13 of the 15 locomotives carrying the names of Yorkshire hunts were allocated to Yorkshire sheds; the remaining two (The **Cleveland** and The **Holderness**) were allocated to Scotland. No D49's were shedded south of Leeds, which had 4 "Hunts" at Neville Hill.

Generally speaking, the foxhunts which comprise Class D49/2 are located in the eastern counties of England served by LNER, from London to the Scottish Border. Obvious omissions from the two ends of the ECML "corridor", are the *Cambridgeshire* and the *Northumberland* hunts, both names having already been selected for display on the D49/1 "Shires". Other omissions include two of the smaller Yorkshire hunts and all of the hunts in East Anglia.

Given that there were eligible names still available, it is surprising that the Class included a number of hunts not in, or barely in, LNER territory, four of them some considerable distance away. The **Albrighton** country lies in Shropshire and Staffordshire, (although the LNER did have a stretch of line connecting Stafford Common with Bromshall Junction, near Uttoxeter), while both The **Berkeley** and The **Cotswold** cover extensive territory in Gloucestershire. The **Cattistock** is located in Dorset and Somerset, close to *Portland Bill*; the **Garth** and the **Craven** lie to the west of London, principally in *Berkshire* and Hampshire which, again, were not served by the LNER. In the north midlands, The **Atherstone** qualifies for inclusion because of boundaries shared with hunts in Leicestershire and Northants, and the passage of the former *Great Central* line through part of its territory.

On the D49's the curved nameplate was fitted over the forward driving wheel splasher surmounted, in the case of the "Hunts", by a cast brass fox which faced forward on each side of the locomotive.

THE CLASS

62700	Yorkshire	62738	The Zetland
62701	Derbyshire	62739	The Badsworth
62702	Oxfordshire	62740	The Bedale
62703	Hertfordshire	62741	The Blankney
62704	Stirlingshire	62742	The Braes of Derwent
62705	Lanarkshire	62743	The Cleveland
62706	Forfarshire	62744	The Holderness
62707	Lancashire	62745	The Hurworth
62708	Argyllshire	62746	The Middleton
62709	Berwickshire	62747	The Percy
62710	Lincolnshire	62748	The Southwold
62711	Dumbartonshire	62749	The Cottesmore
62712	Morayshire	62750	The Pytchley
62713	Aberdeenshire	62751	The Albrighton
62714	Perthshire	62752	The Atherstone
62715	Roxburghshire	62753	The Belvoir
62716	Kincardineshire	62754	The Berkeley
62717	Banffshire	62755	The Bilsdale
62718	Kinross-shire	62756	The Brocklesby
62719	Peebles-shire	62757	The Burton
62720	Cambridgeshire	62758	The Cattistock
62721	Warwickshire	62759	The Craven
62722	Huntingdonshire	62760	The Cotswold
62723	Nottinghamshire	62761	The Derwent
62724	Bedfordshire	62762	The Fernie
62725	Inverness-shire	62763	The Fitzwilliam
62726	The Meynell	62764	The Garth
62727	The Quorn	62765	The Goathland
62728	Cheshire	62766	The Grafton
62729	Rutlandshire	62767	The Grove
62730	Berkshire	62768	The Morpeth
62731	Selkirkshire	62769	The Oakley
62732	Dumfries-shire	62770	The Puckeridge
62733	Northumberland	62771	The Rufford
62734	Cumberland	62772	The Sinnington
62735	Westmorland	62773	The South Durham
62736	The Bramham Moor	62774	The Staintondale
62737	The York and Ainsty	62775	The Tynedale

SHIRES, SQUIRES AND "TALLY HO" CRIERS

A   SHIRE "HORSES"

The D49/1's were named after most of the English and Scottish counties served by the LNER at a time when to travel over any distance – for whatever reason – meant to travel by train.

The fact that the relatively newly-formed LNER chose to name a Class of locomotives after its constituent "Shires" was both a celebration of the size, power and influence conferred upon the Company by the Grouping and a public relations exercise designed to promote what these days would be called a 'corporate identity' by emphasising the contribution of each of the constituent parts.

The "Shires" whose names comprised the Class varied considerably in size and composition, reflecting the diverse purposes for which they were connected to and served by the railway system.

In addition to the express passenger services linking the principal cities and population centres, the LNER provided a wide range of services to coastal resorts and to centres for tourism and recreational pursuits. Many of the areas served by the railway were rich in history and cultural diversity, acting as a magnet for travellers.

Beyond that, the LNER provided a nexus of essential cross-country services linking the many smaller towns and villages which comprised a significant, if not always lucrative, part of the Company's business, bearing in mind that many of the "Shires", particularly those in Scotland, were only sparsely populated.

Besides the transport of people, the railway was very much concerned with the movement of freight between the industrial heartlands of the north, including the shipbuilding and coal mining areas, and the principal ports and distribution centres. Much agricultural produce was also transported by rail.

In 1975, long after steam locomotives had disappeared from the railways, the Scottish "Shires" were absorbed into one or other of the new Regions. A handful of English counties also either "disappeared" or were reconfigured in the local government re-organisation of 1974.

The notes which follow are for the most part written in the past tense i.e. refer to the situation existing when the D49's were introduced into service in the late 1920's.

62700 YORKSHIRE

Yorkshire was the largest county in England, being more than double the size of **Lincolnshire**, the second largest. Administratively, it was divided into three sections viz. the North, West and East Ridings ("thirds").

In addition to its importance as the location of the northern Area HQ of the LNER, the county town of York was, and remains, a major historical and cultural centre for travel and tourism. The importance of Leeds as a commercial centre at the heart of the Yorkshire woollen industry was acknowledged by the LNER in October, 1947, through the introduction of a streamlined train – "The West Riding Limited" – for travel between Leeds/Bradford and King's Cross. Trains to the port of Hull provided connections with ferry services to *Zeebrugge* and the near continent. Sheffield and the industrial hinterland of the West Riding were linked to the midlands and south of England via the former Great Central section of the railway.

The popular east coast holiday resorts, including Whitby, Scarborough, Filey, Bridlington and Hornsea, were all served by the LNER, as were the several mineral spas in Yorkshire. The town of Doncaster, in addition to being the principal centre for LNER locomotive construction and repair, was also the destination for legions of horse racing enthusiasts, as were York, Thirsk and other locations elsewhere in Yorkshire.

In 1974, the county was much reduced in size and divided into the new counties of North, West and South Yorkshire.

62701 DERBYSHIRE

A north midland county of England, bounded on the north by **Yorkshire** and to the south by **Nottinghamshire** and Leicestershire, Derbyshire is largely associated with mining and manufacturing.

The county has also long been an established centre for tourism, associated in particular with the Peak District national park which presents some of the finest hill scenery in England. The character of the landscape ranges from the wild moorland of the **Cheshire** borders in the north west to the parkland and woods of the Chatsworth district. There are several resorts with mineral springs.

Historically, the LNER interest and involvement in the county was always secondary to that of the LMS. In the north-east and north, the former Great Central system touched the periphery of the county, while a branch of the Great Northern served Derby and other places in the south.

662702 OXFORDSHIRE

An inland county of south-central England, Oxfordshire is situated mostly in the basin of the upper Thames, with the Cotswolds in the west and the Chilterns in the south east.

In the late 1920's, in addition to Morris Motors at Oxford, there was a range of manufacturing industries producing predominantly blankets, lace, paper and agricultural implements. Oxfordshire was, however, still mainly agricultural with nearly seven-eighths of the area of the county under cultivation. The dairy industry was also important, due to the availability of rich water meadows for grazing.

Although mostly GWR territory, the Great Central Railway had constructed a branch from its main line at Woodford in Northamptonshire to Banbury.

62703 HERTFORDSHIRE

The county of Hertfordshire – the sixth smallest in England when this locomotive was named – can trace its origins back to Saxon times. Progressive urbanisation, promoted in the last two centuries by the growth of extensive transport networks, has made it largely indistinguishable on its southern perimeter from the greater London conurbation.

Owing to its proximity to the Capital, Hertfordshire has been particularly well served by railways. The east coast main line constructed by the former Great Northern Railway passes through the centre of the county by Hatfield, Stevenage and Hitchin; the Great Eastern (Cambridge line) provided branches to Hertford and Buntingford. The Metropolitan and Great Central joint line was constructed to serve Rickmansworth and suburban lines of the Great Northern the Barnet district.

62704 STIRLINGSHIRE

A county of central Scotland, since 1975 a part of the Central and Strathclyde Regions. The principal towns included Falkirk, Stirling, Grangemouth (now Scotland's second most important port) and Stenhousemuir.

A well-developed coalfield in the south-east served the staple industry; iron-ore, fireclay, limestone and sandstone were also mined or quarried. The ironworks at Carron and Falkirk were an important part of the county's economy. Woollens were manufactured at Stirling and Bannockburn; there were chemical works at Falkirk and Stirling and shipbuilding was carried out at Grangemouth.

Historically, the county played a conspicuous part in the struggle for Scottish independence, being particularly associated with the exploits of William Wallace and *Robert the Bruce*. The three great battles of that struggle were all fought in the Shire viz. Stirling Bridge (1297), Falkirk (1298), and Bannockburn (1314). Beyond that, apart from the disastrous defeat of the Convenanters at Kilsyth

(1645) and the short-lived triumph which Prince Charles Edward won at Falkirk (1746), the history of the Shire is essentially that of the county town.

The southern and south-eastern districts of Stirlingshire were served by the LNER (North British) line from Edinburgh to Glasgow (via Falkirk); a line also ran from Glasgow to Abenfoyle.

62705 LANARKSHIRE

Lanarkshire is a former county in southern Scotland with Lanark, a mediaeval town created a royal burgh around 1140, as the county town. It was in Lanark that William Wallace killed the English Sheriff, William Heselrig, the event becoming the catalyst for the Scottish Wars of Independence. The county was also the scene of the defeat of the forces of Mary, Queen of Scots, at Langside in 1568, while in the seventeenth century, the Covenanters fought several battles in Lanarkshire.

Since that time Lanark has been the site of several local industries, most famously the mills at New Lanark, where the social policies of the philanthropist Robert Owen gained international recognition. With the exploitation of local iron ore and coal in the nineteenth century, northern Lanarkshire, especially the Glasgow and Clyde Valley area, became Scotland's major industrial region: shipbuilding, textiles and engineering were major contributors.

Railway facilities were particularly well-developed in the more densely populated northern part of the county, especially around Glasgow. The LNER (North British) network served a number of towns in the middle and lower reaches of Lanarkshire and its lines to Edinburgh crossed the north-western corner and north of the county.

In 1975, Lanarkshire became part of the newly created Strathclyde Region, with Glasgow as its administrative centre.

62706 FORFARSHIRE

Forfarshire, or 'Angus', was a maritime county on the eastern side of Scotland, bordering the *Firth of Tay*. The principal towns were Dundee, Arbroath and Montrose (all of which were involved in shipbuilding) and Forfar. Montrose was also the local centre for the deep-sea fishing industry. The Shire – now part of the Tayside Region – became known by the name of the county town from the sixteenth century onwards.

Prior to the Grouping in 1923, the county was served by two railway companies, the Caledonian (later LMS), and the North British (LNER) which entered the Shire from the south by the Tay Bridge and followed the coast north-eastwards, sending off a branch to Bervie at Montrose.

62707 LANCASHIRE

This county of north-west England on the Irish Sea became a county palatine in 1351 and a duchy attached to the Crown. It was traditionally a cotton textiles manufacturing region whose administrative centre was Preston. Lancashire was much reduced in size after the 1974 boundary changes, losing the Furness district to Cumbria and much of the south to Greater Manchester, Merseyside and **Cheshire**.

The Lancashire coastline was broken by great inlets, chief of which were Morecambe Bay and the estuaries of the Ribble and the Mersey. Like its traditional rival, **Yorkshire**, the "red rose" county had a number of popular seaside resorts –including *Southport*, *Blackpool*, and *Morecambe* – served this time by the London Midland and Scottish Railway, as opposed to the LNER.

The city of Manchester had several large stations for the various railway companies which served it, including the Great Northern and Great Central components of the LNER. Indeed, the nucleus of the Great Central Railway (which formed part of the LNER in 1923) was the Sheffield, Ashton-under-Lyne and Manchester Railway, incorporated in 1837. The first section of this line (from Manchester to Godley) was opened to passenger traffic in 1841; within 5 years, following the construction of the Woodhead Tunnel, the line was opened throughout, linking both sides of the Pennines.

In 1847, the Grimsby docks and other lines were amalgamated with the original company under the title of the Manchester, Sheffield and Lincolnshire Railway. Thus the M.S.L. was essentially a provincial system linking Lancashire with the East Coast.

62708 ARGYLLSHIRE

Argyllshire was a county on the west coast of Scotland – the second largest in the country -embracing a significant part of the coastal region to the south of **Inverness-shire** and a number of the Hebrides or Western Isles. It is now part of the Strathclyde Region formed in 1975.

Industrial output was relatively scant. Whisky was manufactured at Campbeltown, Oban, Ardrishaig and elsewhere. Coarse woollens were made for local consumption and there was some coal-mining and quarrying of slate and granite. Fishing was, however, the most important industry, Loch Fyne being famous for its herrings.

Owing partly to the paucity of trading industries and partly to the fact that no place in the Shire was more than 12 miles from the sea, the railway system in Argyllshire was not particularly well-developed, the chief means of communication being by steamers plying between Glasgow and various parts of the coast. The Caledonian Railway predominated; a small portion of the North British (LNER) line to Mallaig skirted the extreme west of the Shire.

Before the advent of railways, the county had contained many well-established coaching routes but, by the early part of the twentieth century, coaches ran only during the tourist season, either in connection with train and steamer or in districts still not served by either.

62709 BERWICKSHIRE

Now part of the Borders Region, the small county of Berwickshire formed the south-eastern extremity of Scotland along its border with England. During the long period of border strife, the Shire was repeatedly over-run by the armies of the English and Scots kings, who were constantly fighting for possession and control of the ancient frontier town of Berwick. It was finally ceded to England in 1482.

There are several places of historic interest in this former county, including the Pease (or Peaths) Bridge, 123 ft. high and 300 ft. long, built by Thomas Telford across the deep pass which had been one of the strongest of Scotland's natural defences. Nearby are the ruins of Cockburnspath Tower, at one time a strong fortress and supposed to be the Ravenswood of Scott's "Bride of Lammermoor". Coldstream and Lamberton, being close to the Border, were both once resorted to (like Gretna Green in the west) by eloping couples for clandestine marriage.

Next to agriculture, fishing has traditionally been the most important industry, with the Tweed salmon fisheries being particularly well-known.

The former North British Railway Company monopolised the communications network of the county, serving the coastal districts from Berwick to Cockburnspath, with a branch from Reston to St. Boswells. Express trains on the east coast main line sped through Berwickshire before heading inland across East Lothian on the last leg of their journey to Edinburgh.

62710 LINCOLNSHIRE

The second largest county in England, with a coastline of 110 miles, Lincolnshire was, and remains, predominantly agricultural although fishing and maritime activities have long been significant. The Humber estuary formed the northern boundary of the county with the East Riding of **Yorkshire**; ports on the Lincolnshire side included the small ferry-ports of Barton and New Holland and the important fishing harbour of Grimsby.

Although the extensive coastline generally is low-lying and marshy, on some parts there are fine stretches of sand; Cleethorpes, Skegness, Mablethorpe and Sutton-on-Sea were favourite resorts to which visitors, including day-trippers, were conveyed in large numbers, courtesy of the LNER. One of the most famous of all railway posters, "Skegness is SO Bracing" – complete with prancing fisherman – is an exhortation to travel by train to the delights of this Lincolnshire resort. The city of Lincoln, remarkably rich in history and the remains of domestic architecture from the Norman period onwards, has long been a major tourist and visitor centre.

Three of the companies which came together to form the LNER had lines in Lincolnshire, the principal railway being the Great Northern, its main line passing through the west of the county en route to Newark (Notts.) via Grantham. The southbound stretch between Little Bytham and Essendine (in Rutland) was to achieve lasting fame as the location of Mallard's world steam speed record breaking run on 3rd July, 1938.

The Great Northern had branches from Peterborough to Spalding, Boston, Louth and Grimsby; and from Grantham to Sleaford and Boston, and to Lincoln. The GNR worked jointly with the Great Eastern the line from March to Spalding, Lincoln, Gainsborough and Doncaster, and with the Midland Railway that from Saxby to Bourn, Spalding, Holbeach, Sutton Bridge and King's Lynn. The Great Central Railway connected Lancashire, Sheffield and Doncaster with Grimsby, and with Hull by ferry from New Holland.

62711 DUMBARTONSHIRE

A small county of western Scotland, now part of the Strathclyde Region. The Highland part of the Shire, with its lochs, glens and rugged mountain scenery, was in marked contrast to the more populous and low-lying industrialised area to the south. The Clyde, the Kelvin and the Leven were the only rivers of any importance, the latter flowing out of *Loch Lomond*, (by far the largest and most magnificent of the inland lakes), at Balloch and joining the Clyde at Dumbarton.

The water of the Leven being soft and pure, dyeing and bleaching had taken place along the Vale of Leven since the early eighteenth century. The engineering works and shipyards at Clydebank were world-famous, and at Dumbarton there were others almost equally busy. The then extensive Singer sewing machine works were located at Kilbowie, and the Clyde Trust barge-building shops were at Dalmuir. There were distilleries and breweries throughout the Vale. Kirkintilloch and Cumbernauld were centres of great activity in the mining of coal and ironstone, the former town also being the location for chemical works and sawmills. There was some fishing at Helensburgh and along the Gareloch.

The Shire had interesting associations with Scottish history and national heroes. The captive Wallace was conveyed in chains to Dumbarton Castle, and was taken from there to his execution in London. *Robert the Bruce* died at Cardross Castle in 1329. The Covenanters fled through the southern districts in 1645 following their bloody defeat at Kilsyth. When the Forth and Clyde Canal was being excavated, swords, pistols and other weapons dropped by the fugitives were found at Dullatur, together with skeletons of men and horses.

The populous districts of the county were served almost wholly by the LNER (North British Railway), connecting with train and steamer services run by the Highland and Caledonian Railways to the other more diversified and picturesque areas of Dumbartonshire.

612712 MORAYSHIRE

Morayshire – also known as Elginshire – was a relatively small county on the *Moray Firth*, bordered to the east by **Banffshire** and to the south and west by **Inverness-shire** and Nairnshire. Elgin was the county town.

The county comprised the eastern end of the much larger mediaeval province of Moray and was absorbed into the Kingdom of Scotland by the end of the eleventh century. Macbeth was one of only two Scottish kings who originated from the province.

In 1975, Moray was divided between the newly-created Grampian and Highland Regions.

There used to be woollen mills at Elgin and elsewhere and chemical works at Forres and Burghead, but whisky was the chief product of the area. The deep-sea fishing industry was once profitable and the local rivers yielded large quantities of salmon. Boat building and repair was carried out at Lossiemouth and other coastal inlets.

The Great North of Scotland Railway, (a small company which became part of the LNER in 1923), entered the Shire from Craigellachie in the south east. Branch lines from Elgin ran via Boat of Garten in **Inverness-shire** and Port Gordon in the north east. From Elgin a further branch line served Lossiemouth.

This locomotive was the last in service. Withdrawn in July 1961, it is now preserved.

62713 ABERDEENSHIRE

Aberdeenshire was the sixth largest of the Scottish counties in area. Located in the north east of Scotland, the Shire was generally hilly, (mountainous in places), and had a coastline some 65 miles in length.

The city of Aberdeen was of historical importance from the twelfth century onwards (see Class A1 Pacific No. 60154 *Bon Accord*). Owing to the variety and importance of its chief industries, the "Granite City" was one of the most prosperous in Scotland. Very durable grey granite had been quarried near Aberdeen for more than 300 years; blocked and dressed paving "setts", kerb and building stones and monumental and other ornamental work of granite had long been exported to all parts of the world. Once the predominant industry this had, however, been surpassed by the deep-sea fisheries, with fish trains despatched to London daily. Other significant activities included textile manufacture; paper-making (since 1694); distilling and brewing; ship(trawler) construction; and fruit growing/ conservation.

The Shire was served by the Caledonian, Great North of Scotland and North British Railways (the latter two being absorbed into the newly-formed LNER in 1923). The Great North of Scotland mainline ran via Kintore and Huntly to Keith and Elgin. The North British connected Aberdeen with Stonehaven, Montrose, Dundee and Edinburgh.

62714 PERTHSHIRE

Perthshire, once the fourth largest county in Scotland, is now part of the Central and Tayside Regions. By far the greater part of the county was mountainous, with at least fifty mountains exceeding 3000 ft. in height.

The Shire was famous for its dyeing and bleaching works at Perth. The other leading industries included manufacture of gauge-glasses, ink, muslins, Indian shawls, jute goods, woollens and winceys and boots and shoes. There were tanneries at various locations and quarrying of granite, limestone and slate. In addition, the Shire contained iron foundries, breweries, distilleries, rope and sail works, coach-building yards and brick and tile works. The salmon fisheries on the Tay – Scotland's longest river – yielded substantial revenues.

Perthshire was served by the LNER (ex-North British Railway) and by the Caledonian and Highland Railways, all of which shared the use of one general railway station in the town of Dundee.

62715 ROXBURGHSHIRE

A former Border county of Scotland, bounded on the west by **Berwickshire** and to the south and east by the English counties of **Cumberland** and **Northumberland**. Now part of the Borders Region, it is closely associated with the life and works of *Sir Walter Scott*, who lived at *Abbotsford*, near Melrose.

The county was the main centre for tweed and hosiery manufacture in Scotland. Engineering, iron founding, dyeing and tanning were carried out at Hawick and Jedburgh, while agricultural implements and machinery, chemical manures and fishing tackle were made at Kelso. The salmon fisheries on the Tweed were also of considerable importance. Agricultural activities were concerned primarily with the cultivation of root crops, grain and fruit together with cattle and sheep farming.

The Waverley route of the North British Railway (LNER) ran through the county from near Melrose in the north to Kershopefoot in the south. At St. Boswells branches were sent off to Duos and Reston, and to Jedburgh and Kelso via Roxburgh. The North Eastern Railway (LNER) had a line from Berwick to Kelso, via Coldstream and Carham.

62716 KINCARDINESHIRE

Also called 'The Mearns' (derived from Mernia, a Scottish King), Kincardineshire was a coastal county of north east Scotland sandwiched between **Forfarshire** and **Abderdeenshire**. In the west and north-west, the Grampians were the dominant feature. The coastline consisted mainly of rugged cliffs, ranging in height from 100 ft. to 250ft. and interrupted only by occasional creeks or bays.

The county is now part of the Grampian Region. By an extraordinary reversal of fortune, the town which gave the Shire its name had declined to a mere hamlet by the end of the sixteenth century and when this locomotive was named was represented by only the ruins of a royal castle and an ancient burial ground.

Apart from agriculture, the principal industry was fishing, with Stonehaven as the main centre. The village of Fjndon (pronounced Finnan) gave its name to the well-known smoked haddocks which were first cured in this way at that hamlet. The salmon fisheries of the sea and the rivers yielded a substantial annual return. Manufacturing activities were of little more than local importance.

Prior to Grouping in 1923, The Caledonian (LMS) and North

British (LNER) Railways ran to Aberdeen via Laurencekirk and Stonehaven, using the same metals; there was also a branch line of the NBR from Montrose to Bervie.

62717 BANFFSHIRE

Banffshire, a former county of north-east Scotland on the *Moray Firth*, is now part of the Grampian Region. The North Sea port of Banff was the county town. Banffshire was bounded to the east and south by **Aberdeenshire** and to the west by Elgin **(Morayshire)** and **Inverness-shire**.

The soil was generally rich and productive; oats was the predominant crop but the demands of the numerous distilleries (Glen Livet; Glen Fiddich etc.) kept up the acreage of barley. There was also a considerable amount of dairy farming. Only limited manufacturing took place but sea fishing was carried on at numerous creaks or harbours along the coast. Banffshire streams were well-stocked with trout and the Spey and Deveron rivers were famous for their salmon.

The chief towns of the county were served by the Great North of Scotland (LNER) and Highland (LMS) Railways, providing communication in one direction with Aberdeen and in another with Elgin, Nairn and Inverness.

62718 KINROSS-SHIRE

A land-locked county of east-central Scotland, bordered by **Perthshire**, Clackmannanshire and Fifeshire. With the exception of Clackmannan, Kinross-shire was the smallest of the Scottish counties, from the point of view of both area and population. It is now part of the Tayside Region.

The lower part of the county was generally well-sheltered and adapted to all kinds of crops, chief of which were barley, turnips and potatoes. Tartans, plaids and other woollens, and linen were manufactured at Kinross and Milnathort, which was also an important centre for livestock sales. Brewing and milling were carried on in the county town.

LNER (North British) lines entered from the south and west and ran through the county via Kinross; the Mid-Fife line branched off at Mawcarse Junction.

62719 PEEBLES-SHIRE

Peebles-shire, or Tweedale, was a southern inland county of Scotland, bordered to the north and east by the Lothians – "Edinburghshire" – to the south by **Selkirkshire** and **Dumfries-shire** and to the west by **Lanarkshire**. It is now part of the Borders Region.

The Shire was sparsely populated and predominantly agricultural. Manufacturing of woollens and tweeds was centred on the county town of Peebles and was largely for local consumption. There was also some meal and flour milling.

Peebles was 27 miles south of Edinburgh on the North British Railway; it was also the terminus of a branchline of the Caledonian system from Carstairs in Lanarkshire.

62720 CAMBRIDGESHIRE

An eastern county of England in East Anglia, Cambridgeshire now includes the former counties of the Isle of Ely and Huntingdon and lies mainly in the Fens. It is for the most part flat, elevated only a few feet above sea level, and intersected with innumerable drainage channels.

Cambridgeshire has always been mainly an agricultural county and the land is very fertile. By the beginning of the twentieth century it had become one of the principal grain-producing counties in England. Nearly nine-tenths of the total area was under cultivation; wheat was the chief grain crop, but large quantities of barley and oats were also grown. Dairy farming was concentrated on the south-west of the Shire and much butter and cheese were despatched to the London markets. There was no large manufacturing industry common to the county in general; among minor trades, brewing was carried out at several locations, as were brickmaking and limeburning.

The principal railway serving the county was the LNER, with numerous branch lines of the former Great Eastern centred upon Cambridge, Ely and March. Cambridge was also served by branches of the former Great Northern line from Hitchin, of the LNWR from Bletchley and Bedford, and of the Midland from Kettering. A trunk line connecting the eastern counties with the north and north-west of England ran northwards from March under the joint working of the former Great Northern and Great Eastern companies.

62721 WARWICKSHIRE

A midland county of England which, prior to the creation of the West Midlands Metropolitan County in 1974, contained one of the most highly industrialised regions in the world, centred on Birmingham.

This is yet another county in which the interest and involvement of the LNER could be described as being secondary to that of other companies. Railway communications were provided almost entirely by the LMS (whose main line crossed the county via Rugby, Nuneaton and Tamworth) and the Great Western, which ran through Leamington and Warwick to Birmingham.

62722 HUNTINGDONSHIRE

A former county of eastern England, since 1974 part of **Cambridgeshire**. Among English counties, only Middlesex and **Rutlandshire** were smaller in size.

Huntingdonshire was almost wholly an agricultural county. By the early 1900's nearly nine-tenths of its total area was under cultivation, with wheat, barley and oats the main crops. Market gardening and fruit farming were becoming increasingly important. Dairy farming was not particularly prominent although the village of Stilton, on what was then the Great North Road, had formerly a large market for the well-known cheese to which it had given its name.

The middle of the county was traversed from south to north by the LNER (Great Northern) main line, which entered it at St. Neots and, passing by Huntingdon, exited northwards at Peterborough. A branch line to Ramsay ran eastwards from Holme junction, midway between Huntingdon and Peterborough. From Huntingdon a branch line of the Great Eastern ran east to Cambridge via St. Ives. From St. Ives former Great Eastern lines also ran north-east to Ely (**Cambridgeshire**) via Earith Bridges on the county border, and north to Wisbech with a branch line westward from Somersham to Ramsay.

62723 NOTTINGHAMSHIRE

An inland county of central England, generally low-lying, with part of the south Pennines and the remnant of Sherwood Forest in the east.

Nottinghamshire was, and remains, rich in history, centred mainly around the town and castle of Nottingham, where *King Charles I* raised his Standard at the beginning of the English Civil War in 1642, and around the legend of *Robin Hood*.

Coal was mined chiefly on the south-west border of the county near Nottingham and near Mansfield; the earliest evidence of the working of the Nottinghamshire coalfield dates back to 1259 and by 1881 thirty nine collieries were in production.

Numerous cotton-mills were erected in the Shire in the eighteenth century and there were silk-mills at Nottingham. The lace and hosiery industries were long established in the county, Nottingham again being the principal centre. Light industry and manufacturing made a significant contribution to the economy of the county with cycle (Raleigh Industries) and motor manufacture being particularly important. John Player and Sons employed a sizeable workforce in the tobacco industry at Nottingham.

The main line of the former Great Central Railway (LNER) served Nottingham and Hucknall. That of the Great Northern Railway served Newark and Retford, with a branch to Nottingham and local lines in that vicinity. A branch of the Great Central Railway, formerly (until 1908) the main line of the Lancashire, Derbyshire and East Coast railway, entered the county on the west from Chesterfield, and crossed the Dukeries by Ollerton to Dukeries Junction (GNR) and Lincoln. The Sheffield - Grimsby line of the Great Central crossed the north of the county by Worksop and Retford.

62724 BEDFORDSHIRE

A small county of south central England, mainly low-lying, with the Chiltern Hills in the south.

Traditionally, Bedfordshire has always been a prominent agricultural rather than manufacturing county, nearly nine-tenths of the total area being under cultivation by the beginning of the last century. In the Vale of Bedford the chief crop was wheat; market-gardening was the principal activity in the Biggleswade area, the produce going mainly to London. Factories in Bedford and Luton were engaged in the manufacture of agricultural machinery and implements; at that time Luton was also well-known for the manufacture of straw hats (hence the nickname – "straw-hatters" – given to Luton Town F.C.)

The main line of the Great Northern Railway (LNER) passed through Biggleswade in the east of the county: Luton was served by a branch of the Great Northern. A branch of the Midland railway south from Bedford connected with the GNR line at Hitchin, giving the Midland access to London over GNR metals.

62725 INVERNESS-SHIRE

Inverness-shire, a north-west county of Scotland and largest of all the Scottish Shires, is now part of the Highland Region. It included the Outer Hebrides south of the northern boundary of Harris; of the total land area more than one-third belonged to the islands. The topography was wild and extremely mountainous and was characterized by beautiful scenery. The Shire contained more than 50 mountains exceeding 3000 ft. in height, including Ben Nevis, the highest mountain in the British Isles.

Although the area under cultivation had increased significantly since the mid-nineteenth century, yields were comparatively small, oats being the predominant crop. The hillsides provided good pasture land and were populated by dense flocks of sheep. Highland cattle were also reared in large numbers, particularly in the Western Isles.

The county town of Inverness was the main distribution centre for the Highlands and, during the Summer months, a magnet for much tourist traffic. Its own manufacturing industries were not extensive and consisted mainly of tweed (tartan) production, brewing, distilling, tanning, soap and candle-making. There was a considerable trade with Aberdeen, Leith, London and the east coast generally and, by means of the Caledonian Canal, with Glasgow, Liverpool and Ireland.

One of the last large railway schemes to be completed in Britain was the NBR's West Highland line from Craigendoran, west of Glasgow, to Fort William, opened in 1894, and the daunting Mallaig extension of 1901, a mere 40 miles which took the contractor Robert McAlpine a full four years to complete after much political controversy and a Treasury subsidy of £260,000 (see also LNER Classes K2 and D34).

The Highland Railway (later LMS) main line extended from Perth to Inverness. North of Inverness the line ran to Wick and Thurso, the latter being the most northerly point in Great Britain reached by a main line.

62728 CHESHIRE

Cheshire is a north-western county of England, bordering on the Pennines in the east and bounded in part by the Irish Sea in the west. The coastline is formed by the estuaries of the Dee and the Mersey, which are separated by the Wirral peninsula. The county is low-lying and undulating and mainly agricultural.

From the earliest times the staple products of Cheshire were salt and cheese. The salt-pits at Nantwich, Middlewich and Northwich were in active operation at the time of Edward the Confessor. Twelfth century writers refer to the excellence of Cheshire cheese and in the Civil War 300 tons were requisitioned in one year for troops stationed in Scotland.

The Midland and Great Central (LNER) systems entered the east of the county which was, however, served primarily by the London and North Western Railway (LMS) main line and branch network converging on Crewe and by the Great Western Railway coming northwards from Wrexham.

62729 RUTLANDSHIRE

Rutland, the smallest county in England with an area of only 152 square miles, and a population of less than 20,000 in 1901, became part of Leicestershire in the local government reorganisation of 1974 but was reinstated as a separate county in 1997.

Agriculture was traditionally the only industry of any importance, although there was some quarrying and boot-making. Nearly nine-tenths of the total land area was under cultivation, wheat being by far the most important grain crop. Dairy produce included large quantities of cheese manufactured and sold as Stilton.

The main line of the LNER (Great Northern Railway) intersected the north-east corner of the county. GNR branch lines, together with those of the LNWR and Midland Railway systems served the remainder of the Shire.

62730 BERKSHIRE

Berkshire was a southern county of England whose northern boundary was formed entirely by the river Thames.

Around three quarters of the total land area was under cultivation, the principal grain crops being oats and wheat. Dairy farming was important, as was the breeding of sheep and pigs. The only manufacturing centre of any importance was Reading, which was particularly well-known for its biscuit factories and riverside boat-building yards. The manufacture of clothing and carpets was carried out at Abingdon.

Communications to and within the county were provided principally by the Great Western Railway, whose main line crossed the county from east to west by Maidenhead, Reading and Didcot.

There were no LNER lines in Berkshire.

62731 SELKIRKSHIRE

Selkirkshire, a former county of south east Scotland is now part of the Borders Region.

The predominantly cold and wet climate was not conducive to agricultural production; the rearing of livestock, particularly sheep, was more profitable. Woollen manufactures (tweeds, tartans, plaids, yarn and hosiery) were the principal industries at Galashiels and Selkirk. Tanning, dyeing, engineering, iron-founding and boot-making were also carried on at Galashiels, and there were large vineries at Clovenfords.

The Waverley route of the North British Railway (LNER) passed through the Shire, sending off a branchline to Selkirk at Galashiels, from which there was also a line to Peebles.

612732 Dumfries-shire

A former maritime border county of south-west Scotland on the *Solway Firth,* Dumfries-shire is now part of the Dumfries and Galloway Region.

The surface of the county in general was bare and hilly, but there was some good pasture, particularly for sheepbreeding, and rich arable land, excellent for corn-growing. Manufacturing was of only local importance and confined mostly to Dumfries and a few of the larger towns. Langholm was famous for its tweeds; breweries and distilleries were found at Annan, Sanquhar and elsewhere. The numerous rivers provided excellent salmon and trout fishing.

The LNER (North British Railway) had a short line to Langholm from Riddings Junction in Cumberland, giving access to Carlisle and, by the Waverley route, to Edinburgh.

62733 Northumberland

Rich in history, culture and tradition, Northumberland was the northernmost county of England.

Although the Shire was one of the largest sheep-rearing counties in England, it was above all one of the major industrial centres of the United Kingdom, where shipbuilding, mining and metal working predominated. The Tyne estuary was a region of ironworks, blast-furnaces, shipbuilding yards, ropeworks, coke-ovens and factories for the manufacture of glass, pottery and fire-bricks, from above Newcastle to the sea. There was much activity in all trades concerned with coal mining, the Tyne being one of the most important centres in the world for the coal-shipping trade. There were also several sea-fishing ports, of which North Shields was by far the most important.

Communications were provided almost wholly by the North Eastern Railway (LNER) whose main line entered the county over the famous bridges at Newcastle and ran north by Morpeth and, near the coast, to Berwick before joining up with the North British

Railway system on the mainline to Edinburgh. Numerous branch railways served the district and there were connections westward to Hexham and Carlisle, up the Tweed Valley into Scotland and (by the North British line) up the North Tyne Valley from Hexham.

62734 CUMBERLAND

Cumberland, the north-westernmost county of England (now part of Cumbria) was bounded to the east by **Northumberland**, to the south by **Westmorland** and **Lancashire** and to the west by the Irish Sea. In the south, the county incorporated about one-half of the Lake District, including the highest mountain in England, Scafell Pike, and the majority of the principal lakes.

Agricultural production was limited and was largely confined to the rearing of livestock, particularly sheep. The principal industries of Cumberland were from the earliest times connected with its valuable fisheries and abundant mineral wealth, including coal, iron ore and copper. Carlisle was the centre for a variety of manufactures and there were shipbuilding yards at Whitehaven, also important for coal-mining.

The London and North Western Railway (LMS) entered the county near Penrith and terminated at Carlisle, which was also served by the Midland. The Caledonian, North British (LNER), and Glasgow and South Western lines also served this city, which was an important junction in through communications between England and Scotland. The North Eastern Railway (LNER) connected Carlisle with Newcastle.

62735 WESTMORLAND

A former northern county of England, bounded on the north west by **Cumberland** and now part of Cumbria. The area comprised about one-third of the Lake District, westward from Shap Fell. Rainfall was very heavy, particularly in the west.

Scarcely half of the total area of the county was under cultivation, although the meadow-lands produced excellent grazing pasture for livestock. Manufacturing industry was not significant, due mainly to the absence of any local sources of energy, other than water-power. The principal manufacture was woollens, in one form or another, chiefly confined to the low country in and near Kendal.

The mainline of the London and North Western Railway (LMS) from the south served Oxenholme, Low Gill and Tebay, leaving the county after surmounting the steep gradient at Shap. The Midland main line (also LMS), with a parallel course, served Appleby. A branch of the North Eastern (LNER) system from Darlington served Kirkby Stephen and Tebay, and another branch connected Kirkby Stephen with Appleby and Penrith.

B.   "AFTER THE FOX" ....THE HUNTS

When the D49/2's were named, foxhunting was an established and largely unchallenged part of the English country scene, although not without its critics.

Oscar Wilde referred to the English country gentleman galloping after a fox as "the unspeakable in pursuit of the uneatable". Hunting was gently satirized by the largely forgotten early Victorian author R. S. Surtees, creator of the inimitable Jorrocks, who drew most of his inspiration from observation of hunting in the **Braes of Derwent** country:-

> "Tell me a man's a fox-hunter, and I loves him at once."

> "Unting fills my thoughts by day, and many a good run I have in my sleep. Many a dig in the ribs I gives Mrs. J. when I think they're running into the warmint (renewed cheers). No man is fit to be called a sportsman wot doesn't kick his wife out of bed on a haverage once in three weeks."

And the deliciously suggestive, if politically incorrect:

> "Women never look so well as when one comes in wet and dirty from hunting."

Siegfried Sassoon, on the other hand, in "Memoirs of a Fox-Hunting Man", uses rural pursuits to create a superb evocation of an Edwardian age of endless summers that seemed destined to last for ever.

The point of all this is, of course, that although it is now inconceivable that locomotives could take the names of foxhunts, in the early years of the twentieth century, and beyond, foxhunting was closely woven into the social and cultural fabric of the age and of the Shires served by the LNER.

Hunting with dogs (hounds) goes back to the dawn of time. The Normans brought their hounds to England during the Conquest. Deer, stag, boar, wolves, hares and foxes were hunted; by the eighteenth century hunts were established on geographical lines with members of the local community following either on horseback or on foot.

The training of hounds specifically to hunt foxes came about after the Restoration of *King Charles II* in 1660. Under the Stuart Kings, hunting was seen as a healthy and noble activity – far removed from the squalor, vices and wickedness of the city.

In the mid-1700's Whigs began to caricature the country gentry as ill-educated buffoons whose sole occupation was fox hunting. The political banter which followed gave rise to the name which the hunt gave to its quarry – Charlie – after the Whig Charles James Fox.

Foxhunting has had a marked impact on the tradition, language and culture of the United Kingdom. Everyday turns of phrase, such as being "in the pink" are derived from the hunt (Pink being the way the hunt has traditionally described the colour of its red jackets). The Parliamentary term 'whip' derives from the whipper-in at a foxhunt i.e. someone employed to assist the huntsmen manage the hounds. It is widely claimed that the expression "painting the town red" originated in Melton Mowbray (where the **Belvoir** meets the **Quorn** and the **Cottesmore**) when some young nineteenth century aristocrats went on a drunken spree and literally painted parts of the town centre red.

The Hunts which comprise Class D49/2 include several which could trace their history back 300 years or more. Hunting with wolfhounds in the **Berkeley** country dates from the twelfth century; tradition has it that the **Staintondale** received a charter for hunting from *King John* when he came ashore at Scarborough in 1208. The **Pytchley** is believed to be directly descended from the Royal Hunt maintained by the Plantaganet Kings.

The **Bilsdale** is thought to have been the oldest established pack of foxhounds in England, and was founded by the 2nd Duke of Buckingham (Master 1668 to 1687), who apparently lived openly with the Countess of Shrewsbury after killing her husband in a duel. The **South Durham**, the **Sinnington** and the **Goathland** also originated from the mid-seventeenth century; the **Burton** country was being hunted by foxhounds as early as 1672, although Hugo Meynell, whose family was closely associated with **Meynell** and **Quorn** Hunts, was the first man to breed hounds swift enough to catch foxes in the open.

Not that the foxes were easily (or inevitably) caught. Hunt records make reference to several exhausting encounters of literally "marathon" proportions. In 1770, a fox ran the **Braes of Derwent** hounds for 26 miles before finding safety on board a ship lying by the quayside at Sunderland. In the famous 'Waterloo run' on 22nd February, 1866, the Master of the **Pytchley** Hunt rode no fewer than five horses in a chase which lasted 3 hours and 45 minutes and covered 21 miles; several horses were seriously injured and had to be destroyed. In 1911, the **Fernie** Hunt pursued its quarry for a total of 3 hours and 20 minutes over a distance of 28 miles.

Foxhunting has also been the downfall – quite literally – of many of its human participants, sometimes with fatal consequences. The 2nd Duke of Buckingham, founder of the **Bilsdale**, died of a chill caught while hunting in 1687. Lord Hawke, Master of the **Badsworth** from 1826 to 1869, died as the result of a hunting accident. His successor followed suit seven years later, the result of bursting a blood vessel while blowing his horn. Charles **Fernie**, Master from 1888 to 1919, took no active part in the pursuit after a bad hunting accident in 1906. In a somewhat bizarre twist on the theme of fatality, Captain

Robert Hutton of the **Braes of Derwent** conceived the unusual idea of being buried with all his horses and hounds. Consequently, when he died, so did they, and all were buried together in the garden of his country house.

Many of the country houses – and their occupants – associated with the Hunts which comprise Class D49/2 also feature prominently in the LNER B17/B2 *Sandringham* Class. Successive Earls of Harewood and other members of the Lascelles family were Masters of the **Bramham Moor** Hunt at various times from 1788 to the late 1930's. The 1st Marquess of Zetland was Master of the **Zetland** Hunt from 1876 to 1911, and the hunt kennels were located at *Aske Hall* until that date. The Mastership of the **Belvoir** Hunt was held by the reigning Duke of Rutland from 1750, the date of the Hunt's founding, until 1896. The **Fitzwilliam** was based at *Milton* Hall, near Peterborough, ancestral home of Earl Fitzwilliam, whose family had always held the Mastership.

Away from the 'Sandringhams' the most famous aristocratic association is that between the **Pytchley** Hunt and the Spencer family. Known originally as the Althorp and Pytchley Hunt, with kennels at Althorp, the history of the **Pytchley** is closely intertwined with that of the Earls Spencer, who have been Masters on several occasions. Perhaps the best known incumbent is the 5th "Red Earl" – a member of Gladstone's Cabinet – whose fame and obsession with foxhunting brought Elizabeth, the beer-drinking, cigar-smoking Empress of Austria, to Althorp as a house guest in 1876 and 1878. There is a commemorative portrait of Elizabeth at Althorp, flying over a fence on her mount, riding side-saddle, which was considered the only 'proper' way for a lady to proceed on horseback.

Another aristocratic association which deserves mention is that between the 2nd Duke of **Grafton** and the Hunt which bore his name. The pack was established by the Duke around 1735. He had kennels at Croydon (seat of his friend, the Duke of Onslow), and went to London very early on the days he hunted. After repeatedly complaining about the morning hours wasted in crossing the Thames by ferry at Westminster, his solution was to introduce a

Bill into Parliament for the construction of a bridge, completed in 1748.

Foxhunting may have been lampooned as a pastime of the idle rich, but there is no doubt that it was always an expensive pursuit, requiring the construction and maintenance of extensive stables and kennels to house the horses and hounds.

A day's foxhunting was a full day's occupation, either in the saddle or travelling to a meet. The horsebox was not widely available until the 1930's. For the dedicated enthusiast, hunting represented a huge commitment and not only did the Master need to fork out tremendous sums, but serious foxhunters needed private incomes to afford the time to hunt. Tailors were engaged, boots commissioned, and saddles and bridles made and repaired.

The **Oakley** Hunt originated in 1793, when the 4th Duke of Bedford, one of the wealthiest landlords in the country, established a pack of hounds at Woburn Abbey and stables were built to accommodate thirty six hunters. Both horses and hounds had central heating by flues and the dog kennel alone measured over 400 ft. long, with numerous separate compartments for bitches, puppies and dogs. There were seven hospital rooms dedicated to sick hounds, a handsome house for the huntsman, and apartments for the two kennel keepers. One of the first covered riding schools was also erected.

Hunt country varied in size from the comparatively small territories occupied in North Yorkshire by the **Bilsdale, Derwent, Staintondale** and others to the large expanses of middle-England hunted by the likes of the **Brocklesby** and the **Southwold** in Lincolnshire.

In the early days, the tendency was for hunts to proliferate as the larger territories were broken up and sub-divided. In Northumberland, parts of the **Percy** country were lent to what became the West Percy and Mulvain (Percy) Hunts. The **Hurworth** and the **Tynedale** were formed from the breakup of the Old Raby and Northumberland territories. The **Middleton** was divided into two separate establishments in 1921, as was the **York and Ainsty**

(North and South) in 1929. The West of Yore Hunt was formed originally (in 1932) in country loaned by the **Bedale** in Yorkshire and the **Blankney** resulted from the division of the Old **Burton** country in 1871.

More recent times witnessed an increasing number of mergers, due mainly to the loss of country through creeping urbanisation and the construction of motorway networks. D49 Hunts involved in this process were the **Garth** and South Berks; the **Meynell** and South Staffs; the Vine and **Craven**; the **Puckeridge** and Thurlow; and the **Grove** and **Rufford**. Interestingly, in the early 1940's some parts of the **Braes of Derwent** country had to be given up for a different reason; coal mining subsidence had made much of the area unsafe to ride.

Hunting with dogs was banned by law from midnight on 17th February, 2005.

ISBN 142515869-2